By the same author:

The Race for Trieste
The Defence of Madrid
The Red Army Moves
See It Happen

A TALE OF TWO BATTLES

A TALE
OF
TWO BATTLES

A Personal Memoir of Crete
and the Western Desert 1941

GEOFFREY COX

WILLIAM KIMBER: LONDON

First published in 1987 by
WILLIAM KIMBER & CO. LIMITED
100 Jermyn Street, London, SW1Y 6EE

© Geoffrey Cox, 1987
ISBN 0-7183-0642-2

Printed and bound in Great Britain by
Adlard & Son Ltd, The Garden City Press,
Letchworth, Herts

To all who served in the Div

Contents

PART ONE

PART TWO

Contents

List of Illustrations

The author is grateful to the Alexander Turnbull Library and to Sir John White for permission to reproduce photographs in their collections.

SKETCH MAPS   *Page*

Acknowledgements

In assessing the campaign in Crete and the Crusader battles I have made wide use of the official war histories of the period. Major-General Playfair's volumes in the British series on *The War in the Mediterranean and the Middle East*: Gavin Long's *Greece Crete and Syria* in Canberra's *Australia in the War of 1939–45*: and Agar Hamilton and Turner's *The Sidi Rezegh Battles* from the South African War Histories are key sources. Of particular importance to my task have been D. M. Davin's *Crete* (1953) and W. E. Murphy's *The Relief of Tobruk* (1961) both volumes in the Official History of New Zealand in the Second World War. Davin's work is distinguished not only by the quality of its writing but by the perceptiveness of its judgements at a time when important information, such as that about Ultra, was not available. Professor Murphy gave coherence and perspective to a very confused campaign, and blended this skilfully with first hand accounts of the fighting.

Amongst unofficial books of the period, I. McD. G. Stewart's *The Struggle for Crete* Oxford 1966) is a classic of its kind, all the more remarkable because its author is not a professional historian, but was the Medical Officer of the 1st Welch during the campaign.

On Ultra, Vols II and III of Professor Hinsley's *Official History of British Intelligence in the Second World War* (HMSO) are an essential source, as are Ronald Lewin's *Ultra Goes to War* (Hutchinson) and F. W. Winterbotham's *The Ultra Secret* (Weidenfeld and Nicholson). I am grateful to Paul Weller, of Weller's Bookshop in Cirencester, for giving me access to his personal library on this topic.

For my personal recollections, I have drawn on my diary notes and my letters to my wife.

Mrs Gumpert and Mrs Taylor have shown skill and patience in transcribing my rough drafts into clear typescript, so enabling me to sustain my opposition to word processors.

PART ONE

1. Anzac Day

We arrived in Crete on Anzac Day, 25 April 1941 – some five thousand New Zealanders evacuated from Greece, as the brief campaign there crumbled to disaster under the constant, shrieking assault of the Luftwaffe's dive bombers. Only twenty-six years – a mere eyeblink in the unfolding of the human story – separated this overcast spring day from the one on which, on that other Aegean beach, our forebears had waded ashore through the Turkish fire at Gallipoli. The battle they had fought had found its way into the history books. The one in which we were soon to be engaged would gain its place there too, as the first airborne invasion of all time. Six months later, in the cold wintry desert south of Tobruk, we were to find ourselves again in a central role in another decisive battle, that for the strategic ridge of Sidi Rezegh. Had that struggle gone wrong – as it nearly did – then the way to the Nile Valley would have lain wide open to Rommel's tanks, even more vulnerable than it was to be when he reached Alamein six months later.

These battles of Crete and of Sidi Rezegh were amongst the most significant as well as the most dramatic of World War II. Crete was one of the last actions which the British Commonwealth fought during the time we stood alone, before Russia entered the war. The Crusader offensive of November 1941, of which the battle of Sidi Rezegh was the central action, was the last desert campaign before American support became available. In both of them the part played by the 2nd New Zealand Division, the main fighting force of the smallest nation on the Allied side, under its legendary leader, General Freyberg VC, was to be crucial.

Few if any of us had, however, any such thoughts in our minds on that soft grey afternoon as we stared around us in Suda Bay at the evidence of yet more of the Luftwaffe's handiwork. The masts and funnels of sunken ships showed above the calm water of this great natural harbour, a sight dominated by the long awesome shape of the sunken and abandoned cruiser HMS *York*. Our concerns were more immediate – to get ashore before the Stukas came over again and, in due course, to get back to Egypt and resume the battle on more even terms, and above all with some aircraft of our own side in the skies above us.

Three ships – the cruisers *Calcutta* and *Perth*, and the Combined Operations troopship *Glengyle* – had taken us aboard the night before at Porto Rafti, a tiny fishing harbour just south of Marathon. Their decks were crowded with the men of four battalions of New Zealand infantry, and of two Field Ambulances, and of the staff of Freyberg's Divisional Headquarters. Freyberg himself, with a tiny battle HQ, had stayed to supervise the evacuation of the remainder of the division. A very junior second-lieutenant, commissioned only four months before, I was attached to the divisional staff on the *Glengyle*, and found myself part of the first group to be ferried ashore to organise the landing and the move to transit camps set up in nearby olive groves.

In our landing craft was the commander of the 5th Brigade, Brigadier James Hargest. He was a combative man who did not look the part. At forty-nine his stocky figure was running to fat, and you had to look keenly into his reddish, somewhat pudgy face to see the alert eyes and the resolute mouth and chin. Yet in World War I he had commanded a battalion whilst still in his early twenties, had won the DSO and bar and the Military Cross, and was a Member of the New Zealand Parliament. As we chugged our way towards a small, bomb-damaged jetty a launch dashed out from the shore and circled around us. In it was a red-tabbed officer in British Army uniform. His urgent tones carried clearly across the water. 'Hurry, hurry!' he shouted. 'Get your men ashore and dispersed quickly. The bombers may be over again any minute. All arms except rifles are to be stacked at the pierhead. I repeat, all arms except rifles are to be stacked where we will show you, so that you can move off immediately.'

Hargest's face glowed with swift anger at these words. He saw at once the flaw in this plan. His troops had carried out of Greece every weapon they could – not only their rifles and bayonets, but Brens, mortars, anti-tank rifles, even some heavy machine guns. Once these were out of their hands, they might never be regained. They could find themselves fighting a new battle in Crete inadequately armed. Hargest shouted back at the British officer. 'We will do no such thing. My men will keep their arms, and march off with them.'

The launch circled round, to enable the officer to reply. Whether out of anger or anxiety, his voice rose almost to a shriek. 'We are

Troops evacuated from Greece landing at Suda Bay, April 25, 1941

Parachutists landing .

(*Above*) Parachutists dropp[...]
near Heraklion

(*Left*) Parachutists after la[...]
ing on Crete

under constant attack here. The planes could be back any minute. I am in charge of this base area, and I order you to obey my command.'

Hargest's reply was curt. 'I am not surprised that you are in charge of a base area' – he stressed acidly the word 'base' – 'if this is the way you go on. I tell you my men will retain their weapons.'

But not all did. There was not time to organise New Zealand units to offset the British military police who, stationed on the narrow stone quay which was the sole disembarkation point, continued to order men to dump their heavy weapons. Many did so, and the pile against a dock wall grew steadily. Nor were officers allowed to form up their men in units. The troops were hurried off the moment they landed, streaming along a dusty roadway to a camping area under olive trees at Perivolia on the western outskirts of the town of Canea. Hargest's forebodings were to prove only too well founded. Those units which dumped their heavy weapons were lucky if they later got half of them back.

We slept that night under the olive trees. I had had to dump most of my personal kit at Porto Rafti, but I still had a lightweight sleeping bag which I had bought ten months earlier for use when, as a journalist, I had got away from Paris just before the Germans reached it. It kept me warm in that cold Cretan night, at the end of a day which was made more fateful for us than we realised at the time. For during it Adolf Hitler had signed his War Directive No 28 ordering 'an operation to occupy the island of Crete'.

2. Prelude to Battle

I woke in a grey dawn, with slumped grey figures everywhere, just as they had been portrayed in a big engraving which hung on our High School classroom wall in Invercargill, showing the morning of Waterloo. But this was reality, these figures were soon to stir into men rolling out of their blankets, to ask, 'Where do we draw rations? Who's got the rations?' In their midst a signalman arrived and with quiet efficiency laid a telephone line to the foot of one big tree. The line suddenly made it official, an office, a headquarters, so that the men no longer crowded around, but kept their distance as an officer spoke into the black field telephone, and the show had a head again.

Like every other New Zealander on Crete that morning, I was a volunteer. When the war broke out I had been in Paris, a foreign correspondent for the London *Daily Express*. I had come to Europe in 1932 as a Rhodes Scholar, at Oriel College at Oxford. In 1935 I had secured a toehold in Fleet Street as a freelance reporter, and had gone on to become a foreign and a war correspondent.

Fortune had favoured me, and I had covered many of the most dramatic events of the pre-war years – the Civil War in Spain, the Anschluss in Austria, the Munich crisis from Prague, the last frantic wrigglings of the appeasers in Paris and London to buy off Hitler over Poland. I reported the early weeks of the phoney war from France and from Holland. Between November 1939 and March 1940 I had a real shooting war to describe, when the Russians invaded Finland, and suffered terrible losses in the snow and the forests before their overwhelming power crushed their tiny victim. I learnt one profound lesson from these stubborn Finnish peasant boys in their white snow capes, as they moved on skis to yet one more attack – that it pays to fight, whatever the odds against you. When the German onslaught against the West began in May 1940 I was in Brussels. Once Belgium fell I moved down to Paris, and on 17 June got away from Bordeaux on the P & O liner *Madura*, the last ship to carry Britons from Southern France. When we reached Falmouth I heard on the BBC News that a New Zealand infantry brigade had arrived in Britain, diverted from the Middle East because of the danger to troopships in the Red Sea now that Italy had entered the war. That decided me. A month later, in battle dress and steel helmet, with a Lee Enfield on my shoulder, and familiar New Zealand voices around me once more, I was marching along roads in Surrey, a private in the 23rd Battalion of the New Zealand Army.

It had always been my intention to enlist when war came, even though I could have become a British war correspondent. Arthur Christiansen, the great editor of the *Daily Express*, urged me to stay with the paper, and indeed accused me of letting him down by joining the Army. I rationalised my decision by saying that since in my writing I had advocated standing up to Hitler, it was only proper that I should be prepared to follow the line of my own preaching, and to fight the war and not just write about it. But my true reasons were more fundamental. The ethic of the close-knit community in which I had grown up in New Zealand demanded that, if war came, able-bodied men should go out and fight. There was, too, in that summer of 1940, a further good reason for turning soldier. It looked as if the Germans could land in Britain, and overrun the country. If that happened, it was surely better to have a gun in your hand rather than a typewriter, and, in Churchill's words, 'take one with you'. So I persuaded Cecily, the English girl I had married five years before, to take our two small sons to New Zealand, and then went to the New Zealand High Commission in the Strand and enlisted.

My transition from civilian to military life was abrupt. We had had in my youth a form of compulsory military training in New Zealand, and I had done my ration of night parades, and an annual fortnight's camp in the Territorials – an experience of which my recollections had on the whole been pleasant, particularly on a fine morning in camp at Wainakarua, with the battalion ranged on the brown parade ground, and the sun glinting on our bayonets and on the blue sea beyond. This training was, in the pressures of that threatened summer, deemed enough for me to go straight into an operational unit.

The 23rd and the other battalions of 5th Brigade were camped under pine trees on the edge of Mytchett, and each day we engaged in a series of manoeuvres, being rushed to areas where German parachutists might land, and where we marched and patrolled and mounted mock attacks across commons and heaths and through village streets. The men I was with were in iron-hard condition, and, after months of training, literally fighting fit. I came to all this soft from civilian life, and my first week passed in a blur of fatigue, of aching limbs, sunburn, and frantic anxiety about mastering new weapons like the Bren gun – for in my Territorial days the World War I Lewis gun had still been standard issue. But I survived, and began to savour this new existence.

The change was made easier for me because I was among people from my own part of New Zealand, some of them friends of long standing. The territorial basis for military formations, upon which the British regimental system was largely organised, was, in those less mobile times, an invaluable element in sustaining morale in an army. Men fight better alongside those with whom they have lived – and hope to continue to live – their lives. Under the Mytchett pines I shared a bivouac with a man who had been a boundary rider between two back-country Otago sheep stations. He had lived for

months alone in a remote hut on the Remarkable Mountains, riding
out each day along the ridges which marked the unfenced boundary
between the stations, keeping apart with his team of dogs the sheep
from either station. I had mustered sheep on one of these stations
during a University vacation, and knew not only the terrain, but the
majestic beauty which made such a solitary life not only endurable,
but satisfying. My platoon commander, eight years my junior, was
the youngest brother of a man I had been at the University with. On
my second day in the army I was called upon, as a member of a
piquet patrolling the bivouac area at night, to help arrest a drunken
private from Invercargill with whom my last contact had been a
brief but bloody fist fight behind a sports pavilion after a rugby
match, in which tempers had flared. Dan Davin, who had followed
me to Oxford as a Rhodes Scholar from Otago, commanded a
platoon in the 23rd. I went drinking in a country pub one evening
with him and two of his fellow officers, but never sought to repeat
the process, good friend though he was. Even in the New Zealand
Army, though class distinctions (and they did exist in New Zealand)
were not reinforced by accent or physique, there was a distinct gap
between officers and men – and rightly so. For in war the
obedience which men must give their officers without hesitation in
battle needs to be reinforced by the mystique of authority, a
mystique strengthened by a degree of apartness. Yet it was a strange
– and heartening – experience, when I was given a day's leave,
to return to London to find myself no longer a middle class figure
in a striped suit, able to command a taxi on the expense account,
but a private soldier in rough khaki, caught up at once in the warm
camaraderie of the working class, given free rides on buses by the
conductors and offered free beer in pubs because of the New
Zealand flash on my shoulder.

  In the week that I enlisted, the American weekly magazine *Life*
had featured a photograph of half a dozen airborne German troops
who had landed by glider on top of the seemingly impregnable
Belgian fortress of Eban Emael, and had put it out of action by
attaching high explosive charges to the embrasures and even to the
guns themselves. Under the cowls of their steel helmets they stared
at the camera, hard, relentless, ruthless. I had asked myself how I
would fare if I found myself face to face with such men in a bayonet
fight. One morning soon after I had joined the 23rd Battalion our
platoon was drawn up by the roadside, ready to march off to
company parade, when another platoon came by. It was made up

of men from the West Coast of the South Island, many of them coal miners and bush workers. Studying their weather-hardened, lined, alert faces, under steel helmets, I realised suddenly that they were every bit as tough as these German parachutists, and a great deal more astute and self-reliant, and I felt a surge of confidence that we would, after all, win this war.

My time with the 23rd was brief, for the brigade wanted to make use of my knowledge of German, and of Europe, and sent me off to a British Officer Cadet Training Unit, at Ramillies Barracks at Farnborough, part of the great complex of military establishments centering on Aldershot. So I became an officer cadet in 168 OCTU, with white tabs on the shoulders of my battledress, and a white band around my fore and aft cap.

Our intake was composed in part of older men straight out of civilian life who had joined the Officers Emergency Reserve before the war, and who had been called up because they had specialist skills to offer. They included a number of about-to-be-distinguished men. There was a young barrister, Frank Soskice, who five years later was to become Solicitor-General in the post-war Attlee Government, and who was to become a peer and Home Secretary. One of a pair of dark-haired twins, the Baron brothers, was to win fame after the war as a West End portrait photographer. We had in our ranks a future Master of Balliol, Christopher Hill, and a future Editor of the *Yorkshire Evening Post*, Ewart Clay. Since we were ranged in alphabetical order, I found myself in a squad next to a cadet called Archibald Colquhoun. He was a Roman Catholic, and an ardent supporter of General Franco. Under our voices we would hiss arguments at one another about Spain. When I next encountered him, four years later, at Eighth Army Headquarters in Italy, he was Colonel Colquhoun, in charge of liaison with the Italian Partisans, and as ardently pro-Communist as he had been pro-Franco. An earlier intake at 168 OCTU had included a young classics professor, Enoch Powell.

Our first evening at Ramillies we were assembled under the fierce gaze of our small and peppery Regimental Sergeant-Major, who warned us to keep away from the local whores. 'Them's like oak coffins with brass handles,' he declared. 'All finery and glitter outside, but inside nothing but death and corruption.' With almost equal vehemence he told us to memorise the name of our commanding officer, Colonel Bingham. Two cadets in the previous intake had been Returned to Unit – that dread punishment which hung over our heads throughout the four months course – because they had failed to remember this item of information. A few months later the Colonel made his name known to a much wider audience. He took the extraordinary step for a serving officer of writing to *The Times* complaining of the poor quality of many of the Army's new officers. 'The middle, lower middle and working classes are now receiving the King's Commission. These classes, unlike the old aristocratic and feudal (almost) classes who led the Old Army have never had "their people to consider",' he argued. 'They have never had occasion to think of anyone but themselves. . . . They have largely fallen down on the job. . . . Never was the old school tie and the best it stands for more justified than today.'

The letter led to such an outcry that Colonel Bingham left 168 OCTU and opted to spend the rest of the war as a bench hand in an aircraft factory.

Colonel Bingham's only direct contribution to our training came in two lectures towards the end of the course. The first was on conduct in battle, and he introduced it with the words, 'My great grandfather was the Field Marshal at Balaclava'. The core of his talk was a policy he defined as KBO. 'I found on the Western Front last time, and no doubt you will find this time, that in battle you come up against situations to which there seems no answer. You can't attack. You can't retreat. Even to resist seems hopeless. My advice to you in such circumstances is KBO – keep bashing on. You will be surprised how often something turns up in your favour if you just keep on sticking it out, and fighting on. Don't thrash about looking for an answer which isn't there. Just keep your head down, and your men's heads down, and say to yourself, "KBO".' It was better advice, both for war and for life, than I realised at the time.

Colonel Bingham's second lecture was on how to sail a small boat, a sport of which he was, it seems, an ardent practitioner. It seemed a bizarre subject to teach infantry officers. Yet within a few months I was to find myself anxiously trying to recall what he had said, when it looked likely that we would be trapped in Greece, and escape by a yacht or fishing boat might be the only way out. The Colonel had been more prescient than we gave him credit for.

There were still some weeks of that superb summer of 1940 remaining, and in its hot sunshine we marched out to mount mock attacks across Farnborough golf course, or to dig practice defensive positions in the fern-covered commons beyond. Constantly, but distantly, the air battles of the Battle of Britain were fought out above our heads, as the fighter planes chalked their criss cross lines across the sharp blue sky. As we trudged back at night the search-lights would be thrusting and prowling amidst the clouds, seeking for German planes, whilst above the beech trees half a dozen of our own bombers, laden down with bombs, would make their way slowly towards the French Channel ports where the German invasion barges were massing.

This was the period when the Luftwaffe's attacks were aimed primarily at our airfields. They had had a go at the Farnborough airfield when I was with the 23rd at Mytchett. We had just finished our evening meal about five-thirty when the sound of heavy bombing came from two or three miles to the north of us. Then the sound of planes came closer, and I saw above the oaks which lined the parade ground a formation of Heinkel bombers moving towards us, exactly as I had seen them move three months before on their way to smash the Belgian town of Tournai. But they had only a couple of bombs left for us, and some bursts of machine gun fire which cut the branches above our tents, and riddled one of the big mess marquees, without inflicting any casualties. On Saturday, 7 September, the air war entered a new phase, with the first mass attacks launched on London. Away to the east the late afternoon sky was filled with the steady drone, drone of great fleets of aircraft, so that the air seemed to vibrate as if a thin sheet of metal were being shaken to imitate thunder. We had the afternoon free, and I watched and listened from the incongruous setting of a grassy bank alongside the open air swimming pool at Camberley, where children shrieked and splashed in play, and where officer cadets from nearby Sandhurst (termed merely 162 OCTU for the duration) lay in the sun with girl friends down from London for the day, and someone with a portable gramophone played the hit tune of the moment, Eric Maschwitz's 'A Nightingale Sang in Berkeley Square'.

Were these raids, we wondered, the prelude to the invasion? That certainly seemed to be the case when, just after eight o'clock that evening military police came to the bar of the Queen's Hotel at Farnborough, our favourite off-duty gathering place, with orders that all officers and officer cadets were to return at once to barracks. As we hurried back along the darkening roads, I could hear in the distance a church bell ringing furiously – an agreed signal of the invasion. Back at Ramillies barracks we were told that the code word had gone out warning that invasion might come at dawn the next day. We had been organised to serve as a fighting unit if an

attack came, under our own officers and with a Regular Army
sergeant over each platoon. I had been made one of our platoon's
three section commanders. We were to be held in reserve at the
barracks, whilst the two other platoons in the company marched off
to man a defensive line covering the North Camp railway station.
I still have the notebook in which I wrote down our position: 'No
5 platoon includes station excludes gas works.' A box of live
ammunition was carried into the barrack room, from which I was
to issue fifty rounds per man if the call came. I sat on it and wrote
a farewell letter to my wife, to be posted if I was killed. But such a
possibility seemed a less real worry than the problem of our
ammunition pouches. The regulation army canvas web equipment
was in such short supply that we had been issued with leather
cartridge pouches dating from the Boer War. They were each the
size of an half pound chocolate box, at least two inches deep, of stiff
heavy leather which cut uncomfortably into your chest if you lay
down to take cover or to fire. In a battle they would certainly
jeopardise our movements.

But no invasion was under way. We had been caught up not so
much in a false alarm, as an ill-phrased alarm. The code word
'Cromwell' had indeed been sent out from Army Headquarters in
London. It had been planned as a warning that conditions were
right for an invasion, and that units should therefore move to their
battle stations. But it had been widely and understandably inter-
preted, particularly by the Home Guard, as meaning that invasion
was under way. In many places the church bells had been rung (for
the last time until after Alamein), roads were mined and barricades
erected.

Meanwhile the daytime bombing of London continued. I had
enough of the historian in me, let alone the journalist, to be
determined to see London under the bombing. The BBC gave me
an opportunity. My knowledge of French politics was still sufficiently
fresh for them to invite me to comment on Pétain's new Government,
with the wicked Pierre Laval at its head. I got leave to go up, and
after I had done my broadcast, I drove around the bombed areas of
the East End and the West End with Eric Sevaried of CBS, a friend
from my Paris days, and with his boss, the about-to-be-renowned
Edward R. Murrow. But it was not so much the damage as the quiet
fortitude of the Londoners which was impressive.

I took the tube in the evening to Park Royal, where I was due to
get a lift back to Aldershot. Every station platform was by seven

o'clock crammed with people who had, without any official blessing, decided to use the Underground as air raid shelters. Some lay reading; children were sleeping on mattresses; and the air was thick with the smell of unwashed humanity. In the bar of the pub at Park Royal people were drinking hurriedly. 'They head for home the moment the barrage starts up,' the barmaid told me. Several people with suitcases were eating sandwiches before taking the tube up west to a station likely to have some platform space clear. Gloucester Road, it seemed, was considered to be a good bet. When we got to Virginia Water the anti-aircraft barrage suddenly started up. The guns in Windsor Park sounded like a naval broadside.

I was to spend other days and nights in London that autumn, for we were given an unexpected ten days leave in early October, as they transferred our OCTU from Aldershot to the outskirts ·of Droitwich. I was in the West End on the night when Piccadilly was severely damaged, and St James's Church burnt out. It produced for me a strange experience. Four years earlier Cecily and I had seen, in nearby Leicester Square, Korda's film of H.G. Wells' *The Shape of Things to Come*. It had included scenes of London being bombed in a future war. One sequence showed a crowd stampeding down into Piccadilly Underground Station. One entrance to the station, from North Regent Street, had been exactly reproduced for the film. I was close to that same entrance on this October night, and saw the same – though more orderly – surge of people from the street and down its steps. Had a newsreel cameraman been on the spot, his film would have been little different from that in Korda's picture. Here indeed was life imitating art.

At Droitwich we were well away from any bombing. The mass attack on Coventry on 14 November was simply a white and red glare on the horizon, seen across a landscape of darkened fields and hedgerows. We finished our training in wet Midland fields, with the wind dragging streams of black clouds across the sky, and the rooks cawing in the elms.

There were sunny days too. On one such, with the Malvern Hills forming a grand backdrop, we plotted how we would mount an attack on a lovely old black and white timbered house with 1397 carved into stone above the door, and with a pond with ducks, and a land girl riding home on the top of a load of straw. When the fields became too wet for drill, we paraded in the suburban streets of Droitwich, with housewives staring from their windows, and the sergeants nearly bursting themselves trying not to swear in front of them.

By mid-December it was over, and I duly received His Majesty's Commission and returned, a brand new second-lieutenant in a brand new khaki gaberdine dress uniform with the four stars of New Zealand on its buttons, to Mytchett, where I was allotted to the newly formed 29th Battalion. I spent Christmas with F. G. Miles, the aircraft manufacturer who had designed and built the Miles trainer, one of the main training aircraft for the RAF. He and his wife Blossom had a modern house near their aerodrome outside Reading. Their small son went to sleep on Christmas Eve with a message to Father Christmas pinned up by his bed. It read: 'I am in the air raid shelter, but this is still my sock.' Then it was back to the 29th Battalion in the cold bare gaunt rooms of Farncombe Hall in Surrey. A week later we were enroute to the Middle East.

3. Convoy

The Luftwaffe gave us a spectacular send-off. From the deck of the *Duchess of Bedford*, cruise-liner turned troopship, moored at the quayside in Newport Docks, we watched on the night of 3 January 1941 Bristol and Cardiff blaze. The dark winter night, its blackness intensified by the black-out, was broken by two great ragged areas of light, one away to our left, the other to our right, as the German bombers struck at these two key ports. The reddish and yellow light of burning buildings was reflected from the low clouds, merging with the canopies of the searchlights, and studded with the golden stars of bursting anti-aircraft shells.

The 5th Brigade had embarked that afternoon. The scene of lines of men in khaki greatcoats and the peaked, lemon-squeezer hats of the New Zealand Army, each with a white canvas kitbag stamped with his army number, filing up the gangway was to me suddenly familiar. It was a picture from twenty-five years earlier come to life. For this was the exact scene which had been depicted again and again in the newspapers and magazines of my boyhood, when men in virtually identical uniforms, carrying virtually identical kitbags, had been portrayed on New Zealand wharves, one more draft of reinforcements bound for Gallipoli or Palestine or the Western Front. Now on this Welsh quayside it was as if a news reel, halted

a quarter of a century earlier, had been restarted. The only
difference was that no saddened or proud friends and relatives
crowded these wharves to see us go. Only two pilot officers and two
WAAFS watched us draw out, joined by ATS girls in white aprons
who ran out from a cookery shed to wave.

The next day we were escorted round the Welsh coast and into
the Irish Sea by a destroyer, dark grey, efficient, her guns pointing
skywards, morse flashing from the bridge, weaving in and out
around us. She was a six-funnelled vessel, one of those traded to
Britain under the destroyers-for-bases deal concluded between
Churchill and Roosevelt. But now the White Ensign flew from her
stern, and we were hailed in impeccable and imperious Dartmouth
accents to be told, 'The rest of the convoy is delayed. We are to
proceed to Belfast, and wait there.'

Five days later, in line of five abreast, the thirty liners and
merchant vessels of the convoy were steaming under grey clouds
through the Irish Channel into the Atlantic. Ten destroyers escorted
us on either side, skirting the grey green hills of Ireland to the west
and the high grey hills of Scotland to the east. A battleship and a
cruiser sailed on our northward flank. Overhead Ansons, Hudsons
and Hurricanes watched for submarines and for enemy aircraft.
Amidst all this the great liners, built for luxury cruising, seemed to
move almost protestingly, and the cargo ships proudly. As the grey
Atlantic surge mounted, and the evening brought a band of
turquoise sky above the Argyllshire peaks, it provided a magnificent
spectacle, a Spithead Review moving out to war, radiating
excitement, power, strength and efficiency. 'When peace offers such
excitement, perhaps we shall have it,' I noted in my diary that
evening.

Once we were clear of the dangers of U-boat attack in the North
Atlantic, the convoy's journey round the Cape was for us ten weeks
out of war. We broke the journey only twice, at Freetown in Sierra
Leone and at Capetown. Freetown was a particularly important
staging post now that de Gaulle's bid to take neighbouring Dakar
had failed. At its harbour entrance anti-submarine booms swayed
and tossed in the tide. The masts and funnels of a sunken ship lay
in the minefield outside. Inside, in the wide grey waters where the
river met the sea, another ship lay, listing severely, and a third had
two great holes about the watermark. But I counted another
seventy-nine ships, mostly rusty tramp steamers, safely at anchor.
We were not allowed ashore, but waited in the damp torrid heat

whilst the convoy took on supplies. It was so hot that the polish on our shoes melted during church parade, and the doctors had difficulty in getting a grip on our sweating arms as they gave us our dreaded TAB jabs.

In Capetown the papers were full of accounts of anti-war protests by the Afrikaaner extremists in Pretoria and Johannesburg. But the British South Africans welcomed us warmly, and we alternated swimming at Muisenberg, where the sand was still as white as Kipling had found it, 'spun before the gale', with route marches along the coast road, with the sea very blue on one side and the mist rolling back off Table Mountain on the other. It was the only time in the war when I marched behind a band, and it was exhilarating swinging along in a long brown column, the New Zealanders in our distinctive hats and Tommies in topees. We were soft from our weeks on ship, and sweat trickled down my nose and turned the backs of khaki shirts of the men in front of me black. At one point a black woman carrying a great basket of fruit on her head paused to watch us, and I heard a man behind me mutter, 'By God you couldn't do that on my head this morning.'

When we sailed a band on the quayside played 'Now Is The Hour', which was just beginning to establish itself as an unofficial New Zealand anthem. Its sentimentality, warm but not cloying, exactly matched the moment, and the Maoris of the 28th Battalion sang it in Maori, with their own heart-stirring lilt. As we drew away the waterside and the hillsides of Cape Town twinkled in the sunlight like a chandelier, as people flashed mirrors from their homes and their cars in farewell.

Within a few days the Southern Cross, which had greeted us as we crossed the Equator, once again faded from the night sky, as we sailed back towards the battlefields of the Mediterranean and Europe. Perhaps because we were returning to war, the beauty around us seemed all the sharper.

I noted one late afternoon scene:

An ultramarine sea with a few white waves and a distant, firm-rimmed horizon absolutely clear. Against it the cruisers were dream ships, argosies from some mirage, or – when they were broadside on – like drawings on the sky, unreal, almost lifted off the water. Thin fleecy clouds, purple in their shadows, moved across a sky which was pale yellow and, beyond a clear blue. It was peculiarly light and bright, a light which reminded me of New Zealand. The Bren gunners and the submarine look-outs stared in silence out over the sea. I felt they were as satisfied as I was with this moment of utter beauty.

The long voyage reabsorbed me into the life of the New Zealand I had left nine years before, and gave me my first contact with the segment of my fellow countrymen who formed these first cadres of the remarkable force which was the 2nd New Zealand Division – The Div to all who served in it. These early enlisters were all in the Army of their own free will, drawn to the recruiting offices when war broke out for reasons which were as varied as were their backgrounds. Some were hard-bitten characters, their faces prematurely lined by years of arduous physical work on farms or in forests or on the waterfront or in the relief camps in which, if they wanted unemployment relief, they had to work at road building or comparable tasks. It might not have been very hard work – *Mirimiri rori* – 'stroking the road' was the Maori term for it – but it was enforced work, resented by these proud and highly individual men. In my final year as a student at Otago the dark, bitter gaze of the relief gangs chipping weeds by the roadside would follow me as I walked to my lectures, to study the theories behind the Great Slump. Now the same wary eyes studied me, as I took the platoon for PT, or for training on the Bren gun.

Amongst them were those classed, sardonically, as the One Jumpers – those who had got to the recruiting office just one jump ahead of the police – or the Wife Dodgers. One man in my platoon I had seen twelve years earlier, when he stood in the dock in the Criminal Court in Dunedin charged with the murder of a Chinese prospector in the Central Otago goldfields. As law students we had followed the trial closely, and had debated the rights and wrongs of the jury's verdict, which was guilty of manslaughter. Now, his sentence completed, the man stood, tall and gaunt, as the right flanker in my platoon. Another man had served with the Spanish Foreign Legion, and we exchanged experiences about battles in the Civil War, which I had reported from the Republican side. He was quick to correct me when I suggested that Franco's young aristocratic officers might not have borne their share of the fighting. 'No, they were brave men,' he countered. 'They might not have fought hand to hand themselves, but they knew how to direct fighting – and that, after all, is what an officer's job is.'

But most of those on the *Duchess of Bedford*, whether they were fresh-faced boys or seasoned peacetime Territorials, had joined up out of a sense of responsibility blended in varying degrees with a sense of adventure. Anyway who was to probe or doubt the true patriotism of even the most hardened of the adventurers in our ranks? Some, no doubt, had joined partly because of the chance to see the world beyond New Zealand's shores. These were times before travel became commonplace. On the train taking the first volunteers to camp from Dunedin and Invercargill in September 1939 more than eighty per cent of the men had never been out of New Zealand's South Island, and well over half had never been out of their home province.

Tough self-reliance, and a sense of humour, wry, sardonic, but in no way malign, were two of their strongest characteristics. This showed, in a mass form, when we gathered for our boat drill on our first day of putting out from Newport. The ship was terribly crowded, and units became tangled and muddled as they tried to find their way to the boat stations allocated to them. The decks became a seething mass of men, like a mob of sheep struggling through a gateway. It was a similarity not lost on this force of country-dwellers. Some wit started baa-ing like a sheep. Others joined in, whilst yet others barked like sheep dogs, or whistled like shepherds. Had one closed one's eyes, it would have been easy to imagine oneself outside a New Zealand country saleyard on a busy day. The effect was to turn resentment against an administrative cock-up into laughter, without blunting the protest against inefficiency.

Another example of this bantering comment was to occur when we landed at Suez early in March. It was a day of intense, humid heat. The canteen on the boat had been broken into the night before, and many of the men had terrible hangovers. We were landed by lighter first at the wrong point, and had to be re-embarked and shipped to another quay. By the time we were ranged on the platform of the railway siding, waiting for the train which would take us to camp, everyone, officers included, was drenched with sweat and there was a restiveness and muttering in the ranks which boded ill.

At that moment there loomed into view a figure calculated to precipitate trouble. An elegant British staff officer, the transport officer in charge of the station, appeared on the platform. He was in a garb which the Two Types cartoons were soon to make famous – a khaki shirt bleached almost white with polka dot scarf at the neck, elegantly cut gaberdine trousers, and suede shoes. And he carried something we had never seen before, a fly whisk of white horsehair, which he brandished from time to time. He was the embodiment of a languid English superiority deeply resented by antipodeans of the day.

Oblivious of the effect he was causing, he strolled slowly past the staring troops. My sergeant muttered, 'This looks like trouble' and moved closer to where two of our toughest characters were in line. But a single question from a soldier saved the day. A sharp New Zealand voice rang out. 'Hey!' it called to the officer. 'Hey' in terms half of command, half of query. The officer paused, annoyed but wary, as if he knew that Australian and New Zealand troops had to be handled with care. 'Hey' the voice continued. 'What have you done with the rest of the horse?' The laughter which followed made even the officer grin, and the moment was saved.

I admired, but was never able to acquire, the capacity for a riposte in kind which many of my fellow officers could make to such comments. One instance which stays in my mind came later in the war. Early in 1945 a fifteen from the 2nd New Zealand Division played the rest of the Eighth Army at rugby. With half a dozen ex-All Blacks in the New Zealand side, it was virtually an international, and all the top brass of the Eighth Army were present in the stadium at Forli. General Freyberg's enjoyment of the match was not enhanced by a New Zealand private who had absorbed too much of the local wine, and who shouted ribald and raucous comments from the stand, a few rows behind where the General was seated, with the Army Commander as his guest.

I was sitting next to the Assistant Provost Marshal of the division, a quiet-spoken, ex-school teacher who looked far too slight a figure for such a role. 'I'd better deal with this,' he muttered to me, and walked quietly back to the end of the row where the barracker sat. 'If you go on like that, you'll find that I can shout louder than you,' he said to the drunken private. 'Oh, can you?' came back the slurred response. 'And who the bloody hell are you?' Slowly the APM replied, 'I am the Assistant Provost Marshal.' The shouter was not too drunk to take this in. He paused, and then replied with cheerful dignity. 'Are you? Then you don't even need to try.' In a burst of laughter order was restored, the man kept silent, and the problem solved without animosity on either side.

My first disciplinary problem as a new officer was of a different kind. The first order I ever gave in the New Zealand Army was disobeyed. It was on the deck of the *Duchess of Bedford*, when we were

moored in Belfast Harbour, waiting for the full convoy to assemble.
I had at that time no platoon of my own, but was merely attached
to one, as a spare officer. I took the men of it one morning for
physical exercises, and when I gave the order 'On the Hands Down'
one man, a young tousled-haired boy of nineteen, stood without
moving. I repeated the order, and he stood there, sullen and still.
It was a disconcerting moment. The rest of the squad waited keenly
to my reaction. Did they, a group who had been together for
months, resent this newcomer in their midst? Had my New Zealand
accent been so modified by my eight years in Europe that I seemed
an outsider? Was I dealing with a known troublemaker? All these
possibilities flashed into my mind. But I knew I had to act
immediately, that this was a test I could not fudge. So I asked him
if he were ill. He shook his head and said, 'I'm not going down on
that wet deck.' That left me with no option but to put him on a
charge. He was brought before the Company Commander, and
spent the rest of the voyage in the ship's cells, an unpleasant fate in
the tropics.

Another member of my platoon was of a very different type. This
was a tall, bespectacled corporal called D. P. Costello, an Auck-
lander who had had a scholarship at Cambridge, and had been
a lecturer in classics at Exeter University when the war broke
out. It was my first contact with Paddy Costello, who was in due
course to follow me as Intelligence Officer of the Division, and to
become in 1944 First Secretary of the New Zealand Legation in
Moscow.

The troops travelled in hideously crowded conditions, sleeping in
hammocks slung on the lower decks of the ship. The officers by
contrast had cabins, and we changed into our formal service dress
for dinner in the evening, and played bridge in the lounge afterwards. There was only one woman on board, the wife of A. P. F.
Chapman, who had captained an MCC side which had toured
Australia and New Zealand in the twenties. She was on her way to
a Red Cross post in Cairo. A striking, dark-haired figure, often in
a flame red dress, she stood out sharply amidst the khaki or white
uniforms at the Captain's table.

The most senior officer on board was Brigadier Hargest.
Occasionally during the voyage I would be summoned to his table
in the lounge, to be questioned about what I had seen in Europe
before the war, and during its opening phases. Though I had never
met him in peacetime, he knew my father fairly well, and we had

(*Above* and *below left*) German airborne troops embarking for Crete.
(*Below right*) Seaborne German troops heading for Crete

View from Hill 107. Maleme airfield is on the flat to the right of the cross

Hill 107 from the Tavronitis Bridge

Galatas hills from the Prison Valley

the bond of both coming from Southland, a province of New Zealand as fiercely individualistic as are Texas or Yorkshire.

I found Hargest one day reading Tolstoi's *War and Peace*. It seemed a surprising choice for a man who presented himself as a blunt, no-nonsense farmer. 'I have been reading about this fellow Koutouzow,' he said. 'He is the kind of general to study. He knew that in war steadiness and endurance are more important than any amount of strategic flair. You will find that sticking it out is more important than anything else. We were bombarded sometimes in France for thirty-six hours without a pause, and all you could do was keep steady and try to keep your men steady. Tolstoi knew that – and that's why he portrays Koutouzow as a great general even if, as the book says, "He cannot sit a horse and goes to sleep at table."' Hargest, it was clear, would have endorsed Colonel Bingham's KBO slogan.

I was delighted when, during the voyage, I was given my own platoon. We had a special reconnaissance role, with a three-inch mortar and an extra Bren carrier as part of our armament. But the British and Australian troops were advancing so swiftly in Libya that we wondered if we would ever see service in the desert. Over the radio we heard of the fall first of Bardia, then of Tobruk, and Benghazi, and finally of the destruction of the Italian desert army at Beda Fomm.

4. Maadi Interlude

A shock awaited us when we reached Maadi camp, the main New Zealand base just to the south of Cairo. The 29th Battalion was disbanded, its men being sent as reinforcements to the other battalions of the brigade, and its officers being attached to the 33rd (Training) Battalion for training in desert warfare. It was a bitter blow, keyed up as we were for action, and eager to go into it with the men we had trained and worked with. It was doubly galling when we learnt that the division was under orders to proceed to Greece, ready to meet any German onslaught there.

We also came up against a curious phenomenon, an extraordinary envy and resentment amongst the men of the 4th and 6th Brigades, who had come direct from New Zealand to Egypt, against the 5th Brigade because it had been diverted to Britain. The Glamour Boys, the 5th Brigade were scornfully termed. We were treated as if we had opted out of a hard life in the desert in order to sample the fleshpots of Britain. That the men of the 5th Brigade had had no choice in the matter, that their convoy had been diverted to Britain in mid-1940 because, with Italy's sudden entry into the war, the big liners could not be risked in the Red Sea, within range of Italian bombers and submarines based in Eritrea, made no difference. Nor was account taken of the fact that had Hitler attacked Britain, we might have been caught up in the bloodiest fighting of the war, or that we had risked bombing, and the submarine threat. That counted as nothing against the fact that we had had a free trip to Britain – that seemingly unrealisable goal at the back of every New Zealander's mind in pre-war days. What is more, because General Freyberg had insisted that the New Zealand troops must be held together, to fight as a full division, not as separate brigades, the troops in Egypt had been also denied the chance to join with the Australians in the first, highly successful desert campaign.

This resentment against the 5th Brigade, based as it was on envy, was so manifestly ignoble that it was hard to believe that it was felt by men who, in the weeks ahead, were to demonstrate extraordinary qualities of courage and selflessness and human warmth. Yet feeling against the Glamour Boys ran so deep that for months to come commanders were reluctant to put officers from the 5th Brigade over troops from the other brigades. It was to linger on until the common experience of the Sidi Rezegh campaign burnt away its last vestiges. But it remains a reminder that men in the mass can be curious creatures indeed.

My own resentment at having my first command wrenched from under me was soon offset by the interest of being in the desert, and close to wartime Cairo. Maadi Camp was at a point where the desert reaches the black soil and lush greenery of the Nile valley. On one side of us the desert began to merge into the city's edge, and drab, mud-walled huts and whitewashed flat-roofed shacks straggled out to meet it. On the other side it stretched eastward towards Arabia, white sand alternating with ochre-coloured sandstone sculptured into sudden cliffs, and abrupt small plateaux which stood like islands without seas, ridge upon ridge upon ridge with over it all a pale sky that seemed somehow old and thin. The southern horizon was hemmed in by a bare scarped line of the Mukattam Hills which turned from grey to pink to brown and to purple as the day progressed. Twin minarets showed where this escarpment dropped down to the outskirts of Cairo, whilst away to the east, beyond the green belt of the Nile lands the pyramids were like huge tents in the morning mist. It was spring, and the bugles woke us in the morning to air as sharp as in the Alps.

I shared a whitewashed, bare room in a line of hutments with two other newly commissioned officers, Ted Shand, a farmer from North Canterbury, and John Harper, who worked in a bank at Christchurch, and who was my distant cousin. Within eighteen months both were casualties, Shand killed at Ruweisat Ridge in the summer of 1942 and Harper wounded at Sidi Rezegh. We girded at the midday heat, in which we dug anti-tank ditches or practised attacks on sandy ridges, and at sandstorms which ripped the tarred canvas roof off our sleeping quarters and buried our beds under a sandhill. But we were very fit, and restively anxious to face as soon as possible the test of action.

There was, too, Cairo to explore, only half an hour's taxi drive away, by tarmac road through the eerie Dead City, where tombs built like windowless villas faced each other across dusty streets, for all the world like just another suburb until you realised these streets were empty except for an occasional dog, or a hurrying party of black-garbed men and women.

In Cairo were many British and American war correspondents alongside whom I had worked throughout the pre-war years, and who were now well placed to open up to me the life of this extraordinary city, a teeming Babylon on the edge of the killing grounds of the desert. It provided contrasts which would have stimulated palates jaded with life – and mine certainly was not. I could spend a morning digging anti-tank defences in the desert and – after a change of uniform – spend the afternoon in the Members Enclosure at the Cairo Racecourse, where the Commander-in-Chief of the Middle East, General Wavell, his khaki drill uniform ablaze with ribbons could be seen in a grandstand box with the British Ambassador. The racecourse was a smaller version of Longchamps, with palm trees in its centre, and dark-haired Cairenes and fair-haired English women in Paris model gowns. Through Donald Mallet, who worked with me in Paris, and now had a post as attaché at the British Embassy (and was, I assumed, in some branch of the Secret Service) I was invited to soirées at the home of a Lebanese business man, Abdul Mansour, in a high, cool room with tiled walls and arched windows and marble benches in the wealthiest part of Cairo. Mansour's wife, Madelaine, was a tall, young and radiantly beautiful Frenchwoman, who held court amidst a throng of British and Free French officers in richly varied uniforms – cavalrymen in the crimson trousers of the 11th Hussars, the Cherry Pickers; Scots Greys' Officers with chain mail on the shoulders of their blue uniform jackets; Highland Light Infantry subalterns in tartan trousers; and a few of us from the Dominions in our khaki bush jackets. Gossip had it that Madelaine Mansour had, before her marriage, helped her mother run a pension in Beirut. But whatever her origins, she had an elegance and an easy laughing charm which was the perfect antidote to the rough serge atmosphere of the barracks to which a grubby Cairo taxi took me back, under the huge stars of the black Egyptian night.

Egypt brought one further boon. We were now in regular touch with New Zealand by mail. The New Zealand Army Post Office was very efficient, and right up until the Japanese came into the war, and Singapore fell early in 1942 letters, parcels and telegrams moved smoothly between the Middle East and New Zealand. Cecily and our two boys were now living in a bungalow at Titirangi, just outside Auckland. Titirangi was in those days an area of native bush, not yet suburbanised, and brought her that rich consolation which New Zealand can bring, contact with superb natural beauty. We were able to keep in touch during the remaining months of 1941 more closely than at any time in my army service, for the mails could carry letters at length. When modern technology got into the act, and troops overseas corresponded by airgraph, letters became shorter and inevitably less intimate. It was difficult enough to write fully with the knowledge that a censor's eye might range across your private thoughts. For that reason I hated censoring the men's letters, and was thankful that officers could censor their own, with only the knowledge that some of them would be picked out for random censorship at the rear. But when to this was added the knowledge that what you wrote would pass through the hands of technicians, and would end up as a photocopy, five inches by four – the size of a snapshot – one's privacy felt further invaded.

This postal link mattered a great deal to those of us who were categorised as 'young marrieds', a relatively small group in these early echelons of the 2 NZEF, where many of the men were single, and where most of the married men were older and more senior, with grown-up children. Certainly to me the regularity of the postal services in 1941 was all important. It mattered little that the post could take three or four weeks to make its way along a raider-threatened Pacific steamship route. What was important was to see regularly the handwriting you looked for in the package of letters in the mail orderly's hand.

5. Greece

My period at Maadi was brief. On 6 April came news that the Germans had invaded Greece, and that the Division was in action. After church parade that morning I was summoned to the Adjutant's office and told I was to proceed at once to Divisional Headquarters in the mountains in Northern Greece. General Freyberg wanted a newspaper or a news service started for the New Zealand troops, to counter the rumours which were their only source of information about the world around them. It was not a task I relished. I had joined the Army to get away from journalism, not to practise it in uniform. But it offered the prospect of getting to where the action was, so I hurried away to pack my gear and draw a travel warrant to Alexandria, from where troopships sailed to Athens.

My journey to the front was to prove unexpectedly difficult. I was to spend much of the next three weeks trying to outwit an Army machine which seemed programmed to prevent me carrying out my orders to report to Divisional HQ. In the transit camp at Alexandria I found that my name was not on the list of officers due to board the next troopship for Athens. Somewhere along the line, the necessary instructions had not been given. I got aboard the ship only by arguing that the name of a Lieutenant Mocock on the embarkation list might be a jumble of two names, mine and that of a Highlander, Lieutenant Morrison, who was also awaiting orders. A reluctant Camp Adjutant agreed that Morrison and I might take our gear down to the dockside, and embark if our names were on the full list at the gangway. They were not, but Mocock's was, and to the officer controlling the embarkation I deployed the same argument. With a queue of impatient men waiting to board he let us on, with orders to disembark if a Lieutenant Mocock turned up.

And he did. Half an hour later a small, grey-haired officer with Ordnance Corps badges came into the cabin – Lieutenant Mocock in person. He was a Regular Army officer, a former NCO commissioned after many years' service, an expert in the repair of field guns – and enough of a seasoned old soldier to accept at once our pleas to keep quiet about what we had done. Morrison and I waited anxiously on deck as the ship prepared to sail. To our enormous relief, no commands came over the ship loud speakers calling for us, and we saw the embarkation officer and his military police move away down the quay as the gangway was hauled up. We had outwitted the system, and were on our way.

But on our way to what? As we waited in Alexandria harbour for the convoy to form up Winston Churchill's speech about the fighting in Greece came over the radio. One passage, in which he said that in war we had to take risks, struck at my optimism. It sounded only too clearly like a warning note to the British public that all was not going well. But no such doubts assailed the Australian officers who spread out their maps in the saloon of what had been a cruise liner, with an ornate painted ceiling, and reproductions of Fragonard paintings on the walls. They were studying the routes not only into Jugoslavia, but on into Austria.

The best boost to my morale came from Lieutenant Mocock. In this atmosphere of pre-battle tension and danger – for we were sailing on a route close to the Italian submarine bases on Rhodes – he was normality itself, proudly showing me photographs of his wife and two daughters and of his home in Farnham, with paths the concrete for which he had mixed himself. Dropping his 'Hs' and recovering them with a gulp, and with his face creasing into a smile of recollection, he talked of his family.

'My wife, before she had our first girl, suddenly made a go for peaches. We were stationed in South Africa then, and peaches were cheap there. Bless my soul, she'd buy a box of fifty at a time and they'd be gone in a couple of days.

'On the night when the first girl was born, I'd been up about four o'clock to open the window to chase the cat out of the room. It had got in when I was making her a cup of beef tea. She liked a cup of beef tea and toast in the night. I'd just got back to bed when she dug me in the ribs and said, "I think you had better fetch Mrs Hern now" – Mrs Hern lived up the road and was going with her to hospital.'

Perhaps Lieutenant Mocock too was feeling the strain, and this was his way, by thinking back to his family, of drawing on his inner strength. But it gave me a sense of trust in the future to see him, with his medal ribbons from the last war on his battledress jacket, calmly preparing to endure this new one.

By mid-morning on Saturday 12 April we were off the brown coast of Attica, with the buildings of Athens scattered over low hills. In their midst the Parthenon stood out, white and clear and glowing in the sun. I felt a sudden rush of fulfilment and pride at being in uniform, and a member of a fighting formation, when I caught my first sight of this symbol of democracy and freedom. No doubt it was a naive and over-simplified reaction, but it was one I felt deeply at the time. Perhaps everyone moving towards the front in war looks for symbols from which he can draw reassurance and courage. But in the face of this enduring symbol of human freedom I was glad I had turned soldier rather than remained an onlooker.

Olivia Manning, with the quiet perceptiveness which makes her *Balkan Trilogy* such a remarkable picture of those days, noted this difference between the soldier and the civilian. She saw the New Zealanders in Athens in 1941 as 'tall, sunburnt men who seemed to maintain their seriousness like a reserve of power'. Her heroine, Harriet, wondered what had brought these men to Europe from their remote, peaceful islands. 'What quarrel had they here? They seemed to her the most inoffensive of men. Why had they come all this way to die? She felt, as a civilian, her own liability in the presence of the fighting men who were kept in camps, like hounds trained for the kill. However close one came to them, they must remain separate.'[1]

Piraeus, the port of Athens, was a ruin of smashed quaysides and burnt out dock buildings. A week before a German bomb had hit a British ship carrying TNT, devastating at one blow this key supply port. We were ferried ashore in caiques, those high-prowed, sturdy Greek fishing boats which were to play such a key part in the evacuations which lay ahead. On the small quay where we were landed was a scene only too familiar to me, from Madrid and Finland, from Belgium and from France – refugees in flight. Men and women and some children, mostly well-dressed and middle-class, stood with their luggage waiting to get aboard the ship which had brought us. On their faces were the signs of fear I had learnt to observe during the fall of these other countries, the set faces,

[1] *Friends and Heroes*, by Olivia Manning Heinemann 1965 p. 254

the widened eyes – the eyeballs, it seems, can dilate with fear –
the sense of shame struggling with prudence. An unmistakable
stench of coming defeat was in the air.

The New Zealand base camp was in a dream spot, amid pine trees
by a blue bay looking across towards Salamis. It was on a
promontory at Voula, on the coast south of Piraeus. Today the area
is covered by tourist hotels, but then it was entirely one wide stretch
of pine forest, divided by narrow grassy roadways. I left my bedroll
there, and made my way back to Athens, to the Hotel Grande
Bretagne where, I guessed, the British correspondents would be
staying. Edward Ward of the BBC, alongside whom I had covered
the Russo-Finnish war and the fall of France was there, and we
drove up to the Acropolis and walked amongst its ruins, sharing our
knowledge and our impressions. From him I learnt that the collapse
of Jugoslavia had opened the way for the Germans to outflank the
Allied line on Mount Olympus and along the Aliakmon River in
Northern Greece, and that retreat towards a shorter line at
Thermopylae seemed inevitable.

In the spring sunshine the robust columns of the Parthenon were
honey-brown in the shade and sharply white in the sunshine, and
scarlet poppies grew amongst the white stone outcrop which covered
the top of the hill. We looked across to Mount Hymettus, studded
with pines, and to the snow-capped tops of the mountains beyond,
behind which, far to the north, the fighting was underway. In the
blue bay the white sails of caiques showed, where Greek sailors were
shooting at German mines in the shipping lanes. As we came down
the wide steps from the Parthenon sirens wailed in the city below,
and the guide who had attached himself to us took his departure
abruptly calling, 'Good luck gentlemen. No time for guides now. I
fought in the British Army in the last war and I hope you give the
bastards lots of hell. Lots of hell – you understand, yes?'

Some eight hundred New Zealand troops, reinforcements for the
units already in action, were in our camp under the umbrella pines.
I found myself trapped there, as I had been in the transit camp in
Alexandria, because no orders had reached the camp that I should
go on to Divisional Headquarters. All armies work, very sensibly,
on the principle that reinforcements are sent forward only when
commanders at the front call for them. They alone know what
casualties they have suffered, what gaps in their ranks need to
be filled, what special skills they require. The commander of
the Reinforcement Camp, a former Territorial major from

Christchurch, was deaf to my pleas that mine was a special case, that orders for me to go forward had come from the General himself.

Day after day passed without any order arriving for me to go forward. I sunbathed, swam in the cool, clean sea, watched the German dive bombers come up over the pale blue islands of the Ionian Sea and swoop down, glittering specks in a deeper blue sky, to drop their bombs on Piraeus. I spent my nights on anti-parachute patrols on the nearby airfield which is now the Athens International Airport. We shared the patrols with members of the Greek Home Guard, some of them grizzled veterans of the pre-1914 Balkan Wars, armed with the same old carbines they had used against the Turks and the Bulgars. Each day the radio carried news of hard fighting, and of withdrawals in the mountains to the north, and each day I became more and more determined to find a way forward to the division. But all contact had been lost between the Division in the field and its rear echelons in Athens since the retreat from the Olympus-Aliakmon line had begun.

In Athens there was a New Zealand Army liaison office, set up to co-ordinate the Division's activities with the Greeks and the British Embassy. I was on my way there one afternoon when crowds started to gather in the streets, and newsboys ran through selling special editions of the papers. The Greek Prime Minister, M. Koryzis, had died – he had, it became known later, committed suicide. There was talk of surrender. Shouts rose from the crowds, the blue and white flag of Greece was raised. A dark-haired, beautiful girl, her eyes ablaze, seized me by the arm and said, 'We are being betrayed. You British must stop the Generals betraying us', and I found myself suddenly surrounded by a cheering throng shouting support for Britain. It was clear the whole campaign, the whole Greek venture, was foundering.

On Sunday, eight days after I had reached Athens, I was in the Liaison Officer's office in the city when a weary young officer in dust-stained battledress arrived. As chance would have it, he was from my home town of Invercargill. He was called Bill Good, and we had played rugby for the same team. The Division, he told us, was already back at Thermopylae, badly shaken up by constant bombing. He had brought back messages from General Freyberg, to be relayed to Maadi, and was due to drive back to Divisional Headquarters that evening. Would he take me with him? Certainly, if I wished. He was coming out to our camp at seven o'clock that evening to pick up another passenger, an army doctor. If I could clear the formalities, he would take me.

But I could not clear the formalities. The Camp Commandant not only refused to authorise my going forward without orders having reached him from the front, but burst out in anger at my having made contact with Good without his authority. But I decided that, come what may, this was a chance I would not miss. Our tents were widely scattered amidst the pines. I could pack my gear, and get it aboard Good's car without attracting attention. This I did in the dusk. But to get out of the camp, we had to pass a wooden lodge which served as camp headquarters. At my urging Good swept past that at speed – but not fast enough to prevent my being seen. My last glimpse of the camp was of the Commandant and his Adjutant, their faces furious, standing by the roadside watching us go.

We drove for seven hours, on winding mountain roads, with Good warning us of what lay ahead. 'The planes are the trouble,' he said. 'They are over us all the time, bombing and machine gunning anything or anyone who moves. It's a nightmare.'

At last, in the early hours, a storm lantern set inside an empty, black-painted petrol tin, showed up a sign by the roadside, '2 NZ'. A sentry in a greatcoat gave me a sardonic welcome. 'You've come the wrong way, mate. We're getting out.' I spread out my bed-roll under a nearby olive tree, crushed herbs scenting the grass around me, and slept.

I woke to find that the olive grove was in a narrow coastal strip between mountains and the coastline, with the big island of Euboea to the east. I reported to the Chief of Staff, Colonel Keith Stewart. He gave me the reception I had expected. 'You've taken a bloody long time getting here,' he said. 'And there's no time now for running newspapers' – an idea with which, his tone implied, he had little sympathy anyway. I explained that I could speak German. 'Can you indeed?' he queried. 'Then get over to Lieutenant Bell. There's a German prisoner just been brought in. See what you can get out of him.'

Lieutenant Robin Bell was the Intelligence Officer of the Division, a quiet, courteous former sheep farmer to whom I took an immediate liking. The prisoner was a young motor-cyclist who had been riding pillion with another German when they had overshot the front line, and run into our forward positions. His colleague had been killed, and blood from his wound had stained the uniform of the boy – for he was not much more – whom I questioned. His pocket book was full of photographs of girls, whilst the pocket book of the dead man held photographs of his wife, and of a small boy about the age of my own son.

I felt instinctively sympathetic towards this exhausted youth, but the moment he sensed that his tone changed, and he became surly and hostile, very much the young former Storm Trooper – his pay book showed he had served four years in the SA. So I changed my manner too, and grilled him hard. I had learnt in that moment one lesson about war – that we were now first and foremost soldiers, not humanitarians, and that the enemy were first and foremost the enemy. The only fact of significance which emerged from my probing was that his unit had not expected us to stand at Thermopylae, but had thought we were in full flight towards Athens.

In mid-morning I was summoned to General Freyberg. It was the first time I had seen this man whom I was to spend a great part of the war serving, and who was certainly to be the best boss I ever had. From his World War I record, with his VC won in the bloodiest of trench fighting, and with his aggressiveness driving him on to thrust ahead and seize a key bridge just before the cease fire sounded in 1918, I had expected to find a hardened, indeed coarsened, red-faced figure, an exaggerated version of the burly assertive men, red tabs prominent on their uniforms, who had inspected us as cadets and as Territorials back in New Zealand. But my first impression of the big figure, seated behind a trestle table in a tent – the Greek campaign was to be the last in which command in the field was exercised from tents – was of a huge boy scout. Perhaps his khaki shirt and khaki tie, worn under a battle dress jacket open at the neck, and the boy scout style New Zealand hat on the table beside him, contributed to this. His powerful frame seemed to fill the tent, but his face, with wide-set eyes which studied me sharply, had something boyish about it, alert as well as strong with a hint of humour, even of mischievousness in its lines. It was also the face of a man of keen intelligence. The idea of a newspaper for the troops was still clearly alive in his mind. He told me, 'But this is not yet the time. That will come later. Now get back to your interrogating.' I did so thankfully, for it was much more the kind of thing I had joined the Army to do.

The British position at Thermopylae – one corps against nine German divisions – was untenable. On my third night at Divisional Headquarters we were on the move again, travelling back over the roads I had traversed with Bill Good, in a long convoy of vehicles edging forward in the darkness, as overhead huge fleets of German bombers seemed to shake the sky as they moved on to bomb

Piraeus and other possible embarkation ports. Just before daybreak
we were in the outskirts of Athens, bound for the small port of Porto
Rafti, south of Marathon on the east coast. I had come to know my
way round central Athens during my eight days there, and so I was
given the task of guiding the column through the city streets.

Dawn was just breaking when, to my immense relief, I found the
road sign to 'Marathon', close to the Parliament buildings and
watched for the first time a sight with which we were all soon to
become familiar, that of the grey-green camouflaged vehicles of the
Division on the move. Trucks full of troops, some asleep, some
peering from the backs of their vehicles at the deserted city streets,
moved past, to add our mite to the history of this fabled road.

All that day, Thursday 24 April, we hid amongst the low hills
overlooking the small harbour of Porto Rafti. When I went back
there twenty-five years later, I found that memory had played
a curious trick on me. My recollection had been of a steep hill,
almost a cliff, dropping to a small stone jetty. But no such steep
place exists at Porto Rafti, only a gently sloping hill down which we
filed in the dark, to take our place in the landing craft which ferried
us out to the assault ship, the *Glengyle*.

Towards midday Crete came into view, white mountains on a
blue skyline, arousing thoughts that this must have been how the
migrating Maoris first saw New Zealand from their canoes, as
Aotearoa, the Land of the Long White Cloud, or as Tasman first
saw it, a land 'uplifted high'. And so on the afternoon of Anzac Day
we came into Suda Bay.

6. The Road to Maleme

The next day, 26 April, Hargest was given orders to deploy the 5th
Brigade to defend Maleme airfield, and the area between it and
Canea, the main town the western area of the island. Maleme, ten
miles west of Canea, had an unfinished runway close to the sea
which the RAF used as a base – if used is the word for occasional
flights by a handful of out-of-date machines. But it would be a key
target for any German invasion, as it was closer to the Greek
mainland than the more fully developed airfield at Heraklion, the

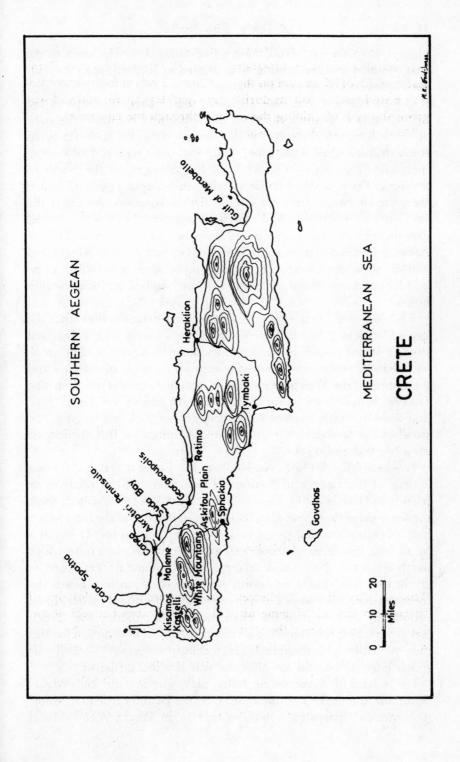

SOUTHERN AEGEAN

Gulf of Merabello

Heraklion

MEDITERRANEAN SEA

CRETE

Tymbaki

Retimo

Georgeopolis

Askifou Plain

Sphakia

Gavdhos

Suda Bay

Akrotiri Peninsula

Canea

White Mountains

Maleme

Kisamos
Kastelli

Cape Spatha

0   10   20
Miles

biggest town on the island, ninety-five miles along the coast to the east. A third smaller landing strip existed at Retimo, roughly midway between Canea and Heraklion.

Whilst Hargest and his staff made their plans, the units of the brigade sorted themselves out in the temporary camps at the back of Suda Bay. All through the day troops straggled into our area, some drunk on the local wine, some just dead weary. Old Cretan men and boys brought sackfuls of big oranges on the backs of donkeys. From a stone house nearby we brought eggs and boiled them in an empty fruit tin over a fire of bamboo. Amongst the survivors were shipwrecked merchant seamen. Their white-haired captain told me that his ship had been one of a convoy sailing for Athens. The coded message telling them to turn back to Alexandria had, by some clerk's error, not included the name of his ship. Alone he had had to continue on his way, to be bombed and sunk within hours.

The next day I was set the task of reconnoitering routes from the assembly areas towards Maleme. Seeking a way towards the coast road, I found myself in the hilltop village of Karatsos. The small square in its centre was deserted except for a couple of old men and a corporal of the Welch Regiment, a regular battalion of which, the 1st Welch, had been guarding this western end of the island. Spic and span in neatly pressed khaki drill and pipe-clayed leggings, he stood at the doorway of a storehouse listening to a BBC broadcast on a big box radio set.

It was a talk by Philip Noel-Baker, the Labour MP and fervent apostle of the League of Nations. Those who had lost relatives or friends in Greece could draw comfort, Noel-Baker suggested, from the knowledge that these men had fallen in defence of the land which had given birth to the democracy we were fighting for. It jarred a bit to hear this from someone well away from this place onto which death from the skies could descend at any moment. Yet I had to admit that Noel-Baker was doing no more than put into words the feelings which had swept through me when, a fortnight earlier, I had caught my first sight of the Parthenon in the midday sun. Noel-Baker was, as it happened, to attract a good deal of criticism for this talk by critics who thought it 'high falutin nonsense' – and was much hurt, as he told me after the war, by this criticism.

I was back in Karatsos an hour later, guiding the 28th Maori Battalion, under their commander Colonel Dittmer, the first Maori to command troops in a modern war – in World War I Maori troops were always under white officers. The Maoris kept up such a rapid pace that I was hard put to keep up with them, and was thankful when Dittmer called a halt, and I could rest by the roadside and exchange memories with a young platoon commander about similar white dusty roads in the pumice country around Taupo. Then it was back to the road along the wide valley at the foot of the mountains, where the grey walls of a prison showed up incongruously amidst vineyards and cornfields, to guide the 21st Auckland Battalion to their place south of Maleme. From under the prison walls a line of boyish Italian prisoners of war stared at us as we trudged by. There were as well civilian prisoners in the gaol. Signing themselves 'The convicts of the Island of Crete' they petitioned Freyberg to be allowed to 'do our little bit in winning this sacred struggle'.

On a ridge between the prison valley and the sea was a hilltop village called Galatas which was soon, by the handiwork of battle, to be one part of Crete whose fate became closely interwoven with that of our distant land. In the evening the Divisional Cavalry moved up the winding dusty road to take up position beyond Galatas. They had lost the Bren carriers which, in this modernised war, had served them as horses, and were to fight now as infantry. They were mostly farmers, brown-faced, weather-beaten men, sinewy and fit, with at their head the huge figure of their commander, Major John Russell. Had the 2nd New Zealand Division run to an élite force, the Divisional Cavalry would have been a candidate for that title. But it was to be one of the great strengths of the Division that no part of it was ever thought of as an élite. Every unit, even those engaged in what are often seen as the less glamorous activities of soldiering, such as supply and ordinance, saw itself as something special, taking pride in its efficiency and its esprit de corps, in its own swiftly developed traditions, its own *mana*, to use the very appropriate Maori word. Yet the qualities which were to give the Division its own special character were never better embodied than in these vigorous and responsible cavalrymen who strode along this white road amidst the olive groves in that gathering April dusk.

The main route to Maleme was the coast road. Along it for the next two days moved a constant stream of troops, some marching in formation, others straggling out, exhausted or footsore, or recovering from the effects of the local red wine which they had got hold of in miraculously short time. At the crossroads where a side road ran up to the hilltop village of Galatas nurses from a nearby tented hospital cheered and waved at the men as they went by. The young military policeman in charge of the crossroads pushed back his steel helmet when he saw me, and came across, hand out-stretched. It was the boy I had had to put on a charge on the wet deck of Belfast four months earlier. He greeted me like an old friend, and poured out a tale of perilous times in Greece, where he had had the task of directing traffic at much bombed crossroads. There was no trace of resentment for how I had treated him, only a desire to share a new found confidence in himself. We shared a common delight at being alive on that spring morning and then, remembering our ranks, formally saluted each other and went about our business.

Another rendezvous with my recent past awaited me further along the road. In the back of a truck heading for Suda Bay were Edward Ward and Alex Clifford of the *Daily Mail* and David Woodward of the *News Chronicle*. They were on their way to take a ship back to Alexandria, leaving, as it happened, Crete as the one key campaign of the war not covered by any accredited British war correspondents other than Robin Miller, a young Auckland journalist attached to the 2nd New Zealand Division.

Later that day I had my first sight of Maleme airfield, soon to play such a huge part in our fate. It was little more than a wide landing strip, lying close to the sandy beach at a point where the stony bed of the now dried-up Tavronitis River widened out to meet the sea. Under pines by the roadside was an RAF camp of a few brown tents. Dense thickets of bamboos – an unexpected plant in this island – and olive trees and lines of vines, thick now with leaf – hid much of the airfield from the road. Only the Bofors guns, terribly prominent in their sandbagged positions, marked the perimeter of the field. The dusty road curved round the southern edge of the RAF camp, past Hill 107, a key feature which overlooked the airfield, and on to a big iron-girdered bridge on concrete piles straddling the stony riverbed of the Tavronitis. Westward of the airfield low hills, covered with olive groves, rose gradually, merging into the more abrupt mountains of a long peninsula thrust like a forefinger northwards towards Greece, providing a sure guide to the route to Maleme for invading aircraft.

Five miles on the Canea side of Maleme, in the coastal village of Platanias, Divisional Headquarters had been set up in a grove of wind-twisted olive trees. At the crossroads in the middle of the village the mayor and his daughter had set out a table with brown bread and white goat's cheese and some jars of wine. Half a dozen officers stood by it, drinking the harsh red wine from small, thick glasses. Their men were resting in the roadside ditches, or packing the wineshop, shouting for omelettes and arguing and drinking the red wine and the sharp, powerful local brandy. Many had their battledress stained or torn, and their small-featured, dark, quizzical New Zealand faces were drawn and thin under the dust and sunburn. Almost all had their Brens and rifles, but only a few had steel helmets, and fewer still had their packs or any personal gear. But you could still see that these were good fighting soldiers. When the officers downed glasses and called on their platoons they formed up by the roadside and moved off at a steady pace, though the weariness of three weeks of fighting and bombardment and retreat was right through to their bones.

By the village well four women watched them go. Two of the women had been drawing water into old rusty benzine tins, but two others had big double handed earthenware jars unchanged in type since ancient Greece. They carried these easily on one shoulder, their strong round breasts thrust out, and their heads dark and erect with the easy dignity of the Caryatids of the Acropolis. They put down their jars to watch another platoon come round the bend of the coast road. It was clearly a good platoon, for it was marching well, and several of the men were whistling. As they tramped in they filled the already excited atmosphere of the village with that electric quality which marching men always seem to arouse. It seemed to be reflected back from the white cottage walls and in the eager eyes of the women at the well. Their lips parted, smiling, and one clapped her hands.

Then I noticed a fifth woman, standing apart. She held a child, a big child, almost too heavy to carry, and her eyes were red and smeared with weeping, and tears were thick on her cheeks, as she stood staring at the marching men. I asked the mayor's daughter, who spoke some French, why this woman wept. She answered almost angrily, 'Her husband and her brothers are away, as soldiers on the mainland. She has not heard of them for weeks. They were fighting in Albania, and are surely prisoners.'

As the troops swung by, they smiled and waved to the women by the well, and the four drawing water waved back. But the woman with child in her arms was silent, and still weeping, as the column strode out towards Maleme. Her face remained sharply etched in my mind. I thought of it later, when the battle was over, and wondered if she had sensed more clearly than we did what lay ahead for these men on the road to Maleme that spring morning.

7. Awaiting Attack

On Tuesday 29 April General Freyberg reached Crete after supervising the final evacuation of Greece. The next morning Robin Bell and I were ordered to make preparations for a conference of senior commanders in a large brick villa on the seashore near Ay Marina. The villa had a big rooftop balcony, covered by an awning looking out onto the sweep of a sandy bay, a place for holidays rather than for war.

On a wooden table we set out the few maps of Crete which were available. General Freyberg and other senior officers were studying them when just before midday a staff car arrived from Maleme airfield. From it stepped the brisk, neatly uniformed figure of General Wavell, who had flown in from Cairo.

When the conference broke up two hours later we learnt that Wavell had appointed Freyberg commander of all British and Greek troops on the island. His orders were to hold it at all costs against any German invasion. Freyberg was the seventh man to be given command of Crete within a period of six months, a striking sign of the low priority which had been attached to this island which had seemed well away from any danger. Now it was the new front line, barring Hitler's progress towards Suez and the oil fields of the Persian Gulf.

Freyberg moved that afternoon into Battle Headquarters which had been prepared for Creforce in a quarry on a hillside above Canea. The task which faced him was unique in the annals of war – to give battle against an airborne invasion. Though the Germans had used paratroops to seize airfields and bridges in Holland and Belgium in the offensive of 10 May 1940 and though glider troops had landed on top of the seemingly impregnable Belgian fortress of Eban Emael, and had knocked it out, these had been subsidiary operations to the main German advance by land. But in the attack

on Crete the airborne parachutists and glider troops were to
constitute the main force. They were to seize airfields to enable
further troops, chiefly from the crack 5th Mountain Division, to be
brought in by transport aircraft. Though there would also be a
seaborne invasion, this was subsidiary to the main attack from the
air, intended mainly to bring in the heavier weapons like artillery
and tanks. Not even in the plans for the invasion of Britain had the
highly trained German airborne troops been allocated anything but
a marginal role. It was in Crete that this new weapon, which was
Hitler's particular pride, was for the first time to be put to full use.
If it succeeded, it would not only bring the Germans the immediate
prize of Crete. It would also open the way for a comparable attack
on an even more valuable island target, that of Malta, the thorn in
the side of the Italian and German forces in North Africa, a constant
threat to Rommel's lines.

Remarkably full information about these German plans was
flowing day and night onto the desks of the Chiefs of Staff and the
Prime Minister in London. It came, as we now know, in the form
of Ultra material resulting from the success of British Intelligence in
intercepting and cracking the codes of messages sent out through the
German Enigma machines. These had an encoding mechanism
which, to the war's end, the Germans believed to be proof against
any code breaker. At the end of the conference in the Ay Marina
villa Wavell had taken Freyberg aside and had told him that
information from a highly secret source would be supplied to him.
It was so secret that it would be relayed to Crete through a special
officer (probably, it seems, someone on the staff of the RAF
commander on the island, Group Captain Beamish). Freyberg was
not to disclose to anyone that he was receiving this information, and
once he had studied it, he was to destroy any message immediately.
Wavell gave Freyberg no indication of the origin of these Ultra
messages, and indeed until late in the war Freyberg believed them
to have come from a British spy planted right in the German
General Staff.

The German Air Force, grappling with Hitler's demand for the
invasion of Crete to be mounted without delay, were prodigal with
their wireless traffic, providing the British code breakers at Bletchley
Park in Hertfordshire with an abundant flow of information. From
this it became clear that airborne attack would be launched against
the airfields of Heraklion and Maleme, and the airstrip at Retimo.
Some 22,750 German troops were available for the attack, to be

carried in 500 transport planes and 70 to 80 gliders. Supporting these would be the overwhelming fire power of more than 600 bombers and fighter planes, who could be sure of sweeping from the sky the tiny handful of British fighters on the island, and be able to operate with impunity as close support for the troops on the ground. Small merchant ships and fishing vessels would bring in the reinforcements of men and weapons to the Canea and Heraklion areas.

To oppose this formidable and superbly equipped enemy, Freyberg could count on some 30,000 British, Australian and New Zealand troops, and about 12,000 Greek soldiers and police. But these numbers were deceptive, for they were woefully ill-armed and ill-equipped. More than half of them – 9,000 New Zealanders, a comparable number of Australians and some five hundred men from the Rifle Corps and the Northumberland Hussars – had all been evacuated from Greece, where all their heavy weapons had been abandoned. Some units had only their rifles. The most basic items of equipment such as trucks, entrenching tools, even cooking utensils were lacking. The only properly equipped formations were the three British Regular battalions which were on the island when the evacuation from Greece began – the 1st Royal Welch, the 2nd Yorks and Lancs, and the 2nd Black Watch. Another Regular battalion, the 2nd Leicester, was to be added before the attack came. Guarding Suda Bay were 2,000 Royal Marines, yet key items of their equipment, like Bren carriers and wireless sets, had to be shared around the Australians and New Zealanders, so that no formation on Crete had anything like its proper complement of arms and equipment. Nor could these deficiencies be made up from Egypt. Constant German bombing of Suda Bay and Heraklion reduced supplies to a trickle. Only six heavy I tanks – the formidable Valentines which had smashed their way into Bardia and Tobruk – reached Crete, enabling Freyberg to station two each at Heraklion, Retimo and Maleme, but these proved to be in poor mechanical condition and, in at least one instance, to have the wrong type of ammunition. The dozen or so light tanks which were landed were, in the words of their commander, 'battered ancient hulks' worn out by use in the Western Desert.

Of the forty-nine field guns brought in, many were captured Italian weapons, some lacking key parts. At Maleme New Zealand gunners devised gun sights from chewing gum and pieces of wood. In the olive groves near Suda were thousands of surplus troops, 'gunners without guns, drivers without vehicles and signallers without the apparatus for signalling'[1], clerks and storemen and lines of communication troops, many without even rifles. The Greek forces were even worse equipped. The 2nd Greek Regiment could list a strength of 930 officers and men, but added 'only 500 rifles'. Even those who had weapons were desperately short of ammunition.

Even more significant was the German command of the air. The handful of RAF fighters at Maleme were to fight one gallant battle against the Messerschmitts of the Luftwaffe in the week before the invasion, but it was an isolated action. Throughout the weeks leading up to the attack, as well as during the battle itself the Luftwaffe exercised complete control of the air. From our first days on the island we had always to be on guard against a sudden raiding fighter, or a reconnaissance plane pin-pointing future targets, or swiftly mounted bombing attacks, part of the onslaught which was to rise to a crescendo as the invasion day approached. When battle was joined, more fire power was to be directed onto troops on the ground than had ever before come in air attack, more intense of its kind than most Allied troops were ever to experience. On fresh troops these pressures would have been formidable. But the troops evacuated from Greece were to a considerable degree in a state of shock from their first and unexpected exposure to attack from enemy planes.

The degree to which the nerves of the men of the Division had been worn raw by air attack surprised me when I finally caught up with Div HQ at Thermopylae. In Belgium and France the previous year, and in Finland, and above all in Spain during Franco's attack on Madrid I had come to regard the sky as an area of constant danger, had grown accustomed to keeping a wary eye overhead wherever you walked or drove, or to watching out for a good ditch or cellar into which to dive should enemy aircraft suddenly loom out of the unseen. But I had been a civilian, in a war zone to observe, not to fight. I had not expected trained and disciplined troops, twenty months after the Nazis had, in Poland, revealed fully the dread weapon of the dive bomber, to have been surprised and shocked when it was turned against them. For these were brave men, some of whom had already manifested their courage in fighting on the ground, hundreds of whom over the months and years ahead were to win decorations for bravery, and hundreds of

[1] *The Struggle for Crete* by I. McD. G. Stewart, Oxford University Press 1966 p 53.

others to merit them. Yet at this this stage many of them seemed to be constantly on edge, staring anxiously skywards, and seeking cover at the first sound of an aircraft engine. They showed the shock of coming up against for the first time an enemy who had complete command of the air, who could seek out and destroy them from the sky, in a form of attack against which they found they had virtually no defence.

The truth is that the New Zealand troops in Greece, like virtually all the British forces there, had been put into battle unprepared for this extra dimension of attack from the air, the dimension which had been added to warfare since World War I. Despite all the evidence provided, with that in Poland reinforced by what had happened along the roads of France during the Reichswehr's thrust to the Channel in May 1940, British training and British equipment had not been modified to counter this deadly technique. In 168 OCTU the method prescribed to deal with air attack could, at best, have been of only partial value against slow moving aircraft of the type employed in World War I. We were taught, when marching along a road, to be prepared, on hearing the warning 'Aircraft Right' or 'Aircraft Left' to move to the verge of the road, one file to one side, the other two files to the other, raise our rifles, and provide an arc of fire above the road designed to deter, or, with luck, hit a plane swooping down on us.

What the War Office training experts did not seem to have taken aboard was that in modern conditions few troops marched to battle, except over the final few miles. They were much more likely to be in trucks. Yet no drill had been devised for firing back from trucks, other than the equipping of the small fifteen hundredweight trucks with a tripod, rather like that used for a movie camera, onto which you were supposed to clip the Bren gun, to fire at the plane. But a Bren gun, with a magazine which held only twenty-eight rounds, offered far too limited and too slow a rate of fire to deal with a fighter plane moving at three hundred miles an hour. In practice, the New Zealanders in Greece rapidly adopted for themselves the tactic which events had taught troops in Spain and Poland and Finland and on the Western front, which was to scatter away from their trucks, and away from the roadside, lying down to present as small a target as possible. Only the very brave or the very rash ever manned a Bren gun on its tripod, which presented an obvious and wide open target to a strafing plane. One of the few who did was Quentin Hogg who, as an officer with the Rifle Brigade in the desert, did just that – and got a bullet through his knee for his pains.

The theory of creating a cone of fire above a convoy of vehicles was a sound one, but it needed more powerful weapons, with a much higher rate of fire, than rifles or Brens. The Germans provided their troops with light anti-aircraft guns and heavy machine guns on special, skywards-pointing mounts for this purpose. In Finland in 1939 I had seen captured Red Army trucks fitted with quadruple banks of heavy machine guns for anti-aircraft work. Yet in our desert training at Maadi, the week before I had set out for Greece, we had been practising the same 'Aircraft Left. Aircraft Right' drill, a process which, in open desert would have been suicidal. The troops who went to Greece found themselves therefore dealing with a form of attack not only outside their experience, but outside their training. It is no wonder that their nerves became ragged under it.

The ironical humour of the Division was soon invoked to offset the strain. The senior chaplain, a bishop in real life, recounted how his driver had protested at his habit of stopping near heavily bombed crossroads to comfort the wounded. 'It's all right for you, sir,' the driver had declared. 'You've got everything jacked up up there if you get killed. But I have to take my chance with the rest.'

Experience proved the best cure to these aircraft nerves. In the fighting which was to follow on Crete the frontline units, held together by discipline and comradeship, and the supply and medical services, busy with their own tasks, came to endure bombing and strafing with remarkable resilience.

8. Before the Storm

Before he could get to grips with planning the defence of the island, General Freyberg had to deal with a more immediate problem. Though he had been left with the physical structure of a headquarters, in the line of dugouts in the quarry above Canea, he had no headquarters staff. His predecessor, General Weston, took his staff with him when he moved to his new, subordinate command of the forces around Suda Bay. Freyberg had to build a staff from scratch, from the men of different formations and indeed of different

armies, brought together largely by chance. It was a fact which
rankled in his mind in later years, and to which I often heard him
refer when Crete was discussed. 'There weren't even clerks or
signallers – only an officers' mess,' he would comment with a rare
bitterness.

He turned to the 2nd New Zealand Division for his Chief of Staff,
taking with him Colonel Keith Stewart. Robin Bell went off to be
one of the Creforce Intelligence Officers. Brigadier Puttick, who had
been commander of 4th Brigade, took over as commander of the
Division, his place with the 4th being taken by Brigadier Inglis, who
was flown in from Egypt, as was the General's PA, Lieutenant
White.

Divisional Headquarters moved back to Galatas. There, in
weather which miraculously remained fine, we slept under olive
trees on the eastern edge of the village, and worked in roofed over
dugouts prepared by the Welch Regiment, which had now been
withdrawn into reserve near Canea. I was given the task of assisting
the senior quartermaster, a former schoolmaster, punctilious and
kindly man, in the task of getting blankets and food, replacement
uniforms and steel helmets, and cooking utensils to the troops.
Many men at first were eating and drinking from bully beef or
cigarette tins. The round tins which contained fifty Player cigarettes
were in high demand, as they made excellent cups.

It was essential work, but I fretted at this staff role, and appealed
to Colonel Gentry, the precise, bespectacled, cheerful New Zealand
Regular officer, who had become Chief of Staff to Puttick, to send
me to a battalion as a platoon commander. The same instinct which
had driven me to get aboard the boat for Greece, and to get to the
front from the reinforcements camp, now impelled me to get
forward to a unit in the field. I wanted to share the strength and
comradeship which I had tasted in those early days in the 23rd
Battalion, and when I had had a platoon of my own in the 29th. But
above all I wanted to gain experience of fighting as soon as I could,
partly to test myself in action, but above all to learn the craft of
fighting in the only way one can, by fighting, since that was the craft
I had volunteered for. I felt like someone waiting to plunge into a
cold river. It was better to get it over and done with than to stand
uneasily on the edge. But there were no vacancies for platoon
commanders, so my pleas came to nothing.

Puttick, promoted now to the temporary rank of general, was a
veteran of the first war, in which he had risen to command a

battalion whilst still in his twenties. He was now almost fifty-one years old, and was a talkative man apt to fuss over trifles. He had plenty of courage and knew his trade. But he was to show little initiative in the battle ahead, and Freyberg was no doubt thankful when Puttick was recalled to New Zealand later in the summer to take on the post there of Chief of Staff.

Another Regular Officer, Lieutenant-Colonel Andrew, had command of the 22nd Battalion, to which had been entrusted the key task of defending Maleme airfield. Andrew was also a veteran of World War I, who had won the Victoria Cross in France. He was a thick-set, reserved man of forty-one, whose deep set eyes, greying hair brushed straight back and a black moustache gave him a fine soldierly bearing.

Equally reserved – at any rate on first acquaintance – was Colonel Howard Kippenberger, who commanded a mixed force of Greeks and New Zealanders holding the hills around Galatas. Kippenberger had led the 20th Battalion in Greece, and had begun already to arouse a remarkable affection as well as admiration among the troops, something which extended beyond those in his own immediate command. I first encountered him, riding with a group of troops in a truck from which I begged a lift, as I went my rounds as a supply officer. He was a quiet, lean figure, in no way assertive in manner, but carrying, even in this dusty crowded vehicle, unmistakable authority, and I phrased my replies with particular care to the questions he put to me.

Those early days of May 1941 in Crete were an interval of beauty and calm, when the stars at night showed large and companionable beyond the dark olive branches, and dawn revealed men in their grey blankets sleeping at the foot of the twisted tree trunks, or beside the heaped earth of their slit trenches. In the afternoon we marched down to the coast, near to the big brown tents of the hospital, to bathe from a white sandy beach. In Galatas the women walked proudly from the well carrying their jars of water, and older men – the young men had all been mobilised – stalked the streets with fierce, upturned grey moustaches, wearing as their ordinary garb the costume in which their forefathers had fought the Turks, with close-fitting knee-boots of soft leather, and baggy trousers and wide sashes at the waist.

The Galatas wineshop had on its walls gaudy posters of the fighting in Albania, with hundreds of Greek and British planes attacking, and Italian troops panicking by rivers deep in mountain gorges. Another, very well drawn, showed women carrying packs of ammunition up a mountain side. The Greek resistance against the might of Italy in Albania had evolved its own symbol – as all great events will – in the worn boots of the mountain troops. These were of yellow unstained leather, with the top four or five holes unlaced, and the laces tied half way down. Tiny copies of these in leather were on sale, and you could buy tiny metal and cloth badges showing a pair of these boots.

In the evenings each family came to its windows, or its doorstep, or strolled in the narrow street, the women keeping carefully shy and apart from the soldiers who prowled the streets, eyeing the dark-haired girls. For all the sense of dangers to come, this was a good time. I was fitter than perhaps at any other period in my adult life, and had an added sense of thankfulness at being here in Crete, for the Reinforcements Battalion with whom I had lived under the pine trees outside Athens had been cut off in the evacuation. Despite a gallant bayonet attack, in which Sergeant Hinton won New Zealand's first VC of the war, most of them had been taken prisoner.

One of the few jarring notes came one evening when a man rushed into the operations room, where I was duty officer, saying, 'Officer, officer, a woman is shot.' On the upper room of the shoemaker's house, a room reached by a ladder, a young woman lay yellow-faced on her bed, with black blood seeping on to the floor in the lamp light, watched by a little girl who sat, with huge staring eyes, upright in another bed. We put my field dressing on the woman's wound. She had been shot by a bullet fired through the ceiling from the floor below by a drunken young New Zealand private who had been firing his rifle by mistake.

The woman kept moaning 'Georg, Georg' as the local doctor administered the only medicine he had, an injection of camphor and water, that cure-all so beloved of Mediterranean doctors of the time. We got her in a truck to the military hospital, and put the soldier, a mere boy with a weak, foolish face, under guard. All the time he protested drunkenly about how brave he had been in Greece. He went off next day to the punishment squad to be worked hard and drilled hard until the attack came – in which the squad fought magnificently. Against a background in which the highly planned killing of thousands was about to erupt this wounding (for the woman survived) of a civilian seemed all the more poignant and unnecessary.

9. The Crete News

On 5 May I was told that I was to report to 5th Brigade Headquarters. Hargest had asked for me to be appointed his Intelligence
Officer. Though I would still have preferred to have been with a
platoon, this promised to be a fascinating job at the heart of the
action. I quickly assembled my kit, which consisted for the most part
only of my sleeping bag and a heavy overcoat tailored for me by
Halls of Oxford. But before the truck from 5th Brigade arrived to
collect me, I was told there had been a change of plan. An order had
come from Force Headquarters that I was to report there instead,
to organise a newspaper for the troops on Crete. It was a bitter
disappointment, and I set off cursing the way in which I seemed to
be perpetually entangled in my newspaper past.

The small quarry in which Force Headquarters were placed was
on a hillside above Canea, where the road wound up from the town
on to the slopes of the high Akrotiri peninsula, which formed the
northern shore of Suda Bay. The headquarters consisted of a line of
dugouts built of stone and set against the rear wall of the quarry with
a low rampart in front. The stone gave them a natural camouflage
which completely deceived the German reconnaissance planes, so
that these headquarters were never bombed at any time during the
campaign. Olive trees nearby provided cover for vehicles, and for
signallers and other supporting troops.

Here I reported to Colonel Blunt, a British Army officer who had
been Military Attaché in Athens, and now combined supervision of
Freyberg's intelligence staff at Creforce with liaison with the Greek
King and his Government, who were installed in villas near Canea.

Blunt took me to General Freyberg's dugout. Seated behind a
plain wooden table which took up half of the cramped space, the
General seemed even bigger than in his tent at Thermopylae. His
orders were brief and clear. 'I want a newspaper to be produced for
the troops that looks like the papers the men read at home.' And he
wanted it quickly. The first number should appear in a week's time
at the latest.

To help me, Blunt offered the services of a Greek journalist, a refugee from Athens, Georges Zamaryas. I found him, a harried young man in a blue suit, seated in a small cafe by the quayside in Canea. Tatty and meagre though its modern surroundings were, Canea harbour that spring afternoon retained much of the dignity and beauty which its Venetian builders had given it. It was small, enclosed by a breakwater of great blocks of stone, with an elegant small lighthouse, and fine yellow stone Venetian buildings rising against low cliffs. Half a dozen Australians were playing pitch and toss at the entrance to a narrow alleyway, with one of them posted as a sentry to give warning of the approach of Military Police. At a table in the grubby corner café a girl in a purple sateen dress and vivid red lipstick watched warily. No doubt she came from what our own Provost Marshal had, in a report on Canea, described as the town's thirty-seven brothels, 'thirty-six of them owner-driven'.

Georges Zamaryas took me off to the printing press of the local evening newspaper, which was in a cavern-like basement room in a street behind the port. The proprietor agreed to print our paper once his own run was finished in the early afternoon. But neither he nor Zamaryas could see any answer to the central – and obvious – problem which confronted me from the outset. How could you produce a paper in English on an island where all printing was done in Greek lettering? There were no founts of English type here, or in either of the other towns on the island, Retimo and Heraklion. The printer confirmed this, with much shrugging of his shoulders and throwing out of his hands.

Blunt had given me another point of contact, a former official of the British Embassy in Athens called Ian Pirie who had a villa in Canea where we could set up our editorial office. The villa was a modern red brick and concrete structure in a small garden in Canea's best residential area. Pirie proved to be a cheerful, cherubic-faced Englishman in his late twenties, wearing a well-cut light grey civilian suit, who was manifestly in some branch of the secret service, engaged in establishing links by caique fishing boat with occupied mainland Greece. He offered me two rooms as editorial offices for the paper, but could see no answer to my problem of how to print a newspaper in English without English type. There seemed nothing for it but to climb the mile-long road up the hill to Force Headquarters and face the unpleasant task of telling General Freyberg that the best I could offer would be a cyclostyled news sheet.

At that moment Georges Zamaryas arrived in a state of high excitement. A caique had just arrived in Canea harbour from Athens. On board were, of all things, two cases of French type which had been intended for a French propaganda newspaper in Athens. We hurried to the quayside, and there indeed, gleaming amid their protective sawdust, were row upon row of virgin lead type in their neat wooden boxes. Within a couple of hours we had them safely housed in the newspaper printing press, and I made my way on foot up the hill to report that we were in business.

Prince Peter, the nephew of King George of Greece, and chief liaison officer between the Greek authorities and Creforce, made available a supply of newsprint, and secured the release from the Greek forces of a compositor called Alexei. In the printing shop we had another overworked compositor called Nikko, and his two daughters, both skilled typesetters. From the Division I gathered in two journalists, Arch Membry and Barry Michael, and a printer, Alex Taylor – later to be joined by three other printers, Ian Bruce, Alan Brunton and J. Gould from the 18th Battalion. I found a woodcarver who cut for us a block for the title *Crete News*. I settled on a format of a broadsheet with six columns, printed on both sides, and with a banner headline which could run right across the top of the front page, based on the format of the Fleet Street popular dailies of the time. We found, too, an English school-teacher called Graham on the island, and brought him in to run a course of basic Greek for the troops in our pages. Another bonus was the discovery of a number of photographic blocks of British troops and ships and aircraft, intended for issue to Greek papers. They provided us with invaluable illustrations.

Our first task was to diss – to sort out – the French type for setting. We discovered one fact about the French language which I had never taken aboard, though I had spent two years as a correspondent in Paris before the war, that the letter 'W' does not exist in French, except in foreign names like Waterloo or Wagram, or in the imported British abbreviation W.C. We overcame this by using 'M' upside down, or the Greek letter omega. The dissing was a laborious task – as was to prove the setting of type – for Nikko and his girls did not read English, and all their work had to be done entirely by eye, without any knowledge of the meaning of the words they were forming. They could work only in the late afternoon and evening, too, when they had completed their own duties for the Canea paper. There was no way in which we could meet the

General's first deadline of 14 May, but I promised delivery of our first number on Friday, 16 May.

By midday on the Thursday all the copy for our two pages had been delivered to the printers, the headlines written out, with Hess's escape to Scotland as a lead story, and with reports of enemy air raids earlier in the week on Suda Bay, Canea and Maleme. But when I arrived at the printing shop in the early afternoon I found the door padlocked, and no sign of compositors or printers. Zamaryas, tracked down in yet another waterside cafe, merely shrugged his shoulders. The owner of the printing shop, he said, had closed it down and departed from Canea. Where to? I demanded. The café proprietor suggested Karatsos.

It was now late afternoon. Onto the quayside drove a three ton truck. I commandeered it, the driver being, I suspect, very willing to get a break from the routine of delivering rations. I told him to drive to Karatsos. There, in the small main square, at the café where I had heard Noel Baker's talk come over the wireless, sat the printer. A furious debate between him and Zamaryas took place, with half the village crowding round to listen. The printer, Zamaryas explained, disliked taking orders from him – Zamaryas. No Cretan would take orders from an Athenian. Conscious that with every minute the chances of publication were slipping away, I sipped the ritual Turkish coffee and argued that it was I, not Zamaryas, who was giving the orders. That seemed to prove an adequate face-saver, and after a further tirade the printer produced the key to the printing works, and still muttering, climbed into the truck with us.

I got back to Canea to find that meanwhile Alexei, the Greek army compositor, had also disappeared. I finally ran him to ground in the army barracks and marched him back to the printers, where grumbling with anger, he set to work. By eight o'clock that night the page proofs were ready for correction. To do this we had to hold a flashlight over the type. The task, carried out with infinite patience by Nikko and his daughters, took two and a half hours. Everything was now ready for the foot treadle printing machine to start the run. We saw the first half dozen copies come off, and went to eat at the waterside café just as an air raid began.

We returned to find the press deserted, with no more copies printed. The air raid had given the printer the excuse to take to the hills. But Alex Taylor, helped by Nikko, could work the press. By two o'clock edition No 1 of the *Crete News*, proudly proclaiming itself The First British Newspaper Published in Crete – Price 2

Drachmas – was bundled up, ready for distribution to the troops throughout the island. With a sense of unbelievable relief I climbed the hill under the star-filled sky, and placed a copy on the doorstep of the villa, half a mile from the quarry, where General Freyberg had his quarters.

We settled down now to a steady routine, based on Fernleaf House, as we had named Pirie's villa. It presented a scene which, had Ian Fleming passed this way, could have been useful to him as a setting for a Bond novel. On the porch burly Greeks, some in army uniform, some in civilian clothes, sunned themselves, carried in cases of machine guns and wireless sets, and cleaned weapons, supervised by a tall thin Englishman who had been a rum runner in the days of prohibition. Another huge British warrant officer with a waxed moustache, had guns strapped all around him – a Mauser pistol at his waist, and a Browning in a leather holster, hidden under his shirt, in his left armpit. Amongst these moved a dazzling Greek girl called Nicky. She was in her late teens, with shoulder-length blonde hair and slant eyes and very white teeth. She had been a singer in an Athens cabaret, and had been brought to Crete by Pirie. She spoke little English, but glided around the house with a puppy-like manner which combined naivety with high octane sexuality, watched with a mixture of envy and admiration and hostility by the three aged women servants in threadbare black dresses. Nicky showed no fear when the bombers struck nearby, but called sadly from the balcony, 'No good RAF. Come along Hurricanos.' But no Hurricanos came then or at any time.

In the midst of this the two sturdy New Zealand privates who formed my editorial staff listened to the bulletins crackling through the ether from a BBC set placed on a table of ammunition boxes, brewed cups of dark brown tea, and argued about the relative merits of their provincial rugby sides. One of them later gave his own picture of Fernleaf House in a New Zealand Army magazine.

One way or another, the place exuded Wodehousianism to a considerable degree. For example, a scene during the pre-blitz period:
Outside Fernleaf House: All the works of a heavier-than-usual raid on Suda Bay. The barrage blazing away madly, all kinds of guns spitting lead and explosive in the air, every degree of noise from the ground-shaking 'crash-boom' of the heavy ack-ack above us to the rattle of guns in front of the house. Stukas of the Luftwaffe slipping over the ridge and setting off for home down our valley, dipping and dodging with seemingly languid indifference to the puff balls puncturing the sky all about them.

Inside Fernleaf House: Two women servants in the kitchen, on their knees praying. A Greek, wearing a tin hat, sprinting smartly out the back door to the slit trench in the garden, where at least one of the English officers was already established. Out on the big front veranda, 'the Majaw' pot shotting at the planes to the accompaniment of his own running commentary: 'Bai jove, this is much better than duck – Ha, I made that blighter turn – Great satisfaction that – Rathaw – Better than duck much. . .' Behind the Majaw the butler (or maybe steward), a big splendidly handsome figure of a man, waiting impassively to pass the tea or the ammunition, as might be required.

The major's comments were sometimes more pungent. Once, as he fired at yet one more Heinkel circling overhead, he turned to me and said abruptly, 'God damn that fellow Chamberlain.'

My own billet during this period had also a touch of the exotic. I shared a room with Robin Bell and a liaison officer, Lieutenant Harry Purcell, on the ground floor of a small roadside restaurant which had been taken over as a mess for junior officers at Force HQ. It was some five hundred yards beyond the General's villa, where the road from Canea climbed into a wasteland of huge rocks, tangled thorn bush and wild lupins on the headland which formed the Akrotiri peninsula. The walls of our room were frescoed with paintings of three large gleaming pairs of legs in shining silk stockings and high heeled black shoes above a frieze of tiny gondolas, an erotic contrast to the peach trees and the stony meadow which ran right to its door. The wilder spirits of Canea for whom this must have served as a modest *maison de rendezvous* had an idyllic spot for their amours, with a view of the long sweep of the coastline towards Maleme, and of the Aegean Sea shading from ultramarine to cobalt to violet and to turquoise. Our appreciation of the view was, however, apt to be marred by the way the rear gunners of German bombers returning from raids on Suda found the villa an attractive target. It was, as Bell put it, disconcerting to have bullets coming in the window and out the door, whilst all we could do was to crouch under the window sill.

General Freyberg, flanked by his ADC Lieutenant John Griffiths, watching the battle from the Creforce HQ dugouts.

Bombing on the Galatas Ridge, viewed from the Creforce HQ. Canea in the foreground

Smoke over bombed Canea

Suda Bay after a Luftwaffe attack. The wreck of *HMS York* is mid-picture

10. On the Eve

Ultra had provided Freyberg with the exact date of the German attack set first at 14 May, then postponed until 20 May. He had disposed his forces to meet an onslaught both from the air and by sea. Around Heraklion in the east he had stationed a predominantly British Army force – the Black Watch, the Yorks and Lancs, and the Leicesters, reinforced by a battalion of Australians. During the battle they were to be joined by the 2nd Argyll and Sutherland Highlanders. They had two Infantry tanks and six light tanks and a scattering of old field guns.

At Retimo the troops were predominantly Australian. Their commander, Brigadier Vasey, had given responsibility for the defence of the Retimo airstrip to Colonel Campbell, a Regular soldier. As a staff officer, Campbell had shown gallantry and enterprise in the attack on Tobruk four months before by going forward into No Man's Land in the dark to mark with tufts of cloth a way through the minefields for the attacking infantry. The area from Canea to Maleme was the responsibility of the 2nd New Zealand Division. Puttick had kept Hargest's 5th Brigade around the airfield and along the coast for some five miles eastwards towards Canea. Around Galatas Colonel Kippenberger had deployed his mixed force of ill-equipped and ill-trained Greeks, 'malaria-ridden little chaps from Macedonia with four weeks service', together with the 190 men of the Divisional Cavalry, and a composite battalion made up of artillerymen and drivers serving as infantry. At Maleme, as at Retimo and Heraklion, two infantry tanks were hidden close to the airfield, and half a dozen light tanks were available under a young lieutenant, Roy Farran. The Welch Regiment were held as Force Reserve just west of Canea, whilst the KRRCs and the Northumberland Hussars were given the task of protecting the rocky headland of the Akrotiri Peninsula, at the neck of which Force Headquarters was placed. Other Greek regiments held the left flank, between the Prison Valley and the high wall of the mountain range.

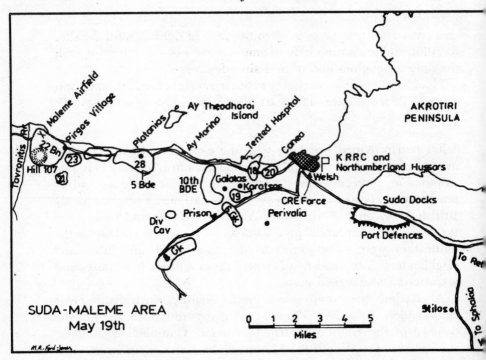

SUDA-MALEME AREA
May 19th

One point in this lay-out particularly disturbed Puttick. There was a gap in the defences of Maleme, along the high ridge which commanded Maleme airfield from the west, a ridge rising above the stony riverbed of the Tavronitis River. He suggested to Freyberg that the 1st Greek Regiment, stationed fifteen miles further west at the small port of Kisamos Kastelli, should be moved to this ridge. But the Greeks were under the command of their own authorities – to Freyberg's annoyance the Greek King, who had come to Crete from the mainland, had insisted on remaining on the island. By the time the permission of the Greek High Command had been secured, invasion seemed close, and the move was not made. This left a gap which was to prove fatal to the defence of Maleme – and of the whole island.

From the second week of May onwards the bombing increased steadily. Every day, as I grappled with the problem of the *Crete News*, the sirens in Canea wailed more and more, as bombers thundered over to attack Suda Bay, or fighters roared in to machine gun the roads. Harry Purcell came back from his journeys to Puttick's Headquarters, or to 4th or 5th Brigade with renewed tales of being chased in his truck by Messerschmitts. With each day that passed the tension seemed to be screwed tighter, until the sky, for all its radiant spring blue, seemed to press down, vibrating with the noise of engines and of anti-aircraft fire.

I had been confined so closely to the immediate area of Canea and Creforce Headquarters that on the late afternoon of Monday, 19 May, I decided to get out and deliver myself the latest edition of the *Crete News* to 5th Brigade. Hargest's Headquarters were in a farmhouse, a few hundred yards inland from the coastal village of Platanias. In the farmyard cooks were busy with black dixies over a wood fire, and a signaller talked urgently into a field wireless set. It was a lovely evening, with the sun sinking behind the great rocky headland of Cape Spatha. Maleme, five miles to the west, had been hard hit by bombing much of the day. Smoke rose from patches of bamboo, staining the otherwise cloudless sky. Hargest walked with me towards a low knoll which looked out towards Maleme. In baggy shorts and khaki jersey, he looked very much the farmer which he was in civilian life as he stared northwards across the sea in the direction from which any airborne attack would come. Then he said quietly, 'I don't know what lies ahead. I know only that it produces in me a sensation I never knew in the last war. It is not fear. It is something quite different, something which I can only describe as dread.'

I did not need to question him on these words. I knew exactly what he meant. His was the reaction of a thoughtful man – and a man of proven bravery – to the extraordinary phenomenon of this period of the war, to the mystique, indeed the mystery which seemed to surround Germany's staggering success in the field. We were in the path of a military machine which had smashed Poland in a matter of days, and overwhelmed France, Belgium, Holland and the BEF in a matter of weeks. The RAF and the Royal Navy had checked it at the Channel, but it had turned south-east and had swept through Yugoslavia and Greece like an avalanche. In the Western Desert only a few German tanks and a previously little known general called Erwin Rommel had been needed to rout the British Army which had, three months before, routed the Italians. Now, this evening, over this golden and blue horizon, these same apparently irresistible forces were massing in an even more novel form to descend on us. I had experienced a year earlier in France the deadening of the will, the paralysis of initiative which had seized a whole nation as its army had disintegrated before these grey

German tanks and grey German planes and grey-clad German infantry. To this was added in Crete the factor that the enemy possessed complete command of the air, denying those who resisted any place of rest or shelter.

I was not surprised that even in a seasoned fighter like Hargest the task ahead should produce this feeling which he defined so accurately as dread. Suddenly the wide tussock plains of Southland under their skies of ragged, wind-torn clouds, which was homeland to both of us, seemed very far away. Then, as the light began to fade, Hargest turned abruptly and led the way back to where his small group of staff officers were gathering for their evening meal.

11. Invasion from the Air

Tuesday, 20 May, was another day of light early mist, clearing to show blue sky overhead. The planes had come earlier that morning, and in greater numbers. From seven o'clock onwards I had watched them from the doorway of our hillside bedroom as they roared in, fighter after fighter with machine guns blazing, and lines of bombers steadily sowing their loads across the olive groves and the hillsides in the wide area spread out below us, between the high wall of the White Mountains and the sea. Away up the coast, where the reddish sand strip which was Maleme airfield just showed in the mist, the Bofors guns were thudding away, baying like huge dogs in a cloud of dust and smoke which grew steadily thicker. The attack reached its climax when five bombers laid a line of thousand kilo bombs along the ridge from Galatas to the tented hospital by the sea. Great brown geysers of earth spouted up, noiselessly for a second, till you wondered what had happened. Then came the noise and the blast, and you knew.

As the bombers which had struck at Suda Bay finished their task, they swooped low across the slope of the hill below us, almost level with where we stood. Harry Purcell shouted to me to bring the Bren gun so that we could have a shot at the next wave. I was struggling with the gun's magazine when, in the valley below, I saw the white of a parachute. I took it to be a pilot bailing out of a hit aircraft. Then other white shapes appeared, drifting in the air above the

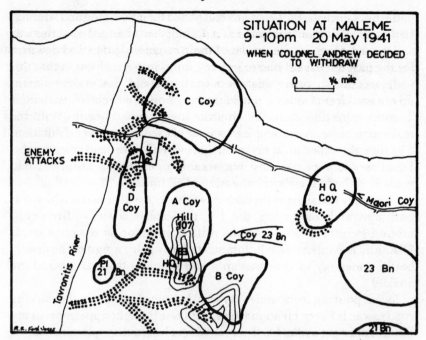

SITUATION AT MALEME
9 - 10 pm   20 May 1941
WHEN COLONEL ANDREW DECIDED
TO WITHDRAW

grey-green olive trees of Perivolia, like white scraps of papers in the wind, like white bursts of shrapnel, like white petals. Under the great yellow nosed Junkers 52s which moved in columns three abreast, from over the shoulder of the mountains, handful after handful of these white shapes were flung into the air.

'Good God, look at that. Right into the olive trees,' Purcell said quietly. Neither of us used the word parachutist, as if we still did not quite believe what we saw, as if we did not want to accept that this was indeed the enemy landing in our midst. Then I shouted, 'There's a plane hit,' as above the edge of Canea a dark aircraft was steadily losing height. But no smoke poured from it, and it was unlike the Junkers and Messerschmitts which still circled overhead. Its wings were much wider, and its body shorter, and silently it curved round and settled out of sight close to the radio masts, and we knew then what it was – a glider.

It all happened swiftly. It took only a minute or so for the parachutists to sway down from the height of two or three hundred feet at which they were dropped. Very quickly they had gone from sight, with only an occasional patch of white to show where a parachute had been caught amongst the trees.

For a moment it was suddenly very quiet. Only one or two planes remained, circling above. With their own men now on the ground, and battle lines unclear, the Germans had halted their bombing and strafing. In that brief moment it seemed as if nothing had changed, that this was still the same lovely valley and mountain range we had looked down on for the past ten days. I had to jerk my mind into a realisation that this wide, tree-filled countryside was now a battlefield, that at any moment up the road from Canea might come grey uniformed patrols with their Tommy guns and grenades, that the invasion had begun. With the realisation came, swamping fear, a sense of excitement, even exultation. The thought welled up in my mind that even if I were dead by midnight, I had seen one of the most remarkable moments in history. I had witnessed the first airborne invasion of all time.

Gradually but sharply the silence was broken with a sound which was both ugly and comforting, the dry, rattlesnake clatter of Bren guns around Perivolia. Bluish smoke drifted up amongst the olive trees. Distantly at Maleme two Bofors started up again, a sign of the deadly battle underway in the vineyards and bamboo thickets around the airfield.

Sweat pouring from under my steel helmet, I ran down the curving road towards Force Headquarters, with one thought uppermost in my mind. I must get a rifle. I had only a .38 revolver, a close quarters weapon which would be of little use in a gun fight amidst these rocks and bushes. There was a small reserve of rifles held close to the Headquarters quarry. The quartermaster had refused to let me have a rifle in the past, but now he relented, though the one he issued to me had its barrel still filled with grease.

I was working to clear this when the planes returned, opening up this time on our area. Machine gun bullets whined through the trees, cutting off twigs and leaves and kicking up spurts of dust on the hillside. Then through a gap in the trees I saw the gliders. One. Two. Three. Four. Five. They sailed in surprisingly fast, swerving straight towards us, soundlessly. They were close enough for me to glimpse faces peering through the windows. My mind seemed unable to take in the fact that these aircraft were full of enemy troops, who at any moment might be amongst us.

Then at the last moment the gliders gave an upward jerk, and swooped towards the hill five hundred yards above us. Within a few minutes Bren carriers of the Northumberland Hussars were moving up the road towards the landing place, their crews with set, tense faces behind their machine guns. They were to find much of their task already done. The gliders had landed in an area of jagged rocks, killing many of the troops in them instantly.

With battle now joined, I had no wish to continue as a newspaperman. This was my chance to switch to the role of Intelligence Officer. The five New Zealanders who were my journalists and printers were attached to the defence platoon, to guard the perimeter of the quarry headquarters, and I reported to Robin Bell, for any duties he might have for me.

The structure of the Creforce Intelligence staff provided a chance for me to do some Intelligence work. Brigadier Blunt, in his role as GI(I) was nominally the head of the I staff, but he had had to spend so much time on his other duties as liaison officer to the King of Greece that the main responsibility had fallen to Robin Bell, who held the post of GII(I). Three British Army captains had been sent from GHQ Cairo, and three other junior British officers were attached as Intelligence officers. They were all able men. One of the IOs, David Hunt, was to finish the war as a highly placed officer of the staff of Field Marshal Alexander. Later, as Sir David Hunt, he was to become British Ambassador to Brazil. The three captains had all been handling intelligence work at a relatively high level in Cairo. Much as they liked Bell as a man, and respected his soldierly qualities, they were restive at finding themselves junior to someone whose experience of Intelligence work had been only at Divisional level, and was relatively brief. They may have also suspected – and resented – that he was the channel through which mysterious information, the exact nature of which was kept from them, was reaching the General. Bell handled them firmly and skilfully, but when the time came he was understandably ready to avail himself to the services of a fellow New Zealander who could speak German – which only one of the others could do – and had had some experience in assessing information. Once it became clear that the Northumberland Hussars had dealt with the glider troops we could put aside our rifles and turn to the task of securing information about the enemy. For the first hour or two of the battle Force HQ was surprisingly quiet, leaving time for the General to study through his binoculars the relatively few signs of battle in the wide stretch of tree-covered landscape below us – the black specks of aircraft circling above Maleme and Galatas, smoke curling up from a burning house or tree, the distant continuing sound of gunfire. With communications disrupted it took time for reports to reach Creforce of the extraordinary battle which was under way amidst the long, neat rows of vineyards and the stands of bamboo and the thick-leaved olive groves of this narrow Cretan coastal strip. The fierce prolonged bombing which prepared the way for the assault did not cause many casualties but left the men around the airfield dazed and stunned, as if they had been through an earthquake. It shrouded the area in dust which was to provide valuable cover for the first waves of gliders. Then came the brief pause, the sudden silence in which the birds could be heard singing, before the air was filled with the thrumming of transport planes. Suddenly, from very low levels, figures swayed down under yellow and green and red and white parachute canopies, and the defenders had to struggle against a sense of unreality to bring themselves to realise that these were indeed the enemy, men who must be killed before they could themselves kill.

Misled by their hopelessly inadequate estimate of the number of British troops on the island, the parachutists and glider troops for the most part came down into areas where they were met with a deadly curtain of fire, where they hung as helpless, clear targets above the troops on the ground. Within a matter of minutes the countryside was covered with the crumpled bodies of dead and wounded figures in grey green parachutist overalls, whilst around them brightly coloured parachutes lay like toy balloons scattered in a garden after a children's party.

From the moment the first parachutist jumped the battle changed swiftly from one in which, by the use of bomber and fighter aircraft, the most up to date and deadly modern weaponry was being brought to bear, into a battle being fought predominantly with small arms, in which the skill of the rifleman was decisive in a way which had not prevailed since the Boer War. In the first few hours after the German troops were on the ground, their aircraft could not be used in their support, so tangled and interwoven was the fighting. Only days later, when clear lines had been established, could the Luftwaffe be employed in all its deadly force as a close support weapon, as artillery directed from above and on the spot.

These first minutes, and hours, and even days were battles of individual men against men. As such they were warfare of a type for which New Zealanders and Australians were particularly well fitted. Many of the men who rose from their slit trenches to give battle around Maleme had grown up in homes where a .22 rifle was part of the furnishings, a weapon used to shoot rabbits, one with which father gave their sons target practice even before they were in their teens. In the bush-covered hills of Southland and Otago deer, introduced from Britain, had bred so abundantly that they provided a natural target on which riflemen could train. My brother and I could get half a crown from the Acclimatisation Society for every deer tail we could bring back, as proof of our kills in the mountains above Manapouri and Monowai. The local Territorial Army Depot would lend us .303 rifles and supply us with ammunition for the task. Not since the sustained rifle fire of the Old Contemptibles at Mons deceived the Germans into believing they were up against machine guns had better marksmen been gathered together than these New Zealanders, and these kangaroo and rabbit-hunting Australians. It is not surprising that the memoirs of the time carry many references to this being 'just like duck shooting'.

In this very first phase, the advantage was very much with the defenders. Not only were the parachutists helpless targets as they swayed down, clearly visible against the sky. They had also to collect their weapons from weapon containers dropped separately before they could function as a fighting force. Their early weapons were, too, mostly only rifles or Tommy guns or light machineguns, which gave them no superiority over the defence. Only later, when heavy mortars became available in substantial numbers – a deadly, indeed decisive weapon against troops who could not dig themselves in – and heavy machine guns were landed – did they outgun their opponents on the ground.

Bit by bit, as the morning progressed, information began to filter back to the quarry above Canea. Freyberg, his massive figure radiating a calm defiance, would turn from looking out across the parapet which ran along the front of the dugouts to study the situation map in the Operations dugout. Gradually the blue circles showing enemy positions covered more and more of the map. 'Parachutists landed here 08.00 hours . . . Three gliders reported here 08.15 hours . . . Parachutes fell here. Believed only supplies,' were messages Bell and his colleagues noted up, as if recording parachute attacks was a commonplace, something done every day, instead of something unknown before on this scale.

One message told of an attack by parachutists on the tented hospital, opposite the Galatas turn-off. They ordered some three hundred of the patients, some in battledress, others in pyjamas or hospital blue, to march with them up the road towards Galatas, where the Germans hoped to link up with other parachutists. But they marched into an area held by the New Zealand 18th Battalion. In the subsequent fighting all the Germans were killed or captured, but some of the patients were also hit – an event which gave rise to reports that the parachutists had dropped some of their men in New Zealand uniforms. These reports seemed all the more credible because they fitted in with the widespread (and false) report of parachutists disguised as nuns dropping on Belgium and Holland a year earlier.

The Northumberland Hussars had done a thorough job of dealing with glider troops on the peninsula behind us, and I was able to take messages to and from the RAF Headquarters in their bombproof culvert without any interference except from the fighter aircraft. These seemed now to be over us every minute of the day, and routinely sprayed the road with machine gun fire when no other target presented itself. Documents taken from the dead on Akrotiri, and from others in the fighting around Perivolia and at the back of Suda Bay began to arrive in some quantity, forming a substantial stack on the trestle table in the intelligence dugout.

Soon after four o'clock in the afternoon, parachute attacks were launched against both Heraklion and Retimo. In both places, but particularly at Heraklion, heavy casualties were caused to the German troops as they parachuted down, and at Heraklion the Bofors guns hit a number of the troop carrying planes in the air. It was clear that the Germans had again completely under-estimated the strength of the British troops on the ground. At Heraklion the invaders were kept well clear of the airfield. One reason was that, unlike the gap left westward of Maleme, British troops had been placed on all the landward sides of the runways, and were able to bring withering fire not only onto any machine approaching the airfield, but onto those parachutists who, having landed further east or west, tried to drive forward to it. At Retimo the Germans were strong enough to seize a hill which overlooked the landing strip, but Colonel Campbell risked his small reserve in a series of counter-attacks which finally recaptured the feature. But he was not strong enough to break through an enemy force which established itself on the road between Retimo and Canea, cutting off the Retimo garrison from its main supply port, Suda Bay. By nightfall, however, General Freyberg could feel that in these two eastward sectors of his command, matters were in hand.

From the sector closest to hand, that from Canea to Maleme, the picture was less clear. So completely had the attack disrupted all communications that information was exceptionally hard to come by. Many field telephones were cut by the bombardment, and machine gunning from the air hindered repair, particularly of those which ran alongside the roads. Runners were either ambushed on the ground or hunted from the air. Wireless sets were few, and unreliable. Platoon commanders had difficulty in letting their company commanders know how they were faring, and the companies had equal difficulty in getting situation reports back to Battalion. Hargest at 5th Brigade had only scanty news of what was happening at Maleme, and could hand little on to Puttick. All that was known at Creforce at dusk was that the enemy had secured a foothold in the Tavronitis river bed, and on the ridge to the west of the airfield, and was attacking Hill 107. Another substantial enemy force had landed in the Prison Valley, and was threatening Galatas. But Hargest was confident that he had the situation in hand, and reported the state of affairs in his areas as 'quite satisfactory', adding that 23rd Battalion and the 7th Field Company were reporting 'hundreds of dead Germans in their areas'. Puttick hastened to pass this on to Freyberg. As that first night of the Battle for Crete closed in the atmosphere at Creforce Headquarters was one of cautious optimism.

12. Fateful Night at Maleme

Bell had taken over the night shift himself, sending the British Intelligence officers off to get some sleep in our roadside billet. I stayed to help him, spreading out my sleeping bag at the back of the dugout. By the doorway stood two canvas bags filled with captured enemy documents, ready for onward shipment to the experts in GHQ in Cairo by a destroyer due to sail from Suda in the small hours. Before turning in to sleep I decided to glance through some of this mass of maps, aerial photographs, paybooks, code books and military papers. This led me to a document which was to have some influence on the battle, and a considerable influence on my own army career.

It was a faded carbon copy, line upon line of close packed typescript, in places stained with blood, of the Operation Order for 3rd Parachute Regiment, the formation charged with the attacks on Maleme, Canea and Retimo. As I made my way through it, picking out the more difficult words with the help of a pocket German dictionary which I had carried ever since my pre-war days as a foreign correspondent, I realised that it set out in considerable detail the German plan of attack. Its importance was underlined by instruction that it was to be burnt once it had been read, and was not to be taken into action. I told Bell of my find, and he took me immediately to General Freyberg.

The General sat behind a bare wooden trestle table in his dugout. On the table lay a hand grenade, ready for use against any enemy intruder. With John White holding a torch for me to read by, I made a rough translation of the order. It not only gave in detail the plans for 3rd Parachute Regiment, but also a summary of the invasion plan for the whole island, including the attack on Retimo and Heraklion. In the Canea area the town was to be surrounded, and then occupied by nightfall. Galatas was to be stormed, and the Canea-Maleme road blocked. The attack was to be pressed on towards Retimo. None of these objectives had been achieved.

Even more important was the estimate of our strength on the island which the document gave. This showed that the German Intelligence was extremely poor. They set the British garrison as no more than 5,000, of whom there were 400 at Heraklion, and none at Retimo. This was roughly the size of the garrison before any of the troops evacuated from Greece reached the island. The Germans had apparently failed altogether to learn of the considerable number of New Zealand and Australian troops from Greece who had stayed on Crete, or of the fresh British units brought in to Heraklion. The total number of British and Greek troops under Freyberg's command was nearly six times this German estimate. Though many of these were unarmed men awaiting shipment to Egypt, some 20,000 were in fighting units. It was these men, hidden amongst the olive trees and the vines, who did such carnage amongst the German parachutists who leapt into what they thought were areas free of troops.

The German knowledge of the terrain was also faulty. They had either not bothered with extensive air photography or had misinterpreted what surveys they had undertaken. Areas full of hazards were marked as suitable for parachutists and gliders. These included the rocky stretches of Akrotiri which had wrought havoc with the gliders I had seen that morning. Moreover the Germans had expected the Cretans to be friendly rather than hostile. From these smudged and grubby pages leapt the fact that we had a much better chance of winning this battle than could have seemed possible twenty-four hours earlier.

I put the document back into the bag for Cairo, and it went off that night. At the same time Freyberg added a postscript to his despatch to Wavell, saying that an important enemy document had been found. It had revealed the main German objectives, none of which had been attained. At the end of his long day the General could seek some sleep with the feeling that the situation was reasonably well in hand.

But it was not. At the very time that Freyberg was studying this operation order in his quarry headquarters, a fateful decision was being taken in the warm darkness at Maleme, a decision which was to lead to the loss of the island. It was taken by Colonel Andrew, Freyberg's fellow VC, who had command of the New Zealand 22nd Battalion, deployed around the airfield. He and his men had had a fiendishly hard day. The stunning aerial bombardment of the area in the early morning had been followed by attacks on their positions from the glider troops who had landed in the Tavronitis river bed, and from the substantial force of parachutists who had landed without opposition on the ridge beyond the Tavronitis, in the vineyards and olive groves where the 1st Greek Regiment could have been deployed. Not only had the men got down safely but their heavy weapons, including mortars and heavy machine guns, had reached ground. With these the Germans had been able to attack across the Tavronitis close to the road bridge, and to bring heavy fire onto the New Zealand positions on the key feature of Hill 107, with its commanding view across the Maleme runway. And always overhead roamed and roared the German fighter aircraft, seeking out targets on the ground. Though the fighting was so entangled that clear targets were few, their constant presence was one more unnerving factor.

Andrew's main problem from the outset was lack of knowledge about what was happening to his companies ranged on three sides of the airfield. He of all the commanders on Crete that day was worst affected by the havoc caused to communications by the air attack. The bombing had severed the field telephone lines linking his headquarters – a trench on the south slope of Hill 107 – to those of his company commanders. The only hope of contact came from runners – that oldest of all forms of military communication. But enough parachutists had survived around the foot of Hill 107 to block the routes for men trying to move through the vineyards and bamboo thickets, and few got through. Andrew, though slightly wounded during the early bombardment, tried during the morning to get forward to his troops, but heavy fire, particularly from mortars, made this impossible. He was able by mid-morning to get a wireless link established to Hargest at 5th Brigade, but he had no wireless contact with his own troops. Either they had no sets or those which they had had been put out of action. On this day of clear, dazzling sunshine Andrew was effectively blinded as to what was happening over much of the area for which he was responsible.

By mid-afternoon he was able, however, to appreciate that the main German thrust was being directed from the Tavronitis river bed, around the road bridge, towards Hill 107. He appealed to Hargest for help for a counter attack, but the Brigadier told him no troops could be spared for this. So Andrew played what he had hoped might be his trump card. He sent into action the two I tanks, backed by his own small infantry reserve, and a group of RAF men who were fighting as infantry. But the tanks proved worthless. One found that its ammunition was the wrong size, and its turret jammed. The other got stuck amidst the boulders of the river bed, and had to be abandoned.

The counter-attack had failed and as dusk fell Andrew was still without knowledge of the fate of his troops on the flat plain at the airfield edge. Lacking any word from them, he assumed the worst, that they had either been overrun or destroyed. The facts were very different. Though they had suffered heavy casualties, particularly amongst the men on the western side of the airfield, they were still holding positions from which they could bring fire onto the runway, and so prevent any transport plane from landing troops or supplies.

Once again Andrew appealed to Hargest for support. Plenty was available, for both the 23rd and 28th Maori Battalion had mopped up virtually all the parachutists in their areas with very few casualties of their own. But Hargest, too, was blinded by lack of information. The telephone lines to his Headquarters were cut. He was too far from the airfield to enable him to get forward to contact Andrew himself – his Headquarters having been established at a point from which he could deal with a sea landing as well as the airborne attack. The weak and intermittent wireless link with Andrew on Hill 107 could give him no clear picture of what was happening. So he sent forward in the dark only two companies, rather than the full battalion which Andrew had suggested – and which the situation demanded.

Andrew found these reinforcements too few for the task in hand, and – still believing most of his battalion was out of action – sought permission from Hargest to retire from Hill 107 to the east. But Andrew found that this ridge would be open to enemy fire once daylight came, and therefore, decided he had no choice but to fall back behind the 23rd and 28th Battalions. Unless he used the darkness to extricate such men as he had left, they would be exterminated by attack from the air and on the ground once daylight came. So, soon after 10 p.m. at the end of this long hard day he ordered a full withdrawal from the airfield.

Of the many crucial decisions taken in this battle, this was to have the most fateful consequences. For at that moment the best chance of holding Crete had been given up – not because of any lack of courage or determination, but because of lack of knowledge. The decisions taken that night of 20/21 May at Maleme stand as a classic example of the importance to any commander of information about the state of the battle he is seeking to control. For based on wrong information, Andrew had made the wrong decision. The position of

his own troops was stronger, and that of the enemy weaker than he
or Hargest had realised. A sharp counter-attack in battalion strength
could have cleared the enemy from the Tavronitis riverbed, and
have destroyed the pockets of parachutists who had survived on the
eastern side of the airfield. By dawn any hope of German planes
having access to Maleme airfield could have been destroyed.

Andrew and Hargest would certainly have acted very differently
had they known how desperate the German position appeared that
night to the German commander General Kurt Student. He had set
up his headquarters in the Hotel Grande Bretagne in Athens, that
luxurious hotel which only a month earlier had housed British
officers and British war correspondents. There, in a shuttered and
curtained room, Student and his staff faced the fact that their plans
had gone terribly wrong. The attacks on Heraklion and Retimo had
failed. At Maleme only a precarious foothold had been secured,
one which could be lost to a determined British counter-attack.
Student's staff officers asked if they should prepare plans to call off
the invasion. He had only a small reserve of parachutists who could
be dropped the next day.

He, like Hargest and Andrew, was unclear about the exact
situation of his troops at Maleme. He decided upon a daring
reconnaissance. He sent off a staff officer, Captain Kleye, in a
Junkers 52 transport plane, with orders to attempt a landing on
Maleme at first light. At worst, if the airfield was under fire, he
might lose a plane and a brave officer. At best he might find that
a gateway into Crete was open. The best from his point of view
proved to be the case. The Junkers touched down on the western
edge of the airfield, and took off again without being hit. To
Student's profound relief – for his job and his reputation were now
very much on the line – this showed that this far side of the airfield
was no longer covered by British rifle and machine gun fire. It gave
him the foothold he determined to exploit by sending in his follow-
up force – the 5th Mountain Division – in transport planes. The
pilots had orders to crashland if necessary, so long as they got their
troops and supplies onto the ground. It was a daring expedient –
and it was to work.

13. 'A Great Responsibility'

At Creforce we woke the next morning to the curious sight of red, green and white Very lights soaring into the mist above the olive and orange groves. Parachutists were signalling for supplies to the planes which already roamed the air above them, or calling for targets to be bombed or areas shot up. With the battle lines more clearly drawn now, the Luftwaffe could be used to the full against our positions on the ground. Throughout the morning the bombing and machine gunning continued at Maleme, in Prison Valley and on the heights near Galatas. It reached a crescendo soon after midday, with a blitz on Piros, the village on the Canea road just east of the airfield. Great clouds of dust and smoke rose, as the bombers dived and circled and dived again. It was an attack as fierce as that which had broken the French lines on the Meuse above Sedan a year before. One aim of this was to prepare the way for a drop of two or three hundred parachutists – Student's last remaining parachutist reserves – along the coastline nearby. Once again the Germans had chosen the wrong place. The parachutists fell into the midst of the Maori battalion, who slaughtered most of them.

Later that afternoon, towards five o'clock, a further, and main reason for this heavy bombing became apparent. A heavy drumming of engines marked the arrival of Junkers 52 transport planes. They came in low down across the sea, black specks moving against the grey rocky coastline stretching towards Cape Spatha. Like great bumble bees they circled above the airfield. Suddenly our field guns – we had nine in all trained on Maleme – went into action. Through my glasses I watched brown earth and dust spurt up. Not a square yard of the landing area seemed uncovered.

Still the heavy black bees circled above. Then one dived. A moment later it was just a black column of smoke winding up. Others tried, and seemed to be hit too. Then one slanted down onto the airfield, and, after a brief pause, took off again in a cloud of dust. I was watching alongside the Australian gunner colonel who was Freyberg's artillery commander on Creforce. 'Seventy seconds to

80

hed in Canea
Creforce

orial Office
leaf House
anea

phone 460

CRETE NEWS

THE FIRST BRITISH PAPER PUBLISHED IN CRETE

THURSDAY
22
MAY 1941

Sunrise 5.18
Sunset 7.52

Vol 1   No 3   CANEA, CRETE   Price 2 Drachmas — Free to troops

VY SMASHES NAZI SEA LANDING ATTEMPT

BIG CONVOY SUNK LAST NIGHT

THOUSANDS OF GERMAN REINFORCEMENTS DROWNED

German convoys packed with troops and heading for the coast of Crete were intercepted and sunk by the Royal Navy last night. The convoys, heading towards the island in the darkness at full speed, were picked out by searchlights. Whole broadsides were fired at them and ship after ship caught fire and sank. Ammunition vessels exploded. The red glow of burning vessels could be seen clearly from the island.

The Navy continued their hunt throughout the night. Thousands of German troops and great quantities of stores, including guns, ammunit, ion and almost certainly tanks were sent to the bottom.

No German ships reached the Crete shore at all.

VIGOROUS BRITISH COUNTER ATTACKS

Ground attack on Crete from the air with the full force of the Luftwaffe and Nazi parachute troops organisation commenced Tuesday morning. Two days later despite heavy air support of the original attackers, we are not only still in possession of the island but have the situation well in hand, and Hitler has already lost a large proportion of the crack parachute troops who landed in such spectacular style, in the sunny calm of that fine day. The British and their allies are fighting with a feeling of certainty now that they are able to deal with these Germans now that they have come down from their aeroplanes.

At the end of the first day of Hitler's attack on Crete we were fully holding our own in all sectors. Counter attacks have been launched in strength against main bodies of his troops still holding out.

Parachute troops were dropped around Canea, Maleme, Retimo, and Heraklion in large numbers and gliders and troop carriers landed at various points. At all points they were proceeded by waves of bombers and machine-gunning aircraft. All three towns were heavily bombed during the day. In all sectors our troops went into action immediately the first parachutists appeared. Late last night when a Crete News representative toured the areas he was told that the situation was well in hand in all parts. Pockets of enemy resistance which had been set up were steadily mopped up during the day. The enemy casualties have already been very heavy.

This is especially important as the troops dropped were the pick of Hitler's parachute troops. It is estimated that at least half of the parachute troops available for the attack have already been dropped.

Canea town was heavily bombed throughout the day but military damage was negligible. At least four bombers were brought down by AA fire during the day. Our own casualties in yesterday's fighting were light. We have captured considerable quantities of enemy material. The prisoners taken have been obviously perturbed by the fierce resistance they encountered. In some areas considerable numbers of Germans surrendered.

TRALIANS PRAISE GREEK ATTACK

CCESSFUL ACTION BY COMBINED FORCE

and Cretan troops, fighting side by side stralians, yesterday gained praise from an an Brigadier.

ook part in a count-   which was complete-   disful, pushing strong   g forces out of a pos-   had managed to seize   he attack the Briga-   in the following

    za and Cretans   agnificently and   aps are proud to   beside them.

REECE

CE MORE

ics, terrible and ro-   r stirred through   Old World by the   of the Greeks and   ghting side by side,   s being repeated, and   r to be back in those   days of the early   h century when By-   n international cru-   store Greece to sov-   dependence.

was once beloved as   impregnable Gibral-   dilisation against the   f barbarism. One of   altruistic of Great   eding phil Hellene   poet Byron. The   n him drew the   nace mountains and   s under the face of   s launched a thousand   the siege of Troy.

THE EYES OF THE WORLD ARE ON US

The battle of Crete is being watched with the greatest possible interest by the outside world. Messages from Egypt yesterday indicated that the eyes of Great Britain, America and the whole Empire were fixed on our fighting. News of the invasion was flashed home to Newspapers in Australia, New Zealand and the United Kingdom at once.

There is every indication that the Germans will endeavour to press home the attack today but with the situation as solidly in hand as it was last night we can feel confident of the result. We cannot give further detail for obvious security reasons. Conditions in Canea, Retimo and Heraklion are normal.

The blunt fact is that by our hard fighting yesterday we knocked their first plan askew. We can do the same again to their second and any other they like to produce.

Greek Humiliations

The Sultans governed the Greeks cleverly through the clergy, but there were intolerable humiliations. Greek boys were compelled to become Moslems and serve as janissaries or household troops at Constantinople, and there were always taxes. In the Greek highlands communities called Kzmatdots maintained some kind of autonomy.

Thus was set the stage for a struggle that lasted for a dozen years and has never really ceased. In fact it is not too far-fetched to say in Greece's counter-blow at the Italians in the Pindus and the Greek victories if good soldiers died has come more in.

Crete News will continue publishing through cut this Blitz as long as the printing press remains undamaged. We cannot guarantee as prompt delivery as in earlier times. We print no news from the outside world because all radios were being used yesterday for the battle. Besides for the present in the outside world, the battle for Crete is the news.

Published in Canea
by Creforce

Editorial Office
Fernleaf House
Canea

Telephone 90

Crete New

THE FIRST BRITISH PAPER PUBLISHED IN CRETE

SATUR[
24
MAY 1

Sunrise 5.1
Sunset 7.5

Vol 1   No 4   CANEA   CRETE   Price 2 Drachmas — Free to troo[

BATTLE OF CRETE RAGES AROUND MALE[

HERAKLION AND RETIMO IN HAND

Retimo and Heraklion are firmly in our hands and mopping up of small enemy detachments remaining is going on. Heavy fighting is continuing around Malame. On Friday German bombers made a heavy raid on Heraklion but did little damage of military importance.

Sixteen enemy troop carriers have already been destroyed on or near the Maleone aerodrome. Others crashed on landing.

This is the latest news of the battle of Crete. Fuller details of Wednesday night's naval action discloses that the enemy convoy which was smashed by the Royal Navy consisted of one Italian destroyer, two transports and over forty caiques. The destroyer was the first vessel sighted. Our ships opened fire on her with pompoms. She replied by firing off five torpedoes. Our ships then fired a six inch broadside at her which caused her to blow up. She did not even have time to fire her guns. The merchant ship was set on fire. Our destroyers then steamed in among the caiques, ramming and sinking them till the sea was full of Germans clinging to wreckage and shouting for help.

Throughout these days our naval forces off Crete have been subjected to heavy and constant attack from the air. One ship was attacked on thirty different occasions in three days. She shot down three enemy dive bombers.

Mr Churchill made a statement in the House of Commons on Thursday about the battle of Crete. He said a British naval force intercepted on Wednesday night an enemy convoy making for the island. We sank the destroyer escort, two transport and a number of boats. Today the enemy made further very much bigger attempts to land an army into Crete.

A convoy of vessels also attacked by destroyers and other light naval units and were in turn attacked by enemy aircraft. No information is yet available as to the result but it is felt that it can hardly be other than satisfactory in view of the naval forces disposed there.

Wave after wave of parachutists were dropped at various points. Some localised successes achieved by the troops at heavy cost to themselves.

The Germans have been concentrating on three strategic points, Heraklion Suda Bay area and Malame. At Heraklion our troops still hold the aerodrome, although the Germans occupied a certain building of the town. An enemy attack on Canea was successfully held up. At Malame the enemy appear to be in occupation of the aerodrome and the area most of it but the aerodrome is still under the fire of our guns. At midnight fall yesterday the situation was satisfactory.

The spirit of the defenders of the island was higher than ever and the British Australian and New Zealand troops, assisted by the Cretans, were rendering a magnificent account of themselves. There

[...] successful night attacks on the enemy. Losses yesterday were even heavier than before.

HESS UNKNOWN

FURTHER
EXPLANATIONS

"The Duke's conduct has in every respect been honourable and proper," stated Sir Archibald Sinclair, on Thursday.

The Duke of Hamilton did not recognise Hess and personally had never met him. It is possible that Hess had seen the Duke at the 1936 Olympic Games in Berlin. Press reports that the Duke had been corresponding with Hess were not true. Letters from Hess had not been received by the Duke or any responsible authority

British submarines attacked an Italian convoy on its way to Libya. One transport, one schooner used for carrying ammunition were sunk. An Italian destroyer was hit and probably sunk.

According to a Buenos Aires there was increasing occasion to take strong action against Totalitarianism and fifth column activity.

IRAQ SUCCESS

In Iraq the resistance of rebel forces is weakening considerably. It is unlikely that he can hold out much longer, despite the fact that an arms supplies have been sent to him from French Syria. Many of these arms were collected by General Waygand who he was commander in chief in Syria.

Colonel Colly, most brilliant French commander in Syria, has joined Free French forces. He crossed the border to Transjordania, it was announced from Cairo on Friday.

On arrival he denounced the Vichy policy of supplying arms to the rebels in Iraq. He recalled the first resolve of all French soldiers to defend the Republic and refused scornfully to Vichy's excuses that German planes made "forced landings" on aerodromes in Syria.

Colonel Colly brought the men under his command with him. He did this by ordering a movement to be carried out which was designed to bring them across the frontier.

RAF

Daylight bombing of German ones was continued on Thursday. Attacks were pressed home despite determined efforts of the ground defences and the German fighters.

A large force was made over Holland. A power station and oil refineries near Rotterdam and in occupied France, were left in flames which were followed by explosions.

During the nineteen raiders were shot down over England. In our defence aircraft were lost, their crews but all made safe.

Among the German raiders were forty bombers with the Heligoland factory. Five German fighters were destroyed.

Nine night fighters and yet bombers driven over the Belgian coast. Five German fighters were destroyed.

WE TAKE VICHY SHIP

NAZI AGENTS IN SYRIA

A French oil tanker en route for Casablanca, in French Morocco has been intercepted by British patrols in the North Atlantic.

Mr Anthony Eden warned Vichy that we will attack any convoy within French territory and hinted that the Germans plan to attack us in West Africa.

Mr Eden said there is no cased and uneasy explanation around in Vichy of the German collaboration of it. There is one could not understand that Vichy collaborated in a policy of re-closing its reserves and on me increasing the disposal of a Police force must move enemy and officer of France's former Premier's Laval and his English White the latter the total positions were developing desperate for the wished said the events war this and the Germans now held on has been able to the same master set here may be found. This could no longer be any distinction between an equivocal and unsuppoistering in the evacuation of our military plate.

The negotiations do read of Vichy reopening my means plans of activation are exemplified by the assist move from the Germans to Vichy Other assisting guaranties Vichy in which the supplies of certain French troops are not liberated in any army to.

Vichy intervention attempts to recover positions occupied to the Free French forces in Africa by saying that at one time had come to re-establish the units of the French in Africa This meant also arming units of the German peaces rendered. The Germans were attempting to play a part by using their motorway "tourists" infiltration. Any forces had already been established in a desirous in this way and a late preparation of personnel of those units German infiltration officers.

ABYSSINIA

Five thousand prisoners have been taken in operations south of Addis Ababa. Our troops lose this week captured 21000 Italian troops including the army under the Duke of Aosta, which surrendered at Amba Alagi and was made up of the remains of two enemy divisions. One hundred dead six hundred prisoners ten guns and five tanks were taken further south. Our advance over which a complete Brigade Headquarters and three colonial battalions. A large points.

Troops ar [...] planes and gliders has been
Allied gun [...] the start of the invasion this [...]

AMERICAS WEIGHT

American war production will not reach its peak until the middle of next year but American is helped to then sir divides its s[...] of this war American and British production will thus overtop German production in [...]

Sir Walter Citrine, secretary of the British Trades Union Congress in his return from his recent tour of the United States and Canada.

"When I arrived in the States I found the public had an exaggerated idea of the effects of the bombing of this country, and my impression had been created that we were almost on our last legs." he said.

"I had to tell people that the suggestion we might be forced to surrender was one I had never heard in Great Britain and that I had had to come to the United States to hear it."

"False ideas of the speed with American industry could be turned over to war production have been created by my statements that aeroplanes could be turned out at short notice as rapidly as taken.

America war production will not reach its peak until the middle of next year is improving. American war planning comprehend and is now settling a red earnest."

"In California I saw huge erecting shed put two months that would take in at least six months complete here. Factory would take 18 months up there in half that time."

Queen Mary, the liner in the world, will turned from the luxury an America ferry as a British troopship been financially very successful. Since the U.S.A.'s gration quota law first itself felt in 1922, no has made so much successive 12 months, the Queen Mary against the very competition.

The people of London lending a sum worthy hub of the Empire, our friends in every land solve that the cause of and freedom shall prevail His Majesty, in a broadcast.

land and clear its men and gear,' he said laconically. It was an ominous proof of German efficiency.

The dive bombers and fighters were onto our gun positions now. We could see them swarming above where the gun flashes showed. Steadily the transport planes were sneaking onto the field, until the line of black dots became a regular ferry service. Every three minutes we could clock one in past the grey tip of the peninsula and watch it move low over the blue water towards the dusty, smoking airfield. It must have been a hideous moment for the German troops in those planes, as they saw ahead of them through the plane windows the inferno into which they had to go. We captured later photographs of a platoon of these mountain troops, taken just before they boarded their plane. They were open-faced, country boys, some grave, one or two smiling. Only the lined face of their officer showed any realisation of what lay ahead.

At Creforce the evidence that at Maleme a doorway had been prised open, that the enemy now had a means, even if at high cost, of bringing in reinforcements and ammunition was observed calmly enough. A major counter-attack to recapture the airfield was planned for that evening. An Australian battalion was being moved from Georgioupolos, half way to Retimo, to hold the coastline west of Canea, releasing the 20th NZ Battalion to join the Maoris in a sweep forward in the dark. The attack would be supported by light tanks under a daring British officer, Lieutenant Roy Farran. It was an attack in force, which should get across the airfield, clear the Tavronitis river bed, and seize the high ground beyond before dawn brought back the German planes.

But our attention in the quarry in this counter-attack was overshadowed by an impending event closer at hand. The seaborne invasion was under way. A flotilla of slow moving caiques, each carrying about one hundred troops, and small steamers, escorted by torpedo boats and by an Italian destroyer was on course towards Canea. It comprised a battalion of mountain troops, an anti-aircraft regiment, field guns and tanks, a formidable and perhaps decisive reinforcement if it got ashore. Ultra had built up full knowledge of the invasion fleet, knowledge which had reached both Freyberg and Admiral Cunningham, the Royal Navy Commander-in-Chief in the Mediterranean. It was now supplemented from another source, a radio intercept unit working close to Force Headquarters. This was tapping both the signals being exchanged by the convoy vessels, and those of the Royal Navy ships waiting to pounce.

One of my tasks during the day had been to carry messages to and from this unit, which was installed in a well-built, roofed dugout cut into the hillside some distance above the quarry. It was led by a tall young Australian, Captain Sandford, the university-educated son of a wealthy South Australian farming family. He was flanked by two tough little British warrant officers. As darkness came, and heavy cloud spread over the sky, and the convoy drew nearer, more and more messages came down the hill from Sandford. Towards eleven-thirty it was clear that the Navy's squadron of cruisers and destroyers was about to close on the enemy vessels some eighteen miles north of Canea.

Bell and I went out to a small knoll close to the quarry which gave a clear view out to sea. Below us the white shafts of our coastal searchlights moved in long, gleaming bars across the harbour mouth and the beaches of Canea. In the wide valley between the coast and the mountains white German Very lights soared into the thick darkness like a firework display. 'There seem to be a hell of a lot of them,' I commented to Bell. The General overheard me. 'Yes, a lot of them – and every damn one scared to death. They are just setting them off to keep up their courage,' he said. His voice carried to all the officers gathered on the knoll, spreading a sense of confidence and experience.

A runner appeared with one more message from Sandford, in his clear, educated handwriting. Bell showed it to me as he took it to the General. The Royal Navy had sighted the convoy, and were moving in for the kill. Suddenly on the horizon away to the north came the flash and thunder of guns, and then the dull red glow of burning vessels. Within a matter of some twenty minutes all was over. Three small steamers and a dozen or so caiques had been sunk and the rest of the convoy scattered. The tanks and other heavy weapons had gone to the bottom. The seaborne invasion had failed.

From our hillside, in the warm overcast night, Freyberg and his senior officers had the evidence of their own eyes for this fact. It was soon confirmed by Sandford's intercepts. The enemy vessels were either all sunk or routed. Brigadier Stewart made some remark to Freyberg which I did not hear. But I heard his reply. 'It has been a great responsibility. A great responsibility.' His tones conveyed the deep thankfulness of a man who had discharged well a nightmarishly difficult task. His comment indicated, I believe, that he felt now the island was reasonably safe. He had reason to do so. The seaborne attack had been routed. At neither Retimo nor

Heraklion had the enemy secured a grip on an airfield. At Maleme, the Germans' one remaining foothold, a counter-attack in substantial force, by the best troops of the New Zealand Division, supported by tanks, was about to go in. It indeed seemed that we had turned the corner. I for one climbed in to my sleeping bag in Bell's dug-out with a feeling of profound thankfulness – indeed almost of disappointment that it had all been over so swiftly.

14. 'The Eyes of the World are on Us'

In war, however, even more than in peace, the best laid plans can go quickly astray. When Harry Purcell arrived at the quarry at breakfast time on Thursday, 22 May, from Puttick's headquarters, his face was grave, and he hurried to report to Brigadier Stewart. The counter-attack had failed. The Australians had been delayed on their way towards Canea by bombing. This in turn had delayed the move of the 20th Battalion towards Maleme. The attack went in late. By the time the 20th and Farran's tanks, after ferocious struggles in which Charles Upham won the first of the two VCs that were to be awarded to him, reached the edge of the airfield, dawn was already breaking. Within minutes enemy aircraft were overhead. The gallant 20th and the Maoris who had advanced alongside them had to abandon all they had gained and pull back to more defensible positions behind Pirgos. Within minutes, the troop-carrying aircraft were again thundering in, disgorging yet more men and supplies to strengthen the Germans on the ground. They were numerous enough to deter Puttick and Hargest from any further attempt at counter-attack. Though few of us realised it then, the final chance to hold Crete had gone. From now on all that remained was to fight a long rearguard action.

News of the sinking of the enemy seaborne forces reached the fighting troops through the *Crete News*, the third copy of which was published that Thursday, 22 May. It was brought out by four of the New Zealanders on my staff (two had been recalled to their battalions) the journalist Barry Michael, and three printers Bryce, Brunton and Gould. When it was clear that they were no longer needed as part of a defence force for the perimeter of Force HQ, they had volunteered to get the paper under way again, even though my intelligence duties held me at the quarry. On the Thursday morning I wrote for them the story of the sinking of the German convoy, and as much as I was allowed to tell of the fighting on the ground. To fill out space, as reception of the BBC News was difficult during the battle, I added two short pieces which were partly editorial, partly explanation for the localised nature of the news we were giving. One read:

THE EYES OF THE WORLD ARE ON US

The battle of Crete is being watched with the greatest possible interest by the outside world. Messages from Egypt yesterday indicated that the eyes of Great Britain, America and the whole Empire are fixed on our fighting. News of the invasion was flashed home to newspapers in Australia, New Zealand and the United Kingdom at once.

There is every indication that the Germans will press home the attack today but with the situation as solidly in hand as it was last night we can feel confident of the result. We cannot give further details for obvious security reasons. Conditions in Canea, Retimo and Heraklion are normal.

The blunt fact is that by hard fighting yesterday we knocked their first plan askew. We can do the same to their second and any other they like to produce.

The other stated:

Crete News will continue publishing throughout the Blitz so long as the printing press remains undamaged. We cannot guarantee as prompt delivery as in earlier times. We print no news from the outside world because all radios were being used for the battle. Besides for the present in the outside world the Battle for Crete is the news.

Michael and his colleagues did an excellent job, with a strong headline across all six columns declaring 'Navy Smashes Landing Attempt'. The page – we had time and news enough only to print one side – was enlivened by two photographs, one showing Royal Navy ships ready for action, another steel helmeted troops holding a line. On Thursday afternoon we got copies out to all the units we could get through to. At least some copies reached the front line, for two were later found in the pockets of Germans taken prisoner or killed. There can be few instances in World War II when troops learnt of the progress of a battle in which they were engaged from a newspaper which was delivered to them in action. Both as a

journalistic product and as a boost to morale this third issue of the
Crete News could hold its head high. I do not know whether General
Freyberg ever had time to scrutinise its contents, but he certainly
knew it had been produced, and saw it as a job well done.

Meanwhile there were prisoners to be interrogated. Three had
been rounded up, hungry and thirsty, from the survivors of the
glider forces which had landed on Akrotiri. One was a big, fair
Saxon who stood rigidly to attention, his finger tips stretched against
his grey parachutist's overalls. When a bomber came over I drew
him under the cover of a big olive tree. He mistook my reason, and
said scornfully, 'Have no fear.' Then its machine guns opened
up, scattering twigs from the tree above us. The Saxon leapt
immediately for cover, saying, 'Look out, look out. *Maschinen
Gewehr.*' The stocky Northumberland Hussar who was guarding
them said, 'What do you think of that? So he's scared too. By God
I'd give a lot to chase some of them up the road with a Hurricane.'

Two other prisoners were glider pilots, just boys of eighteen, who
had been sent to Greece at a fortnight's notice to pilot these
machines. They carried no arms, and wore only mechanics overalls
instead of uniforms. One wept because he thought he would be shot
for not being in uniform. 'So he ought to be,' was the guard's
comment. But they were a valued prize, and were sent to Egypt. In
their shock both pilots talked freely, confirming that the six gliders
– there had been one more than I counted on the first day – were
the entire force launched against this part of Akrotiri, and that all
the gliders from their base had been deployed the first day. But two
officers who were brought in the next day were well drilled, and each
gave only his name, rank and number. To all other questions they
replied firmly, '*Ich weiss nicht*' or '*Ich darf nicht sagen*'. I interrogated
them on the terrace of the villa where Freyberg had lived until the
invasion came. They could see, by the pattern of their bombing,
that the battle was moving steadily towards Canea and Suda, which
no doubt strengthened their stance. When I gave up my attempts to
get anything further from them they stood confidently apart, talking
swiftly and quietly to each other, sure that Crete would soon be
theirs. These were no Nazi thugs, but the pick of the Reichswehr.
One was tall, very erect, a truly soldierly figure.

When I reported this to Bell in Freyberg's presence, the General
reacted abruptly. 'They're not typical,' he said. 'If you had seen the
grey-faced runts who came shivering out of the Hindenburg Line
when we broke it in 1918, you would have seen the true Boche. And

in this war too they will soon be down to those same levels.' It was the swift, instinctive reaction of a leader in a tight corner to demolish immediately anything which could buttress the image of the enemy.

If the prisoners were few, there was an abundance of that other prime source of battlefield information, the papers of the enemy dead. From the bodies of parachutists killed in the first landings, and from those of troops and sailors now being washed up on the shore from the sunken convoy, bundles of paybooks, photographs and letters reached Creforce HQ. This tragic debris of war was a reminder that the enemy, too, was a human being – even if he was intent on killing you.

Alongside propaganda photographs of Hitler there tumbled from these sodden or battered wallets photographs of round-faced, laughing, sunburnt peasant families, of groups on ski-ing holidays, of babies. With them were letters from wives who had had no news, and were sick at heart. One wife was worried by the company which soldiers might keep. The Air Force men stationed in her home town were going around with 'every possible and impossible sort of woman'. Here too were the half finished replies of the men, each expressing that faith without which soldiers could not keep going: 'I will come through all right.'

Across the next four years I was to scrutinise thousands of such documents. I did so always with a conflict of emotion. On one hand I had my share of basic curiosity to learn about our fellow human beings, and here was information such as no novelist could provide. Yet there was also something repugnant about invading, even in war, the ultimate privacy of the individual, to be poring over his most private possessions and his most intimate writings.

15. Canea Bombed

The men of the 5th German Mountain Division who had poured into Maleme linked up with the parachutists and, with massive support from bombers and fighter planes, pushed 5th Brigade back, in bitter fighting, to Platanias and Ay Marina and on along the coast towards Galatas. The parachutists who had gained a foothold in

Prison Valley launched a supporting attack from the south. They had been wide open to counter attack on the night after the landing, 20 May, and both Kippenberger and Inglis had urged Puttick to mount one. But, as at Maleme, too small a force had been sent. Only two companies and three light tanks made what anounted to little more than a raid, and were withdrawn at first light, leaving the main force in Prison Valley intact, though harassed by the Greek troops and civilians. Reinforced now by Mountain troops, this enemy force was now thrusting up the hill towards Galatas.

By Saturday 24 May the front line stretched alone the Galatas ridge, in the middle ground of the great panorama which stretched out beneath us from our vantage point in the quarry. The thought loomed, all the stronger because none of us put it into words, that we might have to retreat over the high mountain wall which rose abruptly, filling the entire southern horizon. Though the road to the tiny south coast port of Sphakia was only some thirty miles long, it wound up the slopes of the mountains in a coil of turns and twists, climbing to a height of some three thousand feet to the pass leading southward. It was hideously open to air attack, and was menaced from the ground. The German Mountain troops were passing along the foot of the range, striving to cut the road behind Suda and block the route of the escape of which no one wished to speak.

Just after two o'clock that Saturday afternoon, the Luftwaffe launched a sustained attack on Canea. It had no military justification. There were no British or Greek troops in the town; it was almost within the grasp of their ground forces; its port facilities would soon be needed by the invaders. Yet for hour after hour throughout the afternoon, and on into the evening, relays of bombers sowed bombs across Canea, like a man punching holes into a sheet of corrugated iron with a spike. Perhaps it was to revenge themselves on the Cretans, who had joined so readily in the fighting alongside our troops, perhaps it was just to give themselves the bombing practice. But relentlessly it went on, a mile or so in front of where we watched from the quarry, as if from a grandstand.

First came the dive bombers, shrieking down, untroubled by any anti-aircraft fire, for none was deployed to protect this civilian target. Then came the Heinkels, and finally long range Junkers 88s. They followed a set pattern, moving over the coast to the west of the town, circling round above the Prison Valley, then moving in to drop their bombs on a run which set them already on their course back to their bases to the north. From the quarry we watched the town disappear into a cloud of smoke, in the midst of which red flames twisted and leapt. The raid must have taken hours of staff work, for the planes roared in as regularly as trains on the London Underground. At one time I counted fifty-four planes in the sky, in two traffic columns, those coming in to bomb keeping to the right, and forming up in line for their dive, whilst those who had delivered their bombs formed up three abreast for the journey home, with their fighters giving cover high above. At times there would be a pause, for ten or fifteen minutes, and we would wonder whether the attack had ended. But then the drone of yet one more wave of bombers would be heard, interspersed with the rattle of machine gun fire as the fighters pursued along the roadways leading from the town the men and women and children trying to flee.

In the midst of this the *Crete News* staff were trying to bring out one more copy of the paper. I had left them at work at midday setting the type in a new location, a small warehouse – no more than a shed – set against the rocky cliff face which rose from the quayside of the old Venetian harbour. It had a big cellar cut into the rock face at its back which provided cover from a direct hit. About five o'clock I was clear of my duties for Bell, and set off back to Canea. The Headquarters defence platoon was moving into position for their night watch around the quarry. One young English soldier, who had become friendly with Barry Michael and the other Kiwis, stopped to look down with me on the sight of the town, covered now in a tall cloud of dust and smoke, with 'tongues of red and yellow flame, writing like gigantic boa constrictors'.[1] All this was set against the blue sky and shining blue sea of a Mediterranean spring evening. The soldier asked if the *Crete News* staff were in Canea. When I told him they were, he said 'Thank God I'm not down there. But then I'm not a New Zealander.' I knew it to be an untrue judgement, for there were no gradations of bravery between New Zealanders or Britons or Australians or Greeks on Crete, only between individuals. Yet his words warmed me as I set my face towards the burning town.

I decided to make my way round the water's edge, where the old Venetian walls had occasional openings and overhangs which offered some shelter, and where the sea offered some check to fire. The first corner I turned brought me face to face with a naked man, dripping wet, arguing with three women on a quayside littered with debris. I saw what it was about when a moment later he dived into

---

[1] *Climax in Crete* by Captain Stephanides, Faber and Faber, 1946, p 100.

the water and started grabbing and hurling ashore fish killed by the bomb blasts.

The printers were all safe, though there were buildings down all around. New Zealand printers, helped by one of Nikko's daughters, were going about their business though all around the benches on which they were setting type crouched or lay terrified women and children. The cellar cave was crowded with people taking shelter. As each attack began, and a string of bombs whistled down, everyone in the cellar turned over, to lie face down, in a single movement, as if they were a trained chorus. Only one girl was hurt, sobbing in agony as friends tugged at her fingers. She had dislocated all the fingers on one hand, it seemed, clasping them in a frenzy of fear.

In and out of this Hogarthian scene wandered a drunken Australian private. He was no doubt a deserter, and no doubt had there been a Military Policeman handy I should have turned him in. But with the cheerfulness of the brave as well as the drunk he would seize each opportunity between attacks to see what new bounty the Luftwaffe had delivered into his hands, and would return with bread and wine and tins of army rations, which he shared around amongst the refugees packing the shelter. All this the people needed, but even more they needed the cheerful indifference to danger which he spread around. The moment a pause came in the attack, he would set out with a whoop on one more foray.

Though we could set the type, and make up the page in the comparative safety of this quayside area, the actual printing had to be done on our old premises, in a side street of flimsy houses and workshops. It was dark and the bombing had stopped by the time we began the printing. There were fires nearby, and several buildings had been bombed out in the same street, but the press itself was intact. Having seen the operation under way I climbed back up the hill to the quarry.

I found the place astir with figures in the dark. Force Headquarters were moving out, to a new place in the olive groves to the west of Canea. There was nothing for it but for me to make my way down to the town again, to warn my four New Zealanders of this move. The whole town seemed now to be a mass of red and black, as the fires blazed and crackled and roared in the still night air. But the quayside between the walls and the water, gleaming and dancing now with red and yellow reflections, still was passable. The little square by the harbour was like a scene from a stage musical set in Ruritania, with the cobbles and massive stone walls and the little café lit up with a rose-coloured, dancing light. Yet the light came from the burning heart of the town, and the square was deserted.

I made my way across it towards the side street where the press stood. A building had collapsed across the entrance to it, and fallen masonry and beams choked its far end. The printing shop seemed to be ablaze. There was no way of getting through to it. I made my way wearily back up the hill to the quarry. It was deserted except for an admirably calm Transport Officer with World War I ribbons, and an equally calm and brave Ellis Waterhouse, one of the British officers of the I Staff, who was manning the one remaining field telephone. It was eerie in the now deserted line of dug outs. German Very lights soared in profusion in the valley below. Close to Canea a French 75mm field gun, one of the few artillery pieces still in action on our side, barked its sharp, unmistakable sound into the night. The gun line, such as it was, was back now in our midst.

I was sitting at the trestle table in Bell's abandoned dug out when Barry Michael and his colleagues suddenly appeared. Their faces were grimy with smoke, their uniforms dusty. Each had a bundle of the *Crete News* under his arm. Michael put his on the table in front of me. 'We got only six hundred off before the building next door caught alight,' he said. 'Have you got anything to eat?'

I had a tin of bully beef in reserve. We shared it, gathered up the papers, and started off on foot downhill when a huge figure loomed out of the gloom. It was the Australian who was Freyberg's CRA. He had discovered untold riches – a half ton truck, still with petrol in its tank, abandoned under olive trees close to the road. We piled aboard, with the CRA driving, and made our way through the smashed streets of Canea. Dust and smoke, lit by the flames, lay like mist across roads where telephone lines sagged and coiled, where bodies lay by jagged bomb craters. A Welch patrol, their uniforms tidy and soldierly, guided us out onto the Suda Bay road. A mile further on we found Force HQ, now just a clump of telephones and an exhausted duty officer at the foot of an olive tree, in an area strewn wherever you looked with the huddled shapes of sleeping men.

16. Of Bombs and Diaries

The next day there were planes over all the time, going for Suda Bay and the roads nearby, spraying our area with machine gun fire as they came and went. But we got a hot meal, and the dark shapes of tanks – the remnants of the squadron of light tanks – amid the olive trees were comforting. At dusk there was one final blitz ending spectacularly as a fighter plane low overhead sent two parallel lines of golden-coloured bullets gleaming across the sky. Then in the dark we marched to yet another site, this time in a clump of big plane trees in a narrow steep gully where the hillside dropped down to the south shore of Suda Bay. The General's tent, well camouflaged, was set up on the edge of a vineyard at the mouth of the gully.

It was here that, as Evelyn Waugh recorded in his diary the next morning, officers of the Commando units who had landed during the night reported to General Freyberg. Waugh's note of the meeting, as of a later encounter with the General at Sphakia, is a warning of the limitations of a daily diary as an historical record, or the way the immediacy and candour it offers can be vitiated by a lack of perspective or background. Waugh describes Freyberg at this meeting as 'composed but obtuse'. Whatever other adjectives might be applied to Freyberg, 'obtuse' is not one of them. I saw him under great pressure, in conditions of exhaustion and strain, on many occasions later in the war, but at no time were his wits other than alert and sharp. What Waugh observed was fatigue, the fatigue of a commander in the eighth day of a battle of a kind never before fought, with his forward and his rearward positions under constant attack from the air. He was moreover a commander who wanted not the minor reinforcement offered by a Commando battalion, but permission to evacuate the fighting men under his command. He wanted to save these men who had fought so superbly in this battle which was now lost, so that they could strike back in another campaign at another time, and not be herded into enemy prison camps. Yet that permission was being constantly denied to him by a Prime Minister in London who did not realise the true situation on Crete and by a Commander-in-Chief in Cairo whose hands were tied by London.

But the virtue of immediacy, as recorded by a masterly observer, is offered in another diary note of that day. In it Waugh records his view of a saturation bombing attack launched on an anti-aircraft gun position at the head of the small gully in which Force HQ had been placed. For over an hour that afternoon a squadron of Junkers 88s, supported by machine-gunning Messerschmitts, attacked this one small target. They worked in relays which suggested that Maleme airfield was now being used for swift replenishment of bomb loads. The gun position was some hundred feet or so above our heads, and perhaps a quarter of a mile away. We had no slit trenches, and could only lie under the three big plane trees and hope. After the first bomb struck I thought I saw a rock thrown into the air at the head of the gully. It came tumbling through the air like a big ash bin – and indeed was a big petrol drum, filled with concrete, which had formed part of the parapet of the gunpit. Had it fallen on us, it would have been more deadly than a bomb. But it caught a ledge of rock fifty feet above, and was hurled aside. Other bombs, as the time went by, hit the sides of the gully, showering us with rocks. But no bombs came into the gully floor, though the branches of the trees above our heads were repeatedly cut through by machine gun fire. Again and again the planes came back, devoting to this one insignificant target so much high explosive that we thought they must have known that Freyberg's Headquarters were here. We had to keep still throughout it, as movement could have attracted the bombers to us. I had time, as we crouched and lay flat, to read a Cambridge newspaper some officer had carried in his kit. The debate in the Town Council about the placing of a new bus stop was reassuringly ordinary.

Waugh observed of this raid that the bombers came round 'regularly and monotonously, like the horses at Captain Hance's' (the riding school near Malvern where Waugh learnt to ride, near the country house he used as the setting for *Brideshead Revisited*).

> Just below us was a very prominent circular cornfield in a hollow, and they used this as their pivot so that they were always directly overhead flying quite low, then they climbed as they swung right, dived, and let go their bombs about a mile away. I do not know what their target was; Freyberg's headquarters had been somewhere in that area. At first it was impressive, but after half an hour deadly monotonous. It was like everything German – overdone.[1]

[1] *The Diaries of Evelyn Waugh*. Penguin Books. 1979 p 500.

Indeed it was overdone, for though the anti-aircraft gun was knocked out, and two of its crew killed, only one casualty was suffered at Force HQ, when Major Queere, a New Zealand staff officer attached to Creforce, got a bullet across the edge of his neck like a slight razor gash. Had we known it, there was an explanation for this overkill. This was the last day on which the German commanders on Crete could call upon the full force of the Luftwaffe units assigned to the campaign. The next day the bulk of the planes were withdrawn, in readiness for the attack on Russia four weeks later. The Air Staff in the Crete operation must have seized this chance to practise the intense bombing of a pinpoint target, just as two days before they had utilised Canea as a target for 'Coventrating' a town in their path.

It was an attack which General Freyberg was often to recall, not so much because of its intensity but because of an incident in its aftermath. He had sought cover from it, not in a slit trench, but under a line of vines in the nearby vineyard, where he sat, tin hat on his head, a writing pad on his knee, as unconcerned as if on a picnic.

'I was sitting in this vineyard', he would on occasion recount, 'with the raid in full progress on the hillside above, when I saw a signaller crawling to me through the vines. I thought that here at last was Wavell's reply to my urgent plea to be allowed to give up this lost battle, and order an evacuation which could at least save some of the troops. But the message said no such thing. Instead it read, ''I am sending you Colonel So-and-so who is an expert in the use of the I-tank in the counter attack'' – and that at a moment when the only I-tanks we had in this part of the island were long since out of action. That was how out of touch both Cairo and London were with the situation.'

The situation was one of defeat. Though the Australians at Retimo and the British at Heraklion had held firm throughout the past week, denying the airfields and Heraklion harbour to the enemy, Maleme was now an open door through which the Reichswehr poured men and supplies. Relentlessly the Germans pressed forward between the sea coast and the mountains. Not even a gallant counter attack by the 23rd New Zealand Battalion and Farran's tanks at Galatas could halt this advance. Yet it was not until the afternoon of Tuesday May 27, with Canea already in German hands and the enemy in the outskirts of Suda, that Freyberg received authority to evacuate the island. It came too late to save the splendid 1st Welch, thrown away in a bungle about orders for withdrawl, the fault of commanders stupefied by fatigue. It was too late, too, for orders to get through to Campbell at Retimo to head for the south coast, so that he was left no option but to surrender. The Heraklion garrison were all taken off by warships, only to suffer from bombing at sea far worse casualties than those inflicted by the parachutists on land.

It was late on that Tuesday afternoon, as the battle entered its second week, that Freyberg and his senior officers drove south, by car and truck, to establish a new Creforce HQ near to Sphakia, the tiny port which was to be the sole embarkation point on the south coast. At eight that evening the rest of us at Force HQ paraded by the roadside overlooking Suda Bay, to begin the long climb up the dividing range. My New Zealand party now numbered six, as Peter McIntyre, the official war artist, and a young signaller had joined us.

We had orders to take only our arms, such rations as we had (I had the luxury of a tin of meat and vegetables, instead of just the tough and salty bully beef) and, above all, our water bottles. All other kit and blankets had to go. My lightweight sleeping bag, which had seen me through the fall of France, and through Greece, I sadly ripped to shreds with a bayonet. I was about to throw away my greatcoat, splendidly tailored by Halls of Oxford, and costing all of nine guineas, when Peter McIntyre took it over. He was prepared to carry the extra weight for the warmth it offered at night. He was to bring it through the retreat, and sell it back to me at Maadi for four pounds, which we each thought a good bargain.

17. Retreat

The climb began for us immediately, as we had to cross a ridge to get to the main road south, which began its serpentine, curling route from a point closer to Suda. When we reached it, and linked up with the main body of Force HQ troops, who had come on from Suda, it was already dark. Yet the white, dusty road was crowded as if with people coming away from a football match, long lines of troops taking advantage of the darkness to move free of air attack. Some were marching in organised units, but many were just streams of individuals, or small groups, trudging along in the darkness, or resting at the roadside, or curling up to sleep under the olive trees. Ellis Waterhouse was with the thirty or so men from Force HQ, clerks and signallers and drivers and men of the defence platoon. They were, like so many British troops of the time, for the most part small, stunted men, a product of the years of bad housing and inadequate food and hygiene. I feared that they would not have the stamina to keep up a good pace. So Waterhouse and I arranged to put three of the New Zealanders, who were all sturdy and very fit men, at the front of the column, and three at the rear, to set and sustain a reasonable pace. He marched at the front, I at the rear.

It was to prove a useful tactic, for it was essential to keep together and to keep marching as it got darker, and stragglers grew more numerous. Voices called anxiously in the darkness, 'Is this the way to the beach? Any water here, digger? Where the hell are you, Mac? For Christ's sake where are you, Mac?'

It was an overcast night, with no moon, and the darkness lay heavily over the road as it wound upwards through the olive trees. The black, jagged wall of the mountain rose ahead of us, very high against the sky. In front and behind were the shapes of men trudging onwards. In the ditches by the roadside, around every farmhouse and every well men were resting, talking little, the tips of their cigarettes moving dots of red in the dark.

At one bend a tank suddenly loomed up in the middle of the road. It was outlined by an eerie glare, which turned out to be an olive tree alight, with four or five others smouldering nearby. This must have been where they had machine-gunned the Australians that afternoon. Beyond was a staff car, burnt out.

Then, distantly, came the sound of a plane. We scattered to the roadside. The plane dropped a flare, a glaring, orange brown lump which descended slowly, lightly up hideously the olive trees and the roofs of a farmhouse and the road and dark shapes at the road edge as far as one could see before it guttered into darkness, and we could form up and move on again.

The Tommies were tiring now, and we had to make longer and longer halts. We had all been on short rations for over a week, and many – myself included – had scouring stomachs. After each halt it became more difficult to get the men onto their feet. Our tactic of having the fitter New Zealanders at the front and the rear was useful in keeping up the pace, but with every mile it became slower and slower.

At Stylos, the first village we reached, we came upon a barn serving as a dressing station. Trucks used as ambulances, marked with crude white crosses of torn cloth stretched across grey blankets, were crowded with wounded men. Others, their white bandages showing in the dark, sat or lay on the edge of the narrow street. The

barn was packed inside from wall to wall with men lying on
stretchers or blankets or sacks. I felt I had seen it all before,
somewhere. Colonel Thwigg, the New Zealand officer in charge,
later provided the comparison. 'It was like the scene of the wounded
at Atlanta in *Gone With the Wind*.' And indeed it was – life imitating
art with a vengeance.

Thwigg had another tale of Crete, which said much not only
about the New Zealand troops of that time, but about soldiers of all
time. About the fifth day of the battle an artillery private drove up
to Thwigg's Advanced Dressing Station with a truck full of
wounded. He said, 'My unit's all knocked to bits – can I stay with
you and drive this truck as an ambulance?' It turned out that he had
a friend wounded in the leg, and he had scrounged the truck from
somewhere to bring him to the ADS, and had picked up the other
wounded on the way.

He drove the truck right through the retreat, and though there
were strict orders that only walking wounded were to be evacuated
– all lying wounded being left to be taken prisoner – the man used
to smuggle his friend aboard at each move. At this Stylos dressing
station the Colonel said, 'You had better keep an eye on your cobber
because I'm not in charge here anymore and they may shift the
wounded to another hospital at any time.' The man replied, 'I've
thought of that. I've moved my mate to that house over there and
I've changed his dressing and found him some rations.' When they
got down near the beach at Sphakia he put the wounded man in
shelter in a cave, and then spent all day driving up and down the
open road, despite the bombing and machine gunning, ferrying
wounded down to places close to the beach.

Thwigg concluded, 'He must have carried his friend all the way
to the beach, because the next time I saw them they were drinking
cocoa together on the mess deck of the ship which evacuated them.
The man who had done it all, who could not have been more than
twenty-five or so, looked suddenly fifty years old.'

Dawn showed us to be moving along the edge of a wide valley,
with the flat ridge of the pass high above us against the skyline, and
the road curving and winding and doubling back and forth towards
it for what seemed mile upon mile. All the way up it were the
moving figures of men, climbing, halting, climbing slowly again.
The daylight gave faces and uniforms and bodies to the dark shapes
of the night, revealing them as walking wounded with bloody
bandages, one man with a bandaged stump of an amputated hand;

as sailors off boats in Suda; as airmen; as Cypriot muleteers; as detachments marching under officers or NCOs; as other men straggling in ragged lines or small groups. Every few yards a figure lay on the roadside in the sleep of the utterly exhausted. Now and then a lorry came along, jammed with wounded, with bandaged men clinging to every corner of it – and a few who looked shamefully fit also grabbing a ride.

All along the road were abandoned lorries and cars, some of which had been hit by aircraft fire, and burnt out, others abandoned for lack of petrol, or because of a breakdown. Some had gone off the road in the dark, tumbling hundreds of feet down to rock filled ravines. Gear spilled out from them – papers, web equipment, mess tins, a paybook, an abandoned steel helmet.

The Tommies in our small unit were close to exhaustion now. It was not surprising, as it was now five o'clock, and we had been on the road nine hours. Soon the planes would be over, and movement would be difficult. Waterhouse decided to halt at a place where olive trees offered shelter, to let the men sleep and rest, and to push on in the darkness of the next night. My New Zealanders were still in good shape, so we left the British party, and carried on on our own, our eyes always on the ridge above our heads. At one point there was a big open well close to the road. We joined the queue at it, and after twenty minutes or so were able to lower our waterbottles into it, and fill them, and drink. It was brackish water, with a brown stain but we drank it thankfully.

On the next stretch, seated on a rock by the roadside, was the surreal spectacle of a girl with blonde hair falling onto the shoulders of her khaki uniform bush shirt, and with her legs in ill-fitting khaki drill trousers. She looked like someone on the way home from a fancy dress party. It was Nicky of Fernleaf House. Her face was crumpled with weariness but her smile was as dazzling as ever. With her were Ian Pirie, in a brand new khaki uniform at least one size too big, and with major's crowns on his shoulders. The admirable plane-potting major, his rifle by his side, was slumped in sleep. They were all close to exhaustion, worn out by the night's march. We chatted for a few moments, and moved on, leaving them to rest.

The climb up the final, interminable serpentine to the top of the pass was a nightmare of fatigue. We had hoped to make it before the planes came, but soon after seven o'clock one flew in a leisurely fashion overhead, the morning sun glinting on its wings, its black Luftwaffe crosses large and menacing. It machine-gunned the road in a desultory fashion. Yet it need hardly have bothered, for the sound of its engine, even in the distance, had been enough to send the lines of climbing men, robbed now of the support of discipline and often even of the presence of friends, scattering among the thorn bushes and the rocks. Just off the road a queue, several hundred strong, had formed at a big well. As the plane appeared the men in it scattered, and then later tried to reform. But many men lost the places they had had, and sat brokenly on rocks nearby, too exhausted even to argue with those now ahead of them. Others, their nerves worn threadbare, shouted hysterically at anyone who continued on the road whilst the plane was still to be heard. Further up, near the summit, two shots were fired, almost certainly by bomb-happy fugitives trying to halt any movement which could attract aircraft.

At long, long last, about nine o'clock, one of what had proved a multitude of false summits proved to be a true summit, and we crested the ridge and looked southward down the other side of the range. We were astonished by what we saw. Instead of a repetition of the steep, pine-clad and olive-clad slopes through which we had been climbing, we were faced with a lush green bowl of fields and trees and white walled houses, encircled by hills. This was the Askifou Plain, a round, fertile plateau set like an oasis in these gaunt White Mountains. We could see the white road leading round the western edge of it, and then climbing away in a new set of hairpin bends into a new range to the south, the last range before the sea.

The sight of this Shangri-la brought an immediate lift to our spirits, the more so since it was so utterly unexpected. We strode off downhill towards the plain. There we reached a well with its lifting gear still in action, offering good clean cool water to drink and to wash in. Nearby was an orchard with long grass. It seemed sensible to get some sleep here, and to push on in the late afternoon, so that we could complete the journey in the dark, free from the planes which must surely be over in their scores at any time now. I needed rest, as for three days past my stomach had been scouring in a condition close to dysentery. Within a few minutes I was deeply asleep.

I woke with a jerk about an hour later, to hear Barry Michael talking in a low voice to one of the others. 'He's exhausted,' he said, in not unkindly tones. 'We could easily push on, but he's exhausted. Yet if we pushed on now we might get to the beach in time to get away tonight.'

I realised they were talking of me. I realised too that if they were fit enough to keep going, as their officer I must keep going too, however exhausted I felt. There was another factor too. There had been no planes overhead since we had crossed the pass. The roads,

which I had expected to have been made impassable by enemy
aircraft during the day, were remarkably open. So I pretended to
sleep for another ten minutes, and then bestirred myself, looking
around, and said, 'I think we should risk the planes and push on.'
Barry Michael had meanwhile found a ration dump that provided,
of all things, a tin of pineapple. We ate that as if it were ambrosia,
and set off on the remaining twelve miles to the sea.

There were two ways southwards out of the Askifou Plain. One
was by the main road which wound up over the final range,
climbing back up to a height of some 2,500 feet in yet one more
series of bends, before plunging down towards the sea. The other
route, a dusty road no more than a track, led from the floor of the
valley towards the mouth of the Imvrotiko Ravine, cleft like an axe-
cut through the mountain wall. I opted for the second, not because
I knew of its nature, but because it avoided the option of a further
climb – and that on a road open to machine gun fire.

The first part of our route lay through a narrow valley, on either
side of which hills covered with pine trees rose steeply. There, in
mid-afternoon, enemy aircraft swooped on us, spraying the road
and hillsides with machine gun fire. In rushing for cover, we split
up, Michael and McIntyre climbing the hill on one side, and the
others and myself on another. When the attack finished some ten
minutes later I could find no sign of Michael and McIntyre, and
after waiting for a while had no choice but to push on with the
others. We came out onto a small plain – not much more than a
large clearing – beyond which showed the narrowing entrance to
the gorge. Here a New Zealand captain flanked by a couple of
soldiers stopped us. 'This is a gathering point for New Zealanders,'
he said. 'You'll not get off in a small party. They are taking only
the fighting formations. What battalion are you from?'

I explained the men were from the 18th, but were now with me at Force
HQ. 'The 18th are in the first gully to the left,' he said. At that moment
the sound of returning planes could be heard. The captain moved smartly
to the cover of a clump of rocks. I had to make an instant decision. 'You
will have a better chance back with your battalion,' I said, and the four
moved off quickly towards the side gully.

I plunged on into the narrow shaded entrance of the ravine alone,
troubled by my decision. Had I thrust them on a course leading to
a prison camp? That anxiety remained at the back of my mind until,
ten days later, I was able to establish that all six of them had got
safely off. But I needed now all my wits about me, for the path

through the ravine was menacingly lonely and silent, as the sheer cliffs rising on either side grew taller and taller, and closed in ever more narrowly. What if it proved a blind alley, if I came to a barrier which would force me to climb the high walls on either side or retrace my steps? I dared not contemplate this possibility but strode on, sometimes at a half trot. It was well into the evening now. I hung ever more firmly onto the strap of my rifle, slung over my shoulder. At last, at about seven in the evening, the defile began to open out, and its walls to lean back, disclosing a magnificent display of purple rhododendrons. Then I rounded a bend to see the sea, deep blue in the late evening light, clear and serene, stretching to the horizon beyond which lay, distantly, Egypt and safety.

At the end of the ravine I came out into a village. Around its well sat a group of Cretan civilians. They eyed me warily – and eyed, all too interestedly, it seemed to me, the rifle I was carrying. I kept it slung over my shoulder as I drank, and filled my water bottle, and asked the way to Sphakia. They spoke swiftly among themselves before one pointed out a rough track leading westward. How far was Sphakia? Three, four kilometres, they said.

The light was going now, and I hurried as fast as I could, with the sea on my left and, towering above, on the right, high rocky slopes rising steeply towards pine covered heights. I had gone about two kilometres when I was faced by an officer in Marine uniform, his hand on the butt of his revolver. 'Where the hell do you think you are going?' he said. 'To Sphakia.' 'Well you can't,' he said. 'No one is to move on these slopes during the daylight. Do you want to bring every bloody German plane down on us? The orders are clear. No movement by day – and anyway no individuals are allowed into Sphakia, only formed units. I've a good mind to arrest you as a deserter.'

I protested I was from Freyberg's headquarters, and had orders to report there. He paused, weighing me up in case I was a Fifth Columnist or a German in disguise. Then he said, 'His headquarters aren't in Sphakia. They are in a cave up on the right hand side of that wadi' – and he pointed to a shallow gully running down from the slopes above us. I set out up it, and just as dark fell I came upon a group of caves set into the hillside, two with stone barricades set across the entrance. They looked like a setting for the legend of Cyclops. In one cave I found Robin Bell. In another were the General and Colonel Stewart. In a third, smaller cave were several British officers from Creforce, including three of the British Intelligence officers. They had come across by truck, and were well installed, with some rations and a bottle of sherry. I drank thankfully a glass of sherry, ate a couple of slices of bully beef – all my stomach would take aboard – and lay down on the cave floor to sleep, secure in the knowledge that no bomb or bullet could reach us in this natural anti-aircraft shelter.

I slept, however, only brokenly, for the night proved cold. My legs, in thin drill shorts, were bitterly cold. I regretted my overcoat, which indeed – he later stressed – kept Peter McIntyre warm on the hillside where he and Michael were spending their night.

18. A Trip to the Rearguard

The next morning, as I thawed out in the sun, Bell told me that a first wave of a thousand men had gone off overnight – the night of Wednesday, 28 May. A further six thousand would go this evening, Thursday. Force HQ would be amongst them. Bell was to carry off a briefcase of General Freyberg's papers, and that I was to come with him, with orders to take over the case, and see it delivered to Maadi, if anything happened to him.

These headquarters caves were some two hundred feet below where the road over the mountain ended abruptly at least a kilometre from Sphakia. Its final stretch, cut across the mountain side, petered out in a waste of rocks. By a small margin of about a mile – a margin across which at least a workable track could have been cut by engineers during the previous winter – the use of the road as a means of evacuating the wounded, and of bringing up rations and water from Sphakia had been lost. Now a line of abandoned trucks and cars and motor cycles stood at the road's end as a monument to this blunder – and as a useful pinpoint for the German planes which, from daybreak onwards, came and went in relays.

But we were out of sight in the caves, and in the intervals of the air attacks could sun ourselves with our minds eased by the knowledge that by midnight we should be aboard ship. In the early afternoon this swiftly changed. Bell called the British Intelligence officers and myself into one of the caves, and said one of us had to carry a message back to General Weston, who was in command of the rearguard, on the heights above, and then take on another message to Brigadier Vesey of the Australians, on the Askifou Plain.

We all knew immediately what this meant. To climb the two thousand feet and more, on the winding, bombarded road to the heights, and make one's way the eight miles to the Askifou Plain, and yet get back in time to rejoin Force HQ before they moved off to the beach at seven that evening was virtually impossible. It was beyond the strength of a fit and fresh man, let alone anyone who had marched over the mountains and who was weakened, as I was, by several days of something close to dysentery. Yet not to get back in time meant that you became a straggler, a loner who would never get through the cordon thrown around the Sphakia evacuation beach. Whoever had to take on this task took on also a major chance of being left on Crete. Aware of this, Bell had four pieces of paper folded in his hand. One was marked with a cross. Whoever drew it was to take the message.

I unfolded my piece, and stared with disbelief at the pencilled cross on it. It was, I thought, if not my death warrant, at least a warrant for many years in a prison camp. Hastily I collected the written orders which I was to deliver, and set off up the slope to where the line of abandoned vehicles marked the end of the road – and marked for me the beginning of this long trek back once again over this nightmare route.

Among the vehicles by the roadside were a couple of motor cycles. I had never ridden one, and because machines were in short supply, and were needed for operational duties in the summer of 1940, we had not at my OCTU been put through the usual officers' course in the use of motor cycles. I tried to get these started, in the hope I might get at least a few hundred yards on one of them, but without success. All I attracted was a chorus of abuse from the woods by the roadside, which were crowded with bomb-happy troops.

I could drive a car, but none of the abandoned trucks or cars would start. So I set off up the road on foot. An Australian private, his head bandaged, sitting in a roadside ditch called to me, 'Why do you walk?' as casually as if we were on Bondi beach.

'I can't find anything to ride in,' I replied.

'There's a truck up there that will go. I've tried it. I've got a garage of my own back home, and I know about cars. The steering on this one is bad but he will go.'

He took me to the truck, and got it started. We could hear a plane in the distance. This roused the troops hidden in the trees to renewed curses and threats, and one shot whistled close to us. The Australian was furious, and let off a stream of oaths and obscenities which even the toughest Australian quayside could seldom have heard. Magically it quietened the shouters. He turned the truck round for me, handed it over, and returned to his ditch. New Zealanders are traditionally at odds with Australians, but no human being ever did me a better turn than that Aussie that afternoon.

The front wheels were wobbling crazily, and twice it lurched to the edge of a sheer drop with only inches to spare. I made up my mind I would drive fast even if I went over the edge, calculating I could jump clear just in time if that happened. Bend after bend miraculously went by, as the truck climbed in minutes what would have taken hours on foot. At one point I came round a corner to find myself facing a truck coming the other way, with Harry Purcell clinging on beside the driver. I missed them by inches, without time even to reply to Purcell's astonished wave. After three miles one wheel – fortunately on the inside – gave a final lurch and came off. I abandoned the truck, and went on on foot. I had been joined now by three Marines. They led me to a unit headquarters in a culvert under the road. On the roadside was a Morris staff car, the first type of car I had ever owned. Beside it stood an army driver, ashen-faced and shaking. He was clearly shell-shocked, and was refusing to drive the car any further. I offered to take over as driver, since the Marines were heading for Weston's headquarters.

At last I saw Weston, up on a hillside supervising the line his Marines were taking up. I clambered up to him, secured his signature for the message, scrambled back to the car and drove on to Imvros, the village at the southern exit from the Askifou Plain. In a house here I found Brigadier Vesey, every inch the tall, slack-limbed, nasal-voiced Australian of the cartoons, his conversation liberally sprinkled with 'bloody'. He was cheerful and unhurried, asked me about conditions at Sphakia, and the terrain in between, and took me out to the village edge to show me, through binoculars, the first German units advancing over the pass into the head of the plain. 'Tell your General we can hold the bastards for at least twenty-four hours,' he said, as he in turn signed the receipt for the orders I had given him.

It was now after six o'clock. I returned to the car, thankful I had it, for there was no way in which I could get back to the cave on foot before the beach party set out. But the car refused to start. The petrol gauge showed either that it had used its last drop to get me to Askifou, or that someone had siphoned out the petrol whilst I was with Vesey. To complicate matters German planes reappeared, and began machine gunning the road. Trucks were moving along it, carrying men I recognised from the 23rd Battalion, and the Maoris. I waved my arm, in an effort to get a lift, but none stopped. They moved swiftly on, partly because of the machine-gunning but partly from fear that if they slowed down they would be swamped by the stragglers who now moved along both sides of the road in a constant stream.

My car partly blocked the road. As yet one more fifteen-hundred-weight truck approached, stragglers filled the rest of the route. The truck slowed down. Two Maoris jumped out, pushed the car clear but thrust me back as they clambered aboard. Then I heard a shout from within the truck. 'Let him on,' it said. It was the young Maori officer beside whom I had marched on the first day, when I had guided them towards Maleme. Hands grabbed me, and I fell thankfully amidst a pile of gear on the truck floor.

The Maoris halted at the crest of the range, where they were to form a new defensive line. This left me some two miles short of the caves, but it was downhill all the way. I ran much of it, watching as I went a bomber raid on Sphakia. I counted fifteen planes coming in in groups of three abreast, their bombs thudding down around the tiny harbour. It was nearly dark as I reached the road end, and clambered down the track to the caves. There I handed over to Colonel Stewart signatures of Weston and Vesey for the orders they had received. The Force HQ troops were drawn on the wadi nearly ready for the march to the beach. I had made it just in time. Waterhouse's unit was amongst the waiting men. He had brought them over the pass, across the Askifou Plain, and up the final stretch during the previous night. They had hidden in the trees until this evening. It was a piece of unostentatiously responsible leadership, which had brought these often puny but brave signallers, orderlies and clerks through in good shape. I never saw Waterhouse again after that evening, but I hope he had a good war. He deserved one.

As the last light faded, Puttick and Gentry and two or three other officers of the New Zealand Divisional Headquarters came down the hill towards the caves. Freyberg went forward to meet them. Puttick saluted and said, 'We did our best. We did all we could.'

Then we were off, formed into columns of threes, with strict instructions to keep in formation and allow no stragglers into our ranks. We passed through the cordon of guards on the edge of Sphakia, and lay in the darkness waiting for the wounded and the troops ahead of us to be embarked. It was a strain, watching other figures in the dark moving forward, and wondering whether word would come back that the ships were full. Sometimes a wounded man would not be able to keep up with his friends, and he would cry out, 'Charlie, Charlie, for God's sake wait.' The badly hit ones, cried, 'Christ, where's the beach, where's the beach?' They were a black procession stumbling, limping and staggering on towards the shore.

At last we were off down the slope through the narrow village street, and in the small bay clear Navy voices in cultured Dartmouth accents called, 'Come on, come on, get a move on. Hurry up there, hurry up.'

Then we were on the landing craft, and there was the inside of a ship again and cocoa and bully beef sandwiches, just as we had had coming off Greece. We were on the Australian cruiser HMAS *Perth*. An engineer officer gave me his berth. I left my ·303 rifle with him. He wanted it for shooting kangaroos back home. It is unlikely ever to have served that purpose. Six months later the *Perth* was sunk by Japanese bombers off Java, and was lost with all hands.

German bombers did their best to anticipate this action the next morning, when, under a grey sky, we came under attack. We lay on the wardroom floor as the guns thumped and barked above us. The man next to me clutched his rosary and prayed and, for the first time in a decade, I prayed too. One bomb hit the ship, putting the foremost boiler room out of action, and killing eleven men, seven of them evacuated soldiers. A second raid brought several near misses. But by early afternoon we were safely within range of the RAF fighters from Egypt. We took a muster roll of the men crowded on the decks below. Amongst them were a number from the Commando units which were supposed to be forming the rearguard.

The next morning we were drawing into Alexandria, past the shameful dark grey French warships lying at anchor, with our own escorts pulling aside to their berths, and the tang of the desert on the offshore breeze.

19. Crete: A Battle Evaluated

A considerable literature has emerged about the battle of Crete during the past forty years, arguing about why the battle was lost. The struggle was so finely poised during its opening phase that it lends itself to the type of debate much favoured by historians, the 'if only' theme. If only General Freyberg had placed troops on the ridge above the Tavronitis before the battle; if only Hargest had mounted a full scale counter-attack on the enemy around Maleme on the first day and the first night; if only Puttick had done the same in the Prison Valley; above all if only Andrew had held his ground on the night of the 20/21st, instead of yielding Hill 107 and the eastern edge of the airfield to the enemy; if only the counter-attack on Maleme on the night of the 20/21st had been launched in time for it to be completed before daybreak; if only one further counter-attack had been tried the next night: any one of these actions might have provided the extra straw to tip the balance in our favour.

These decisions appear all the more puzzling because General Freyberg went into this battle very fully informed, through Ultra, about the strength and plans of his enemy. Winston Churchill has declared that 'at no moment in the war was our intelligence more truly and more precisely informed'[1]. One of the chiefs of British Intelligence at the time, F. W. Winterbotham, has stated that 'Freyberg was in possession of the most detailed plans of the enemy's proposed operation that were ever likely to be available to any commander'[2]. Yet Freyberg left a gap in the Maleme defences along the river above the Tavronitis, and held all the battalions of the New Zealand 4th Brigade back in the Galatas-Canea area. They were well placed to deal with any seaborne invasion, but Ultra had made plain that there would be no attack from the sea on D Day, and that the forces coming by ship were back-up units and weapons which could be landed only once a port had been captured. Maleme was clearly the main objective, and even one of the 4th Brigade battalions would have provided an invaluable reinforcement around the airfield.

The failure to garrison the Tavronitis ridge was to provide the parachutists with their one safe landing place near Maleme. This was such a manifest tactical blunder that considerable attention was paid to it by both the inquiries held in the Middle East in 1941 into the loss of the island. Certainly it was a strange error for an experienced commander like Freyberg to have made. He indeed agreed to move the 1st Greek Regiment to the ridge from the small port of Kisamos Kastelli, fifteen miles further west, but cancelled the plan - so it was stated at the time - for fear that they would not have time to dig in and prepare their positions before the attack came. Yet this ruling was made a week before the assault began.

---

[1] *The Second World War* by Winston Churchill Vol III p. 240 Cassell and Co 1950
[2] *The Ultra Secret* by F. W. Winterbotham, Weidenfeld and Nicholson 1974
[3] *Ultra Goes to War*, by Ronald Lewin, Hutchinson p. 158.

The men could have marched the distance overnight, even if trucks had not been available – and many trucks could have been diverted for this key purpose – and a day's digging would have given them protection enough.

A clue to the reasons for this baffling lapse has been provided in the recently published volumes of the *Official History of British Intelligence in the Second World War*. These make clear that strict rules were laid down for the use which commanders in the field could make of information reaching them from Ultra. So valuable was Ultra to the war effort at the highest level that no commander was permitted to make a move based on information from Ultra alone. 'Though Headquarters could take it into account in framing operational orders to lower commands, such use of the intelligence was permitted only when it could be made to seem that it had been disclosed by other sources like reconnaissance or low grade Signit'[1] – Signit being the Services term for information gained from the interception of enemy signals. 'The possession of Ultra', it was ruled 'should never be jeopardised by a tactical operation which might arouse the enemy's suspicions.'[2]

For some commanders these were relatively easy requirements to meet. When the GOC Malta learnt from Ultra that an Axis convoy was setting out from Italy for North African at a particular time, and on a particular route, he could send out a reconnaissance aircraft or a surface vessel to secure a sighting which would mislead the enemy as to the source of his information.

The spectacular victory of the Royal Navy at Cape Matapan in March 1941 was possible because Admiral Cunningham had learnt from Ultra that the Italian fleet was at sea. But he could not move to engage them until after a Sunderland flying boat had duly reported a sighting. Montgomery at Alam Halfa and Alamein in 1942 had a free hand in the use of Ultra material, because his reconnaissance aircraft were constantly over the Axis lines, and RAF fighters could keep the enemy from observing too closely any moves of British troops. Freyberg on Crete had virtually no such alternative sources which could provide cover for the copious information he was receiving from Ultra. He had no air reconnaissance. Pirie and his MI6 operation at Fernleaf House could provide only dribs and drabs of news, smuggled out of Crete

---

[1] *Official History of British Intelligence in the Second World War*, by Professor Hinsley. HMSO 1981. Vol. I p. 571.
[2] Hinsley, op. cit. Vol II p. 643.

by caique under cover of darkness. Freyberg could hope – but do no more than hope – that the Germans would assume that we had agents in Athens who would get some information to us. But these sources were quite insufficient to meet the very clear and rigid requirement that he must not base his actions on the use of Ultra alone. He did not know the source of Ultra but he did know it was a source that had to the protected at all losts.

General Freyberg was a punctilious, rigorously trained soldier who would obey his orders faithfully. This could well have led him to interpret this ruling about Ultra as preventing him from moving the 1st Greek Regiment to the Tavronitis, or from transferring one of the battalions of 4th Brigade to Hargest's command to garrison that key ridge. He had to assume that such a move would be observed by the German Storch spotter planes which prowled low and often above our positions on Crete. They would be likely to pick up any digging of slit trenches by new troops west of the Tavronitis. It is noteworthy that not only along the Tavronitis, but elsewhere in the Canea-Maleme sector no major changes in the dispositions of the defending forces were made after Ultra material began to reach Crete. Freyberg had to face the possibility that by making such redeployments he would be in direct contravention of the orders given him about the limitations on the use of this most secret-and highly vulnerable-information.

The accuracy of this view is difficult to prove. Both Freyberg and Wavell, the two men who knew the full story of those days, are dead. Both died before the security clamp on Ultra was lifted in 1974. No records were kept, for security reasons, about the use of Ultra in Crete. But the thesis fits the facts closely. Further confirmation comes, too, from the reluctance of General Freyberg to enter into controversy about Crete during his lifetime. He made surprisingly little effort to defend his actions in the face of often hostile comment from historians. This could well have been because he could not refer to Ultra. He could not adduce in his own defence evidence which would have imperilled what was still one of the most closely guarded secrets of the war. His – and Wavell's – hands were tied by the very instrument of top-secret intelligence which was providing such abundant warnings of what was to come.

Even after gaining their foothold on the Tavronitis ridge and in the riverbed the Germans had only a tenuous grip on the western edge of Maleme airfield by nightfall on 20 May. They were equally vulnerable in the Prison Valley. Yet in neither area was a counter attack in any strength mounted by Hargest or Puttick, leaving Andrew to believe that he was so exposed that he had no choice but to withdraw from Hill 107, at a time when his forward platoons still commanded the airfield with their fire. This was a formidable list of errors to be made by seasoned and brave officers. I believe the reason can be stated in five words – German domination of the air. At no other time in the war did one side not only have such complete air supremacy, but was also able to exploit that supremacy so effectively. During much of the campaign in Italy the Allied air forces controlled the air space virtually as completely as did the Luftwaffe over Crete. But we were unable to utilise this advantage to anything like the same degree in Crete as the Germans did. For one thing the German troops in Italy had plentiful and efficient anti-aircraft defences which could deter low level bombing and strafing. For another they had the equipment and the materials with which to dig defences and fortifications which provided a defence against bombing and machine gunning. They had the transport – which we did not have on Crete – to move men and supplies under the cover of darkness. On Crete, except for the handful of Bofors guns around the airfields, and the more powerful but scanty 3.7 anti-aircraft guns at Suda Bay, we had no anti-aircraft protection at all. Worst of all, there were few entrenching tools. Once the troops had been forced to leave their prepared positions around Maleme, they seldom had the means to dig slit trenches, as they fell back from ridge to ridge towards Canea. An occasional shovel or their bayonets were the only tools available to scrape some cover in the stony soil. Otherwise they had only low stone walls or the trunks of olive trees as protection. Once the lines of battle were clear, after the first confused stage, the enemy Storch reconnaissance planes could circle overhead, directing onto our positions the waiting Stukas and Messerschmitts. The obliteration of the anti-aircraft position above Force Headquarters on our last afternoon near Suda was merely a demonstration of what was being meted out, hour after hour, day after day, to the front line troops. The battle of Crete was a masterly demonstration by the Luftwaffe of close support from the air for troops on the ground. By the latter stages of the war, when we had developed the Cabrank technique, with half a dozen Hurricane fighter bombers on call to hit targets at will, the Allies had developed a comparable system. But the model for this was in full operation three years earlier, in Crete.

Quite as deadly as this direct impact of the enemy aircraft on the battle field – perhaps indeed even more deadly than it – was the effect of constant attack from the air on the minds of the men, and above all of the commanders, of this sense of being hunted by machines every minute of the day. This worked in two main ways. The planes severed communications, so robbing commanders of information essential for them to take the right decisions. At the same time it wearied them, numbing their powers of decision, inducing apparently inexplicable errors of judgement.

In particular these factors need to be borne in mind in evaluating Andrew's decision to pull the 22nd New Zealand Battalion back from Maleme on the night of 20/21st. Not only was he tired, but he was blinded by lack of information. With his telephone lines cut, and his runners ambushed, he needed above all that most modern form of battle field communication – the wireless. But there was no wireless contact between Andrew and his company commanders. There were not enough sets for this. This shortage of a modern army's most basic form of communication was one of the worst gaps in the equipment of the defenders of Crete. A hundred more Mark II wireless sets could have saved Crete. Indeed half a dozen of them – enough to maintain contact around the airfield of Maleme, might have tipped the scales. As it was Andrew was throughout the first day and night of the battle deprived of knowledge essential to him. He was not so much a man fighting with one hand tied behind his back, as a short-sighted man whose glasses have been smashed – able to deal with events close at hand, but blinded as to those at a distance.

It is also possible that Andrew and Hargest thought too much in World War I terms, of holding a defensive line. Certainly the line to which Andrew ultimately fell back at Maleme was stronger, in terms of resisting a land attack, than was one with his units scattered around the edge of the airfield. Yet the issue at stake at this stage of the battle of Crete was not one of holding lines, but of denying the Germans the use of the airfield. They had virtually no more parachutists left to drop. Only by securing a runway on which their transport planes could land reinforcements and supplies could they avoid defeat. In the same way neither Andrew nor Hargest – nor Puttick – appears to have appreciated that in the air age the pace of fighting had greatly increased, that counter-attacks in a battle in which the enemy can be supplied and supported from the air had to be swift and immediate. Campbell at Retimo, with the experience of the winter campaign in the Western Desert to draw on, had learnt this lesson, and applied it. Prince Rupert rather than Koutouzow was the better guide to the opening stage of the battle for Crete.

Yet these factors, though considerable, were outweighed by another – the mental impact of intensive and prolonged attack from the air. Heavy bombing and strafing not only physically and mentally shook nerves as well as smashed bodies. It also drained away mental energy, inducing a lethargy and exhaustion which inhibited the consideration of issues and the taking of decisions. All three men who made the key decisions during those first three days and nights – the dour Andrew, the coolly quiet Hargest, the loquacious Puttick – were men of tested valour and endurance. Yet the two in whose hands the power to counter-attack rested, Hargest and Puttick, reacted with a fatal slowness which was at odds with their fundamentally aggressive characters, whilst Andrew showed an uncharacteristic pessimism. Constant air attack might not kill many men, if they could shelter in slit trenches. But it could numb thought. It could weigh like lead on the powers of decision, weakening the will not through fear but through mental fatigue. It could induce the feeling which Hargest had called dread, a dread which inhibited initiative – and particularly initiative in a situation which was unclear. The decisions taken by Andrew on the night of 20/21 May were taken by a man who had not even a roofed dug out or cellar in which to consider his options and discuss his moves. He had been in the open, lying or crouching in a slit trench, at best able occasionally to stretch his legs amidst rows of vines. Part of his mind was always having to engage itself with watching for a swooping fighter plane or a whistling bomb.

'Half the mistakes since 1918 have been the work of tired men,' Stanley Baldwin had said to Ramsay MacDonald in 1932, when he excused himself from a Cabinet meeting on the grounds that he was too weary for his judgement to be of use. If a politician in the security and comfort of Whitehall could feel like that, how much more did this truth apply to the soldier in the field faced by an enemy with complete domination of the skies? That was the element which made the fighting in Crete unlike any that British or Dominion troops had experienced before.

One further question poses itself. Why did General Freyberg not intervene to urge Puttick and Hargest to take more urgent measures more quickly? All his instincts must have directed him to that end. If ever there was a man imbued with what Marshal Foch defined as the most important of all soldierly qualities, a burning desire to engage the enemy, it was Bernard Freyberg. Had indeed he not been drawn away to Creforce, but had been left in command of the 2nd New Zealand Division, who can doubt that – having restrained an initial impulse to seize a rifle and bayonet and set about any Germans in the neighbourhood himself – he would immediately have sought every chance to counter-attack? Yet from his eyrie in the quarry he left Puttick, certainly throughout the first day, to fight his own battle, refraining from interfering with the decision of the man who had succeeded him as commander of the 2nd NZ Division.

One reason for this may lie in the background to Freyberg's assumption of command of the New Zealand troops in the Middle East. Though a New Zealander by birth, he had been a serving officer in the British Army, not the New Zealand Army, when in the autumn of 1939 he had been given this command. He had been promoted over the heads of the top men of the small New Zealand Regular Army, and over other veterans of World War I, like Hargest. This must inevitably have produced some tension into his relationships with his immediate subordinates, though he worked hard to remove it. This could, however, have led him, once he had yielded command of the division to Puttick, to be punctilious in leaving to his successor the maximum freedom of action. But an even more potent reason for Freyberg's stance on that first day of the battle lies in the breakdown of communications. Not enough news of what was happening on the fronts reached him for him to be able to intervene. Though Creforce, from its vantage point on the hill above Canea, appeared to have a grandstand view of the battle, it was an illusory view. Most of the fighting was hidden amongst the olive groves and the vineyards. Where it was in the open, as at Maleme, it was too distant to be reliable. At this highest level of control, as at the level of the platoon of 22nd Battalion around the airfield, the battle of Crete is a classic example of the importance of intelligence in war.

The Germans for their part were monumentally ill-informed about both their foe, and the terrain. They had underestimated the total strength of the British forces six-fold, and set the British fighting strength at a third of its effectiveness. They misread their aerial photographs, sending their gliders onto broken and impossible ground on the Akrotiri Peninsula. They believed that the Cretans would be at worst neutral, or perhaps even friendly. That these fiery islanders would see the German attack as an attack on them, and see the British, Australian and New Zealanders as allies who had come to their aid, and in no way as intruders who had dragged their island into an unsought battle, was an idea that Berlin never entertained. This misreading may account for the brutal bombing of Canea during the battle, and for the hideous reprisals on Certain resistance fighters later.

The Askifou Plain from the North

Creforce HQ Cave at Sphakia

(*Above*) Sphakia from t[
The road in 1941 finish[
amid the pines, (top ce[

(*Left*) Faces of exhaust[
Survivors landing from [
at Alexandria

German intelligence at this stage of the war was often poor – though there were exceptions, as with their detailed knowledge of the defences of Fort Eban Emael in Belgium, which enabled them to execute one of the most daring and decisive attacks of the war. So swift and shattering had been the German victories in Poland and France and the Low Countries that any defects in intelligence had not mattered. The battle had been won. It is the weaker rather than the stronger combatant who has to scrutinise closely the strength of his enemy. It was noticeable that as the war developed, and Germany was forced back onto the defensive, its military intelligence improved. By the time of the campaign in Italy in 1943–4 it was very good. German success in the early battles at Cassino owed much to the constant interception, by the Reichswehr, of telephone calls between our front line troops and the higher command.

When the battle of Crete got under way this imbalance in information, which had been greatly in our favour, swung swiftly the other way. Once the first confusion of the landing, with its massive slaughter of parachutists, had subsided, the Germans gained quickly a clear tactical picture of the situation. Their reconnaissance aircraft could wander at will along the front, pinpointing targets. They had from the outset an abundance of wireless sets. Their signallers could lay telephone lines without risk of these being cut by bombing. The reverse was the case within our positions. Telephone lines continued to be put out of action by bombers. The shortage of wireless sets became more acutely dangerous during the withdrawal, and was a major factor in the muddle which led to the loss of the 1st Welch Regiment. Nor was the gathering and assessing of information within the 2nd New Zealand Division either at brigade or divisional level, at that time adequately developed. The role of brigade or divisional Intelligence Officers was not seen first and foremost as that of knowing about the enemy. They were seen rather as additional reconnaissance and liaison officers. It was to take at least one more major battle before Intelligence at all levels in the Division was given clearly its two main tasks – to learn everything possible about the terrain and about the enemy.

Crete was for the Germans very much a Pyrrhic victory. The casualties to the parachutists were so great that Hitler was never again prepared to launch a major airborne attack. The sacrifices made by British, Australian, New Zealand and Greek troops in the vineyards and olive groves did not prevent the capture of Crete, but they may well have saved Malta, which would otherwise have been a tempting target for Student's highly trained forces. And Malta was to a large degree the key to the war in the Western Desert. From its airfields, guided by information from Ultra, a handful of British bombers and torpedo-carrying aircraft was to cripple Rommel's supply lines. Indeed the battle of Crete may have brought an even greater dividend. It delayed the German offensive against Russia, certainly by ten days, perhaps even as much as three weeks. This meant in turn a delay in the German advance on Moscow. The upshot was that the Reichswehr tanks and troops were caught on the outskirts of the city by the onset of early snow, enabling the Russian's most potent ally, General Winter, to come into the field. With these gains accruing to the Allied side, the loss of Crete, though a bitter blow at the time, cannot be classed simply as another defeat.

Indeed it can be argued that had we won in Crete, we would have faced such formidable problems as to give victory an equally Pyrrhic quality for us – and for Cretan people. British troops badly needed for the desert fighting would have had to be held in the island throughout the rest of the war. Supplying them would have provided a costly drain on shipping. Canea, Retimo and Heraklion would have been open to the German bombers based on the mainland, and would have paid a high price in civilian casualties and in material damage. These costs would have far outweighed the reprisals, cruel and numerous though they were, which were inflicted by the Germans on the Cretans who had helped or continued to help the Allies. As it was, we were able to tie down German forces on the island, and to inflict upon them such ignominies as the kidnapping of their commander, General Kriepe, in 1943. Cretan loyalty to the Allies never wavered throughout the darkest periods of the war. This brought one valuable by-product to the island. It developed only one Resistance movement, instead of the divided forces of Left and Right on the mainland. The civil war of the immediate post-war years never raged in Crete. Its people had been too firmly united by the common struggle which began on 20 May 1941.

Perhaps the best way to evaluate the battle of Crete is to see it for what in fact it was, a final rearguard action of the campaign in Greece. As such, it was highly successful, inflicting such heavy casualties on the enemy as to blunt his further advance in the Eastern Mediterranean, at a time when Syria and Iraq could have offered enticing further targets. For those who were engaged in it, the battle was to remain an enduring experience, reflected in the fact that each year at Galatas on 20 May veterans from New Zealand, Australia and the United Kingdom gather for a memorial service and parade. They meet to mark not a battle won, but a battle lost – but lost after such a hard fight that it can be recalled with pride.

PART TWO

PART TWO

20. A Strange Sort of Leave

I had been back at Maadi only some forty-eight hours, and had barely had time to draw a new uniform and acquire some new kit, when I was summoned to see Peter Fraser, the New Zealand Prime Minister, at the British Embassy in Cairo. He was en route to a War Cabinet meeting in London, and had played a part in getting the Royal Navy to send an extra cruiser, HMS *Phoebe*, to take off more troops from Crete on the last night of the evacuation.

I had not encountered Fraser before, but he was a Scot of a type very familiar in the parts of New Zealand settled by Scottish immigrants – a tall, gangling, balding man with a high forehead, and heavy-lidded eyes which looked out keenly and watchfully through gold-framed spectacles. I had met his counterpart many times among shepherds on back country sheep stations, or schoolmasters in Invercargill. He was, he said, very concerned about the lack of information reaching New Zealand about the activities and indeed the fate of the New Zealand forces in the Middle East. The defeats in Greece and Crete had come as a great shock to the New Zealand public. He wanted me to take charge of the public relations of the 2nd New Zealand Expeditionary Force, which comprised not only the fighting division, but all ancillary troops in Egypt.

It was the last thing I wanted to do. I had joined the Army to be a soldier, not a publicist. Had that been my wish, I would never have moved from the very well paid role of a British War Correspondent. Was I never going to be able to make my escape from journalism into soldiering? Had I made the effort, and gone through the arduous training of an infantry officer, to find myself now doing a press job at a much lower level than that which I had given up when I enlisted?

I decided, on instinct, that Fraser was a man with whom I could be frank. So I told him that not only did I want to remain a soldier in the field, but that I thought I ought to remain one. I had in the years before the war constantly urged people to stand up to Hitler.

117

Now that this had happened, it seemed to me only proper that I should accept my share of the risks which this involved.

Fraser had with him Carl Berendsen, Head of the New Zealand External Affairs Department, one of the country's most senior civil servants. Berendsen had no time for my objections. 'He is a soldier, under military orders,' he said to Fraser. 'He should be ordered to do this job.'

Fraser shook his head. 'No, I would not do that,' he said. 'I respect his view.'

I suggested a compromise. Could I do the job on a temporary basis, for a month, during which I could reorganise the Public Relations service within the 2 NZEF, and then return to the division? Fraser agreed, and went on to question me about Crete. I stuck to the one point on which I was sure – that by comparison with the Spanish Civil War, or the Russo-Finnish War, or the German attack in the west a year earlier, no troops had ever before been brought under such sustained and deadly attack from the air.

I was impressed by this big man, in his ill-fitting tropical suit, and the sharp mind behind this gawky countenance.[1] I wrote to my wife of him a day or two later:

> He has an appalling lack of method. I should love to have five minutes of watching the War Cabinet sitting in London now. But he has one characteristic of a great man. He can see issues simply and clearly . . . He is also prepared to speak his mind. He saw the issues of Crete with remarkable clarity.

I was to have further chances of studying Peter Fraser at close quarters later, when I served for a time in the New Zealand diplomatic service. They confirmed these first impressions. There was about him a touch of greatness of a kind which is rare, even in men who become Prime Ministers.

I was clear in my mind about what was needed to get the public relations problems of the 2 NZEF sorted out. The New Zealand public needed more news about what their troops in the Middle East were doing, and the troops needed more news about what was happening at home. The first, the flow of news to New Zealand, had

---

[1] So too was Sir John Colville, Churchill's Private Secretary at the time. He notes of Fraser, in his wartime diaries (*The Fringes of Power*, Hodder & Stoughton, 1985, p. 413), 'once his shyness was overcome, gold shone, and he was seen to be a sincere, unassuming and deep-thinking statesman.'

been hampered in Greece and Crete by the capture, with the Reinforcements Battalion in Greece, of Bert Hall, the official war correspondent. But a very good replacement was at hand in Robin Miller, the young Auckland journalist who had covered the Crete fighting with courage and skill. Had his despatches been passed through the censorship more quickly half the problems which concerned Peter Fraser would have disappeared. All that was needed was a sensible and flexible system of censorship which would enable Miller to write as fully as was compatible with security about any future campaigns. I urged that he be confirmed in his job, and given the maximum scope. He was to fulfil admirably this trust placed in him. I recommended, too, that film cameramen should be attached to the division in action.

For the troops in Egypt, the answer lay in a Forces' newspaper. The *2NZEF Times*, appearing on a weekly basis, and looking, with its headlines and general layout, very much like a New Zealand daily, met this need. It rapidly became an excellent small newspaper in its own right, one of the best of the many soldiers' newspapers of the war.

When I had got this sorted out, the fatigue of Greece and Crete suddenly hit me. I applied for leave, got a lift to Palestine in an RAF press relations car (my links with the journalistic brotherhood were operating once again) and settled into an hotel on the sea front in Tel Aviv, which struck me for all the world like a Jewish suburb of Vienna transplanted to the Mediterranean.

It did not prove a restful leave. The Allied invasion of Vichy-held Syria was under way. On my first night in Tel Aviv I was literally blown out of bed by a bomb dropped by Vichy bombers. The bomb fell immediately outside the hotel. Fortunately I had the windows of my room open, and they survived, remarkably, intact. But the blast shook the jerry-built hotel so severely that one leg of my bed collapsed, throwing me to the floor. A few days later I faced another hazard. I began to develop a very sore throat. I had reached Jerusalem by then, and my throat became so painful that I reported to the military hospital. They took a swab, and put me into a ward to await a report from the laboratory. Among the other patients was Quentin Hogg, recovering from the leg wound he had received when, in the desert, he followed the drill and stood up to fire at a German plane. I felt bound to tell him that I had canvassed and spoken against him during the post-Munich by-election in Oxford, which he had won on a Chamberlainite ticket. We were continuing the argument the next morning when a doctor and a bevy of nurses appeared in the ward. I had diphtheria, they told me, and must be moved at once to an isolation hospital. Everyone else in the ward must have an immediate injection to ward off any infection. My last sight of Quentin Hogg was of him, face down, waiting as a sister approached one of his bare buttocks with a hefty syringe.

The isolation ward was in a small building in the grounds of the army hospital set up in the Hospice of St John, in a building on the crest of the hill east of the Old City constructed specially to house Kaiser Wilhelm I on the visit he made to the Holy Land before World War I. From my bed an immense vista stretched away below me, where the road to Jericho wound down through the red hills of Judea to the grey streak of the Dead Sea. It was the road where the Good Samaritan encountered the wounded traveller and where Lot's wife had fatally looked back. Here it was my turn for my buttocks to be attacked by syringe, as the newly discovered anti-biotic, M & B (these were pre-penicillin days), was injected into me four times a day. It worked swiftly. The acute pain in my throat eased. I had a bedside radio through which I could listen to short wave programmes from all over Europe. On it, early on a Sunday morning, I heard on the Deutschlander Sender from Berlin military music, and then an urgent yet measured announcement. The Reich had invaded Russia. The Geman army thumped out the same stirring music which I had heard broadcast as the Reichswehr in pre-war days moved into the Rhineland, then into Austria, and Czechoslovakia. It was followed by the sharp tones of Dr Goebbels denouncing the evils of Bolshevism, and saying that all along the western frontiers of the Soviet Union the Reichswehr was advancing swiftly.

I felt a profound sense of relief. We had held the line against the Nazis and the Fascists until others had been drawn into the fight. Whatever the outcome of the struggle now being waged on those vast plains of European Russia and the Ukraine, Germany's strength must be worn down, if not defeated. There was hope too not only that the war would surely be won, but that Soviet Russia might emerge at the end of this struggle not only a wartime ally but a friend of Western democracy, might find its own harsh system modified by the experience of the effort against a common enemy. This second hope was to prove unfounded, but it welled up strongly in my mind on that sunny morning high in the hills of Judea.

My diphtheria cleared reasonably quickly. I was fortunate that it had developed when I was close to a hospital. For in the same hospital was a British army officer who had been paralysed in his legs as a result of developing diphtheria during the fighting at Karen, in Eritrea – and continuing for days with it undiagnosed. He would recover in due course, we were assured, but it would take many weeks. For me it was only a matter of a month before I was graded as convalescent.

Jerusalem in 1941 was a good place in which to convalesce. It was free of virtually all tourists except soldiers on leave, and not yet marred by harsh white modern buildings. From the hospital grounds we looked across the Valley of Jehosaphat to where the old city walls rose abruptly from the bare brown hillside. It was just as Vincent Sheean had described it a decade earlier, 'a small jewel of a city, white roofs and domes serried in order up and down hills beneath a startlingly blue sky'.[1] I could walk down from the hospital to the Garden of Gethsemane, with its cool trees and paths and shrubs and be the only person there except for an old monk tending the flower beds. At evening one could walk for more than a mile along the ramparts of the old city walls. In the souk in the Old City a wealth of fabrics was on sale. I bought for Cecily a length of yellow-striped Damascus heavy silk – not sheer silk, but a silken worked cloth; seven yards of a blue striped cloth; and three cummerbunds; and a length of Persian brocade – all for less than ten pounds. All made their way, via the Army Post Office, safely to New Zealand.

Through Christopher Holme, the Reuter correspondent in Jerusalem, I made two Arab friends, George and Katy Antonius. George was a Christian Arab, of Syrian origin, who had been educated in Alexandria and at Cambridge, and had served for many years in the British Government service first in Egypt and later in Palestine. Now he had come forward as a leader of moderate Arab opinion, striving to prevent what he saw as a nightmare future for Palestine if, after the war, the British yielded to Zionist pressure and allowed the Jews to flood into the country.

His wife Katy was in her mid-forties, the embodiment of the liberated, well-educated Arab womanhood of the inter-war period. Dark hair, every wisp of it combed into place, framed an open, wide-browed, candid countenance. She had a questing, somewhat sardonic gaze, as if relishing her freedom from the veil, still

[1] *In Search of History* by Vincent Sheean. Hamish Hamilton 1935, p 371

obligatory for so many of her race. She was even more avidly an Arab nationalist than was her husband. When she took Holme and myself to picnic on the coast near Haifa she ensured that her driver, manifestly an Arab in his burnous, drove through the busiest streets of Tel Aviv. From the depths of her long black car her eyes blazed hostility at the Jews in the streets, who looked back with equal hatred. There was an irony about the small beach flanked by the ruins of an old Crusader Castle, where we bathed, and ate our lunch watched by a score of ragged Arab children. For this was Athlit, where in the Jews were later to beach their main transport bringing illegal refugees to what was soon to be Israel.

George and Katy Antonius lived in a big villa on the road between Jerusalem and the hospital, serving lunches of hot tasting olives and roast pigeon and rice and tomatoes and grapes and Mount Carmel wine, and gathering together for drinks in the evening British army officers and reserved and hesitant Arab writers and teachers, who always seemed deeply worried – and indeed with reason – about what the future held for them.

The other good friend I had in Palestine was on the other side of the invisible but very real barricades. This was a Jewish girl whom my wife and I had known in Vienna in 1937, as Rosa Mazur. She was now married and called herself by the more truly Jewish forename of Rachael. Rachael Hubner was in 1941 a corporal in the British ATS, eager and elegant in her neat khaki uniform with its two white stripes, very much a citizen of the new city of Tel Aviv. We went swimming at Jaffa, where the Mediterranean surf rolled in in surprisingly high breakers. She represented the emerging Jewry which George and Katy feared. When the fighting developed in 1948 Rachael Hubner put her British military training to use, and emerged a decade later as Israel's first woman general.

To complete my convalescence the army banished me from these more exotic spots to a camp of wooden hutments just behind the sand dunes at Nathanyia. It had been a barracks for the only remaining horsed cavalry formation in the British Army, the 1st Cavalry Division. This had gone into action on its horses for the last time in the Syrian campaign, and was now to be mechanised. Some of its mounts were available to us, and I spent agreeable hours in the early morning riding through the olive groves with an English officer called Neville Heath. He was awaiting repatriation to England, not because he had been wounded, or ill, but because, it was rumoured, of something shady to do with missing mess funds.

I never saw him again, though I recognised him immediately when his photograph appeared in all the English papers in 1945, when he went on trial for a series of viciously sadistic murders. He was found guilty of them, and hanged.

By mid-August I was passed as fit, returned to Egypt, and was immediately sent on an Intelligence course at the Kasr El Nil barracks in the heart of Cairo. I had been appointed Intelligence Officer on the Divisional Headquarters staff, working under Robin Bell, who had been promoted to the post of GIII(I), the army abbreviation for Staff Officer Grade Three, in charge of Divisional Intelligence. Though I still hankered for experience as a platoon commander, this was, I realised, a dream job, a key post at the heart of the division, working through Bell to General Freyberg himself.

21. Wartime Cairo

Amongst the lecturers on the Intelligence course was the eccentric and able Colonel Wintle, who had gained fame by commandeering, without any authority, an RAF plane when France was collapsing, had flown to a Brittany airfield and brought away key equipment necessary for the British arms programme. He was himself a pilot, and was later to get into trouble for flying a light aircraft between the towers of Tower Bridge. He began his lecture brusquely. 'If you look in the Encyclopaedia Britannica you will find it lists three types of Intelligence – Human, Animal and Military. There are many who would rate them in that order.' His main object was to urge us to use common sense in the gathering and interpreting of intelligence. He told how, when the rearmament drive got under way in the late 1930s, British Intelligence in Whitehall had enlisted his help to find the whereabouts of a Canadian who, in World War I, had been an important cryptologist, decoding German messages with uncanny skill. The man had left his home in Canada some years before, and his whereabouts were unknown. The Canadian police could find no trace of him. The FBI had no record of his being in the States. Could Wintle tackle the problem?

'I did,' he said. 'I looked in the London telephone book. There were three people of the Canadian's name and initials listed. The first of them proved to be our missing man. No one in Whitehall had dreamt of doing anything so obvious.'

For the three weeks of this course the officers on it stayed in a small hotel nearby, a gloomy six-storied Victorian building where every room seemed to open onto a foul smelling inner well. It was a place to keep out of, so I used my off duty hours to explore further this lush, garishly strident city whose life I had glimpsed before I went to Greece.

On Gezireh Island, across the Nile from the Kasr el Nil barracks, was the main British sporting club in Cairo, the Gezireh Club, one of that string of clubs which were a key element in Imperial rule, providing a place of relaxation for the British soldiers, administrators and businessmen – and by their exclusiveness underlining the strength of British power. Gezireh was the most exclusive club in Cairo, its membership entirely British except for a handful of Anglophile Egyptians and Lebanese immensely proud of their entry to this place apart.

You drove to it by the wide bridge across the brown Nile, with the yellow stone Kasr El Nil barracks hot and steamy by the water's edge, with the clothes of the other ranks hanging from the windows, and officers sipping drinks on the terrace of the officers' mess overlooking the river. On that terrace Kitchener had paced, planning his campaign against the Mahdi in Sudan, and Lieutenant Winston Churchill had sipped his drinks whilst waiting for the river steamers to transport them up river to the battle of Omdurman. Now your ancient taxi honked its way past trams and army lorries, past the donkey carts with their flat sideless platforms crowded with squatting black crows with veils, the Moslem women to whom these carts were the local bus. Upstream the high sailed feluccas moved slowly with their loads of grain or cement or stone, each vessel with two men working, steadily and slowly, a huge oar at the stern.

On past the new stadium, and the public gardens where plump young Egyptian girls and plump young Egyptian men in grey suits and red fezzes walked on the lawns between great banks of flame flowers, and veiled nurses watched plump olive-skinned children play around the shrubs – agreeable outer regions for those who could not enter the club itself. Then came the gateway, with a white-gloved Egyptian policeman chatting to the drivers of taxis parked under the notice – Gezireh Sporting Club – Private Property – Members Only – Drive Slowly – Watch Out For Prams. On up the long straight drive, with the chock chock of polo mallets and the thud of ponies' feet from the field on the left and people strolling from the squash courts in white shorts, racket in hand, towel around the neck.

You went through the hall straight onto the terrace beside the swimming pool. Beyond stretched two cricket fields (or, if it was winter, hockey and football fields) and through the trees you could glimpse the grandstand of the Gezireh Racing Club. You found a table – the terrace was seldom overcrowded – drew up a wicker chair, ordered your drinks from the white-robed, green-sashed negro suffragis, and studied the people around you.

The men in the pool, brown-skinned and muscular, were at first sight those you might see in any pool anywhere. But a second look would show that the scar just under the shoulder of the boy diving now – for he looks no more than a boy – comes from no casual accident. It was done by a Vichy French bullet in the grey June dawn at the Litanes River in Syria, when the Commandos landed too far north, and the French had their machine guns onto them the moment they reached the beach. That tall thin man next to him, his face marked with a calculating disdain, is a former Monte Carlo playboy who now commands – with rash courage – a tank troop; that wide-shouldered fair man surging up and down the pool like an Olympic swimmer is an Australian war correspondent who was just that – an Olympic swimmer. The three men nearby, their skins burnt almost black by the desert sun, are South Africans, one with a healed bayonet gash in his thigh.

On the far side of the pool the mothers sit under their wide white hats, the thin white English mothers, looking out to where their children play in the shadow of the tamarisk trees, to where little boys in floppy grey hats ride on a donkey, beside which runs a great white-robed Egyptian ready to catch them if they slip. On this side the tables are filling up. A brigadier with a purplish face and red tabs, and an array of last war ribbons to justify the base wallah's job he assuredly has, is peering amorously at the nurse at the next table. She looks like a flushed nun in her white summer uniform – or her severe grey habit if it is winter – and in her starched collar and cuffs. Her face is plump from too much time spent in too many hot wards tending to too many wounded. She would no doubt like adventure, and excitement, and above all romance, but she has little chance, for she is due back on duty at seven that night. She stares with interest mixed with envy at the dark-haired Egyptian girl who has just come in, a girl with a long white face and carmined lips and long idle red-tipped, very white hands, and eyes as black as her black hair, in which is braided one white flower. She moves to a table where two other girls, who look as if they were her sisters – they are not, but all Egyptian girls look alike in this setting – are sitting with a group of young British officers in beautifully tailored gaberdine uniforms. The officers rise to greet her with a maddening, confident ease which annoys the old brigadier and the nurse, who looks wearily at the figure of the brigadier's friend who is making his way towards them – a bespectacled man in his forties who is something in the quartermaster's department, and who was a prep school headmaster in civilian life.

The voice of one of the young officers carries confidently across the terrace: 'All right. We'll call for you at nine. And Charlie will book a table at the Continental', and as they move away the girls draw closer together and talk eagerly, in low voices.

On the nearby ground the cricket match is drawing towards its close. From deck chairs around the ground men and women clap the play, or call 'Well played. Well played' and white-robed suffragis carry tea. On the verandah two groups of Egyptians play bridge, one of them glancing up from his cards to watch closely his young wife, who is having tea at a table nearby with a young Scots Guards officer, whose red fly whisk and cap lie on the chair beside him. The Egyptian is not sure whether his wife is having an affair with the officer, or with the young Druze prince who is in town from Damascus. He knows something is afoot, and though it does not worry him greatly, for theirs is an arranged marriage beneficial to both sides, he likes to know. He won't make a fuss unless it all becomes too open, but he likes to be the first to know.

In the hall a small group is reading the news from the ticker tape. Reuter messages from the desert, telling of fighting in which these men's friends and colleagues are engaged, to which they may return tomorrow or the day after, pour from the machine, side by side with the Stock Exchange prices from London and New York. It is close to six o'clock, and the men's bar by the doorway is getting crowded. Better to get a taxi and move across to Shepheards if you want a chota peg in some comfort before dinner.

Shepheards Hotel belonged to the era when famous hotels were not only grand, but distinctive, a world away from the mass-produced international skyscraper hotels of the jet age. I had envisaged it, for some reason, as being on the edge of the desert, and was surprised to find it jammed in the heart of Cairo, facing onto a narrow street which robbed its celebrated, wide stone terrace of all dignity, as the yells of street vendors, the blare of taxi horns and the rumble of lorries echoed amongst the buildings. But inside it was dignified to the point of being sombre. You moved into a lofty central lounge as dark as a cathedral, lit by stained glass windows set high above arabesque columns and pointed arches. In this ecclesiastical atmosphere army officers and their girl friends sat on couches set so high that the girls' legs dangled, their shoes just off the ground, as they sipped tea in the late afternoon. At other tables Egyptian families, with slim girls in white dresses grouped round portly matrons in satins and brocade sipped tasteless Cairo lemonade from tall glasses. Upstairs the bedrooms opening off the wide corridors were vast and high ceilinged, with brass-topped bedsteads and bell pushes to summon the silent suffragis who never came or when they did never brought you what you asked.

Shepheards was the great meeting place for officers during the 1914–18 war, a background sketched in many memoirs of that time. But in this war its Victorian ponderousness seemed to weigh heavily on the spirits of most of the men seeking relief from the aridities and pressures of soldiering. Yet it had its faithful patrons, particularly from amongst the officers of the more aristocratic regiments of the British Army. From its terrace you could watch cars draw up, still thickly covered with desert dust, and with sand trays and camouflage nets and shovels tied to their sides. The porter, green baize apron over white robes, would lift down the bedrolls and valises from the top of the car, whilst the officers, their knees dusty in their shorts, their faces sunburnt and their eyes eager, would follow into the lobby to begin their leave. Leave. What visions, what dreams were conjured up in that one word – and, as often as not, what disappointments.

Much more to modern taste than Shepheards were the establishments of Signor Groppi, who had brought to Cairo two European style cafes. The smaller Groppis was part indoor cafe, part courtyard, and part a long bar housed in a building through the middle of which grew a huge magnolia tree. Once you had fought your way through a horde of small boys crying 'evening baber' (the Arab tongue seems to find the letter 'p' particularly difficult) and out of date copies of *La Vie Parisienne*, you found yourself in a setting little changed since the days, a generation and a war earlier, when T. E. Lawrence came here, to sip chocolate and try out his Arabic. Now, against the usual background of officers in khaki, these inescapable extras in this wartime Cairo scene, can be seen some of the varied figures drawn to this feverish city. That thin dark girl who makes her way to a table on the bar terrace is a Rumanian, technically an enemy alien. But she is the mistress of a British Army officer who brought her here from Bucharest when the Balkans collapsed. She is bitter because he gives her little money, and because the British security services regard her as a spy, which she is not, but is just a girl who fell for a man and grew tired of him, and is trapped by the war. She would like to go off with the young Frenchman who meets her here every day, but she cannot. If she quits the protection of her British officer, out she will go.

At a table in the garden are two Egyptian girls whose gleaming, well-tended hair is so dark that it seems to have shades of blue in it. They have fine features, and delicate complexions, and sip their drinks nervously, as if they should not be here. Nor should they, according to the habits of their families and their faith. They are Copts, Christians by religion, members of a race which claimed to have been in the Nile Valley before the Arabs arrived, descendants of the Ancient Egyptians of the Pharaohs – and indeed there is something in their faces of the fineness portrayed in the bust of Nephertiti, now hidden away in a Berlin bunker against our bombing.

And this fair woman who comes in, wearing a black French haute couture dress with that added grace which every Greek woman seems to have. She is Greek, but from Alexandria, not from Greece. Her husband is a wealthy merchant there, and she returns to him this weekend. For though she wears black, and has that sudden strained look of the widow, her husband is alive. It is her lover she is mourning, that young British cavalry officer who met her here regularly until a week ago, when he was recalled to the desert, and his death.

The other Groppis, half a mile away in Suleiman Pasha Street, is bigger, a long room of marble walls and mirrors, with a patisserie offering rich French cakes and pastries, and at the far end a dancing area which is a favoured resort of sergeants and above. The girls come independently, in groups of two or three, wearing garlands of fresh, heavy scented jasmine around their necks, the white flowers glowing against their dark skins. Many will have another spray of jasmine in their dark hair. Almost all will wear white, which shows up their lithe figures, and the sergeants and the pilots and young officers wend their way through the close packed tables, and

(*Top*) Troops bathing at Baggush prior to the Crusader offensive

(*Centre*) Crossing the frontier wire

(*Right*) Captain Robin Bell

General Freyberg confers with his Brigadiers inside Libya. Left to right: Colonel Gentry (with glasses); Brigadier Hargest (full face); Brigadier Miles; General Freyberg; Brigadier Barrowclough

Digging in on Sidi Rezegh

bow stiffly and ask in their awkward French '*Voulez vous danser?*'

At one time the British Army, concerned that officers might spill secrets into the champagne glasses, started its own night club, called the Trocadero, where all the girls were vetted for security. It was theoretically for members only, but you could get in easily enough if you gave your name as Captain Smithers – which was the name of a genuine officer at GHQ in Cairo. It worked well as a technique until one night when the Military Police inspected the register, and discovered that seventeen Captain Smithers had clocked in. But when the great flap came in 1942, with Rommel only fifty miles away at Alamein, the Trocadero was closed down, never to reopen.

The really knowledgeable had in any event long preferred the night club on the roof of the Continental-Savoy Hotel. It was here, during my stint at the Kasr El Nil barracks, that old war correspondent friends would take me to dine on their copious expense allowances. It had a touch of genuine glamour. You made your way through the throngs of men in khaki and naval blue and air force blue grey in the lobby and took the elevator to the Roof Garden. There in the moonlight tables were set under the open sky. Soft lights gleamed on white cloths and silver and glassware, on the polished buttons and badges of dress uniforms, on bracelets and earrings and necklaces. Some of the women in evening dress wore, like the girls at Groppis, garlands of jasmine. But these were girls of a very different type, the truly rich. Here were the slim, red-finger-nailed girls from Gezireh, and wives of diplomats, and English girls in the well-tailored khaki of the fashionable Motorised Transport Corps, and an occasional Wren from Alexandria in her trim naval blue. The floor show was indifferent – the team of women acrobats included a grandmother and her grand-daughter – except for one famous belly dancer, the great Fatima, swaying with her face rapt and absorbed, and her heavy earrings and gold bracelets jangling.

From the edge of the roof top you could look out over the city below. Purplish-blue lights showed in the darkened streets. From one of the blocks of white buildings would often come the slow, slow incantation of an Arab song, a reminder of the other teeming, truly Arab world into which we did not penetrate. The moonlight would show up the gaunt cliff on the city edge, where Napoleon had camped for nine months, discussing philosophy with his savants and seducing his bugler's wife. The cannon balls from his guns could still be seen in the walls of the mosque which rose against those dead hills where the desert begins. In that desert, under this same moon, men were sleeping beside their tanks, or moving cautiously on patrol, peering out at the shadows among the camel thorn, rifle in hand, fingers ready to move toward the safety catch at the least sound. Since the fierce tank battles of Battleaxe in June a lull had settled in, on the frontier and around besieged Tobruk. But even here, on this languorous roof top, we knew that it was only a lull before a further storm which will encompass many of us.

22. Western Desert

I rejoined the division at Helwan, in the desert beyond Maadi, a few days before we were due to move to the Western Desert. My first task was to learn to ride a motor cycle which in those days was the only means of transport for the Intelligence Officer of an infantry division. It was a sensible enough plan in well-roaded areas like Western Europe, but – as events were to prove – hopelessly impractical in the rough, rockstrewn, sand-clogged ground of North Africa. Within a couple of days my skills were put to the test, as we set out in a long convoy of vehicles across Cairo and out along the Mena Road, past the young cypress and eucalyptus trees with their last caress of green, and past the pyramids, huge and aloof, into the open, dun-coloured desert. We slept that night in the desert south of Alexandria. The next morning, at the junction of the road to Alexandria, red-capped British military police directed us onto the black bitumen roadway leading westwards, past a big wooden notice reading 'Western Desert: Danger of Air Attack. Convoys Keep 150 Yards Distance'.

At a railway halt marked El Alamein we looked across the wide stretch of stone and sand, shimmering now in the haze, southwards to where the men of the 5th Brigade were working on defensive positions. With Greece and Crete in mind we kept a wary eye skywards, but there was no sign of any enemy planes, and near El Daba two Hurricanes appeared, comfortingly overhead. By late afternoon we had turned off the road, and after a final stretch along a rock-strewn and sandy track, where my motor cycle slewed and jolted and twice cut out on me, we reached our destination on the

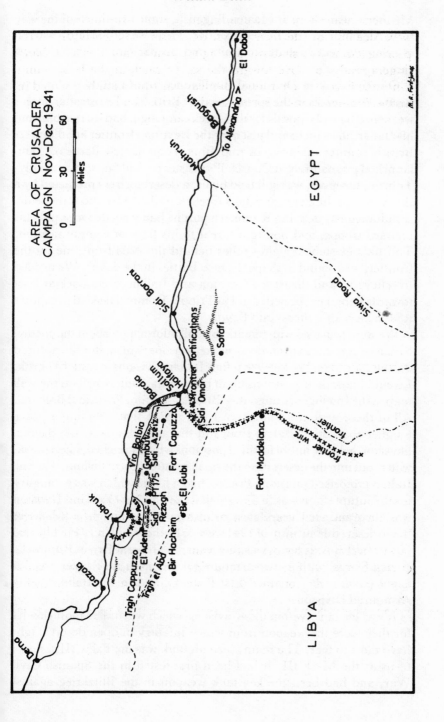

AREA OF CRUSADER
CAMPAIGN Nov-Dec 1941

Miles
0   30   60

M.R. Fielding

El Daba

To Alexandria >

Baggush

Matruh

EGYPT

Siwa Road

Sidi Barran

Sofafi

Frontier Fortifications

Halfaya
Sollum
Sidi Omar

Bardia

Via Balbia

Frontier Wire

Frontier

Fort Madalena

Fort Capuzzo

Bir El Gubi

Bir Hacheim

Fort Capuzzo
Sidi Azeiz
Gambut
Sidi Rezegh
Pt175
El Adem
Tigh el Abd

Trigh Capuzzo

Tobruk

Gazala

Derna

LIBYA

Mediterranean shore at Maaten Baggush, some two-thirds of the way from Alexandria to the Libyan frontier. There we settled into a warren of camouflaged dugouts, to train and prepare for the next desert campaign.

Our first task in Divisional Intelligence was to study the enemy. Rommel's attacks in the spring, against British and Australian forces weakened by withdrawals for the Greek campaign, had carried him and his Italian allies up to and just over the Egyptian frontier at Sollum. A British counter-offensive in mid-June, code-named Battleaxe, and launched prematurely at Churchill's insistence, had failed disastrously. Tobruk, however, was still held by us, a desert fortress protected by a thirty mile perimeter of anti-tank ditches, barbed wire and minefields, simultaneously denying Rommel a port he badly needed to supply his forward troops, and posing a threat to his lines of communication. Tobruk's existence, eighty miles behind the Axis front line on the frontier, was bound to shape the next battles in the desert. We needed to relieve it, and thrust the German and Italian forces back at least towards Benghazi, or better still to Tripoli. Rommel needed to capture it, as a base for a thrust into Egypt.

We were provided with remarkably full information about the enemy. Much of this came from documents, prisoners or material captured during Battleaxe. We knew that four Italian divisions invested Tobruk. I would mark their positions up in blue chinagraph pencil on the wall map in the Intelligence dugout – Brescia, Trento, Pavia and Bologna. All of these were from northern Italy, a sign that they might prove tougher than other Italian troops in the past. Another, the Savona Division, held the line of fortified positions which stretched, like a break-water, out into the desert from the small frontier post of Sollum. The one Italian motorised division, Trieste, had a name which was an augury for the future, for it was in Trieste that the 2nd New Zealand Division was, three and a half years later, to finish its war – though few who were in the desert this autumn of 1941 were to be there still in 1945. The real power in this Axis army was, however, in General Erwin Rommel's Afrika Korps, with its two armoured divisions, 15th Panzer and 5th Light (soon to be renamed 21st Panzer), and in the Italian Ariete Armoured Division.

It was the tanks within these divisions which we studied most closely, for they were the weapon from which infantry in open desert might have most to fear. The main German tank was the Pzkw III, known to us as the Mark III. It had been first tested in the Spanish Civil War, and had been the key tank weapon in the Blitzkrieg against

Poland and France. It was a cruiser tank, built to range widely, with a speed of 28 miles an hour, and with a 50 mm gun which outranged the guns on even the fastest British cruiser tank, the Crusader. British tank experts, wincing from the experience of Battleaxe, in which one third of our faster cruiser tanks, and two thirds of the more heavily armoured but slower Infantry tanks had been lost, were inclined to give the German armour an edge over ours. Yet the margin of German superiority, in a tank-v-tank battle, was slight. The Germans themselves had a great respect for the Matilda I tank, which had not only three inches of armour plating on its front, but a thin protective layer of concrete as well. It was – and looked like – a moving gun emplacement. What the experts had not realised was that the damage to our tanks had been done less by German tanks than by German anti-tank guns, and in particular by the 88 mm anti-aircraft gun, which in the open desert the Germans used as an anti-tank gun. Its 16 pound shell could smash through any British tank even at ranges of over a mile.

The relative qualities of tank against tank were not however our primary concern, even though they were soon to prove of deadly importance to us. What we had to study was how to protect ourselves against attack from the Mark III, when launched against our infantry on the ground. On the face of it, the prospects were not very good. The two-pounder anti-tank gun, which was the main British anti-tank weapon of the day, would be effective against the Mark III only at short range. Because of this a few 75 mm guns were added to the Anti-tank Regiments, but they – like the two-pounders – had no armoured protection, and were easy targets for the enemy guns. More and more it became the view of General Freyberg, and the big, quiet-spoken Brigadier Miles who commanded the New Zealand artillery, that we might well have to use our field guns, the superbly efficient 25 pounders, in an anti-tank role. But that made for supply problems, for it involved carrying heavy armour-penetrating ammunition, as well as the usual high explosive shells.

We were also provided from GHQ in Cairo with remarkably detailed information not only about the structure and armament of the Germans and the Italians, but about the names of their commanders, down to quite a low level. All this information I studied as if I were preparing for an examination, trying to master the organisation and lay-out of the enemy, the power of their weapons, even the outline of their tanks and guns in silhouette as we might – and indeed soon did – see them against the horizon. I discovered that as an Intelligence Officer I had to think in very different terms from when I had been a journalist. Watching Italian tanks in the Casa del Campo at Madrid in 1936, or German tanks moving into Austria in 1937 or into the Sudetenland in 1938, I had been primarily concerned with them as a spectacle, as something to describe and depict. I paid less attention to the strength of their armour plating or the size of their guns than to searching for similes which could bring the scene to life for my readers, or for the significant detail which would enliven my description, such as the skis strapped to the back of the tanks on the road to Innsbruck, or the flowers decorating the gun barrels of the tanks escorting Hitler into Karlsbad. But now what mattered was whether the Mark III had the new 50 mm gun, rather than the old 37 mm, or whether the Mark II had reinforcing armament bolted to its sides.

The other key subject we had to study was the topography of the area in which we were likely to fight, the Libyan Desert. The word 'desert' conjured up pictures of great, undulating sand dunes, patterned and sculptured by the wind. Such a desert did exist in North Africa, in the Sahara to the west, and in the Great Sand Sea to the south of Libya. But the desert in which the battles of World War II were staged was a bare, flat plain tufted with camel thorn, with wide acres of barren rock scree, stretches of soft sand, and shallow twisting wadis. Its most important characteristics, in the stretch between the frontier and Tobruk, were the northern escarpments, in which the flat inland plain fell away in a series of abrupt cliffs. At Sollum and Bardia these formed the actual coastline, dropping sheer to the blue Mediterranean. But west of Bardia they ran some ten to twenty miles inland, in a sort of false coast line or coast lines – because there were in places a series of these escarpments – descending to a flat corridor beyond which a jagged series of wadis met the sea, indenting the entire coastline eastwards from Tobruk.

The Divisional Engineers made a plaster model of the desert between the frontier and Tobruk. It showed at a glance how significant a feature was the main escarpment in any battle for Tobruk. The south-eastern segment of the Tobruk perimeter – the area through which the Australians in February 1941 had stormed the fortress – was overlooked by the escarpment, particularly from a point marked on the map as Sidi Rezegh. It was named after an Arab saint whose small white tomb stood on the escarpment edge. Freyberg needed to take no more than one look at this model to confirm in his mind what he had already deduced from his study of maps – that the key to the relief of Tobruk was the Sidi Rezegh escarpment. So long as the Germans and Italians held it, they could direct the fire of their artillery against any relieving force approaching from the east, or against any attempt by the Tobruk garrison to break out. If we could seize it, we could direct our own fire to give cover to our forces in a link up.

That plaster model showed how false was the doctrine, then prevalent in the thinking of the strategists of the British High Command, that in the desert ground did not matter. They argued that what counted was mobility; the skills of deploying and manoeuvring fleets of tanks; and the relative qualities of the tanks on either side, the thickness of their armour, their speed and reliability, the range and penetrating power of their guns. Yet the reverse was the truth. Because the desert was so flat and open the least rise or promontory or ridge became of great importance. It provided a point of observation, a place which could enable the fire of guns and mortars and machine guns to be directed across the surrounding flat ground, where there was usually no cover other than hastily dug holes, or a low rampart of easily shattered stones. A ridge twenty or thirty feet high could give a view for miles, and was the equivalent of a low hill in the ordinary European landscape. In this setting the eighty feet or so of the Sidi Rezegh escarpment was the equivalent of a mountain range.

This indifference to the possession of particular points in the desert, apart from the manifestly important Halfaya Pass, up which the coast road from Egypt climbed onto the inland plateau near Sollum, derived not only from loose strategic thinking, but also from a careless use of words by those who wrote or spoke about the Western Desert. It had become dangerously fashionable to speak of war in the desert as being like war at sea. Countless words were expended comparing armoured divisions and motorised units in the desert to fleets sweeping across the oceans. This reinforced the idea that ground did not matter – for fleets at sea were seldom concerned with which particular stretch of sea they were engaging the enemy in. It also tended to produce a false equation between warships and the tanks. Tanks were described as the warships of the desert, a concept which strengthened the idea that armoured warfare was essentially a battle of tank against tank. This was not how the Germans saw it. To them a tank – however deadly it might be to infantry – was highly vulnerable to artillery fire, and needed to be surrounded by a protective screen of field guns and anti-tank guns. Had the eloquence expended on comparing the desert to the sea – and Churchill himself was one of the foremost users of this metaphor – influenced only the general public, it would have mattered little. But it influenced also the planners of battles, with dangerous, and at times disastrous results.

In one respect, however, the similarity between the sea and the desert was close. This was in the art of navigation. Finding one's way across wide stretches of open desert, with few natural features to rely on, called for a knowledge of how to navigate by compass. The theory of this was straightforward enough. You worked out on the map – the British Army's ordnance survey had produced excellent detailed maps of the Western Desert – the route you wished to follow, and measured the compass bearing on which it lay, and the distance. You then lined your vehicle up on that bearing, ran the appropriate number of miles on your speedometer, and – theoretically – there you were.

In practice it was far less simple. Though tanks had sophisticated gyro compasses, the rest of us had to rely on the ordinary hand held oil-bath compass, or at best the more ingenious sun compass. The problem with the regulation army issue oil-bath compass was that its reading was distorted by any surrounding iron or steel. Since the trucks in which we travelled were almost entirely made of iron or steel, you could not trust a compass reading taken from the driving seat, or anywhere in the truck's interior. You had to stand in front of your vehicle, free from any such interference, and line it up exactly on the bearing you wished to follow. But once you climbed back on board you could no longer trust the reading the compass gave. When to this distortion was added the jolting and lurching of the vehicle, the need to make constant detours round drifts of sand or broken stretches of rock of impassable wadis, keeping on course could be very difficult. And the mileage shown on your speedometer could itself be distorted by the many unavoidable detours. The most practical method was to pick out some feature on the horizon on the bearing on which you wished to travel, and drive towards it, halting at intervals to re-check your bearings. At night this could be done by picking a star, fairly low down towards the horizon, and running for twenty minutes towards it – the maximum time within which it would not have markedly shifted its position. You then halted, locked a new star on your bearing, and continued.

A sun compass was easier to operate, and more exact, but such compasses were few in number, and restricted to only a few men in each formation. It depended on a series of discs prepared by Army ordnance, each for a particular area, and each covering a period of three or four days. You placed the appropriate disc, like a gramophone record, over a centre shaft on a small flat platform fixed on the mudguard of your truck or car. This produced a sundial with, instead of the hours, the marking of 360 degrees around its edge. The cards were designed so that the shadow cast by the sun would provide a specific and exact bearing, according to the time of day. The advantage of a sun compass was that it was not distorted by the metal of the vehicle. You still had to make allowance for rough ground and detours, but it was a remarkably accurate instrument, on which you could run for considerable distances without the intermittent halts necessary with a magnetic compass.

Desert navigation, particularly at night, was certainly sufficiently complicated to call for a good deal of practice. This was difficult for me to get, as a motor cycle was little use for this purpose. So rough was much of the desert surface that on a motor cycle you could make only very slow progress. You were too close to the ground to pick out points by which to steer. And navigation was in any event a two-man job, calling for one man to navigate and another to drive. My only chance to practise at all was to borrow the 15 cwt truck belonging to the Intelligence section, or to hitch a ride with one of the liaison officers, who had sturdy 8 cwt small trucks, called pick-ups. But this was not often possible.

Riding a motor cycle in the desert was in any event a nightmare. When we went out on our first major manoeuvre, with an approach march across thirty miles of desert at dusk, and a dawn attack, it was like riding along a dried up river bed, with jagged rocks, or great slabs of stone, or stretches of soft, boggy sand, or camel thorn bushes which a truck took in its stride, but around which I had to swerve and slew. It was impossible to keep up the same pace as the trucks, and I fell further and further back, my every muscle in my arms, shoulders and back aching. Finally the clutch cable broke. I sat alone in the dark, watching the vehicles of the column disappear over the horizon, and wondering what I should do if this happened in action, not just on manoeuvres. Fortunately a maintenance truck, itself lost, came along, and picked up me and my cycle. I helped them steer a course to where the force was due to camp. When, exhaustedly I arrived at the Divisional Headquarters position, having covered the last half mile on foot, I found Bell waiting impatiently for me. As part of the exercise, a bundle of documents purporting to come from the enemy had been prepared by Corps. Evaluating these, and preparing an estimate of the forces supposed to be opposite us, was my task. I got it done, though my hands ached so much from their jolting that I could barely hold a pencil.

To arrive on the job too weary to do it properly seemed to me a hell of a way to run an Intelligence service, and I argued that the IO's motor cycle should be replaced with a pick-up truck, like those used by the liaison officers. Colonel Gentry, who was Freyberg's chief of staff for this campaign, reacted with a rather amused disdain, as if implying that these would-be intellectuals of the I branch could do with a bit of toughening up. So my battering continued, even though I developed a constantly ulcerated mouth and severe toothache, which led to my having a molar removed. Yet though I always fell well behind the column, particularly on night marches, I gradually acquired a type of motor scrambling skill which enabled me to finish the course, even though occasionally I would reach one site just as the Headquarters were preparing to move to the next, and would wearily have time just to gulp a mug of tea before kicking my cycle – how I detested that untrustworthy brute – into life again.

For these manoeuvres, two dummy forts had been constructed deep in the desert, similar to those which the Germans and Italians had built along the frontier, with anti-tank ditches and barbed wire and dummy minefields. One was named Sidi Clif, (the Division's Chief Engineer had been George Clifton) and Bir Stella (Stella being the name of the main brand of Egyptian beer). Onto these the guns would bring down a curtain of live shell fire, behind which the infantry would race forward in their trucks and Bren carriers, force a breach in the defences, through which 'tanks' – trucks had to serve this role, for no real tanks were available for these exercises – would pass and fan out to attack the rest of the defences from the inside. Even in practice the sight of a fleet of two or three hundred trucks, looming bigger and bigger in the dust cloud they threw up, and of carriers, machine guns blazing, swaying and bucking on the rough ground, was a formidable one. With real tanks in the forefront, as would be the case in battle, it would be a sight to test the nerve of the Germans, let alone the Italians. Yet our own troops in the trucks knew too that in the real thing their soft skinned vehicles would be an easy target in the open desert, and practised intently at debussing swiftly and spreading out for the attack.

This manoeuvre, of trucks carrying troops to within a few hundred yards of their objective, was to be characteristic of the Crusader offensive, and was to take place more often during it than in any other desert campaign. It was a sign of Freyberg's skill as a trainer of troops that he foresaw this, and prepared the division for it. This concern to ensure that the one-time civilian army under his command should acquire thoroughly the basic skills of war, was not shared by any means by other commanders. The two South African brigades were to go into Crusader with virtually no training in Western Desert mobile warfare, and were to suffer heavily in consequence. Freyberg's attitude fitted in well with the high sense of individual responsibility which marked the men of the 2 NZEF.

New Zealand life at that time, still largely rural, tended to throw men and women on to their own resources, and the Kiwis of 1941 approached war not only as an adventure, but as a job to be well done. In Freyberg they had a leader who saw as a primary task the need to train them rigorously for that job.

In the Chevrolet three ton truck, used for carrying both supplies and troops, Freyberg saw an excellent instrument for mobile warfare. Even though it was not armoured or protected in any way, it was strongly built, and mechanically reliable. It was the great workhorse of the Allied armies in World War II, and played a major role – which the Russians took care never to publicise – in the logistics of the Red Army, to which it was supplied in great numbers. Freyberg in later years would often comment that the three tonner was as important to victory in the desert as the Sherman tank. To the infantry man, it was not just a vehicle, but to a considerable extent his home. In its sand coloured desert camouflage, with the white fernleaf on a black background which was the 2nd New Zealand Division's insignia painted onto its front and rear mudguards, it was the centre point of his section or his platoon. Under its high, canvas-covered canopy, were stowed his blankets, his spare gear, the tools and weapons of his trade. From its open back he stared out at the roads along which he travelled towards war, and from it he prepared to leap, bayonet fixed, into action. Like its counterpart in the air, the Dakota, and the mass produced Liberty ships, the three-tonner was one of the ways in which the vast industrial power of the United States was to prove decisive in this conflict.

Another piece of desert equipment which has not been given its due by the historians was the Benghazi burner. This was a two to three foot high piece of steel tubing, looking like the barrel of a mortar, made out of the light steel of benzine tins. Inside its outer casing an inner casing was welded on, and then closed at top and bottom, so as to provide a tube which, between its outer and inner layers, had a space into which water could be poured. This was done through an opening in the top which could be closed by a screwed cap. A handle was then attached to one side of the tube, making as it were a tall jug which held water between its outer and inner skins. The metal jug was then placed upright in an open pan containing an inch or two of petrol. A match dropped down the open centre of the tube produced a fire, the intense heat of which would simply boil the water held between the outer and inner surface of the tube. It was an ingenious way of exposing the maximum surface of the water to heat, so harnessing the fierce but brief heat of the flaring petrol. A Benghazi burner became part of the equipment of every vehicle in the 2nd New Zealand Division throughout the rest of the war. I used one to make my breakfast tea on the pavement of the Via Veneto in Rome on the day that city fell in 1944. Ten years later the scorch marks could still be seen on the kerbstone outside the Excelsior Hotel, amid the papparazzi and the film starlets of the era of La Dolce Vita.

23. A World Apart

As these weeks of training and preparation went by, the desert began to exert its subtle grip on our minds. I was not deceived by my first impressions of it, which were of drabness and monotony. It shared these qualities with other areas which had come to exercise an attraction for me like the wide tussock covered stretches of Southland and Otago, or the grey manuka and brown fern hillsides of the pumice lands around Taupo, before they were tamed into green and fenced cow farms. It took time to accustom oneself to the limited palette of the desert's colouring, with its browns and yellows and greys, so that when I marked my map in red or blue chinagraph pencil the colours seemed like a shout amidst silence. Our khaki uniforms, and the ochre paint on trucks and tanks, and the carefully devised greenish brown of the camouflage nets which we threw over the trucks, to remove the telltale dark shadows, fitted into this general monotone.

There was not much beauty in the military areas close to the coast, with their rutted tracks, and dumps and airfields and camps, and rusty benzine tins, and storms of grit stirred up by lorries. But a few miles inland you were in virgin desert, with scarcely a tyre track on its surface, mile upon mile of clean stone and sand and stunted bushes, an area not yet poisoned by minefields and barbed wire or churned up by tank tracks. Across this we could race in our trucks, covering fifty to sixty miles a day without seeing another living person, filled with a sense of space, and solitude, and freedom and of direct and fulfilling contact with the earth on which we slept by night and into which, we well knew, we would soon have to dig for our lives by day. On all sides there was only this immense plain, broken by an occasional low ridge, or a cairn, or the hump of a bir, where stones surrounded the entrance to a cistern cut into the rock centuries earlier, to gather in the rare winter rainfall. In the evening the least fold or curve in the desert's surface would be marked by

purple shadows, sharp and distinct after the shimmering haze of the
midday. In the midst of this silence and stillness it was easy to
understand how, out of another desert only a few hundred miles
further east, had come three great religions.

In this autumn of 1941 the Western Desert was literally a world
apart. No civilians lived there. Even the wandering Bedouin had
been moved away by the Egyptian authorities. There were no
women. Not even nurses were allowed west of the Alexandria turn-
off. There were only the armies, transforming this into an area
dedicated to men striving to kill one another, enhanced only by the
great arc of the sky in the morning and the stillness of noon and
multitudinous stars that stared down at night.

I lay in my bedroll and stared up at those stars on many nights,
but one in particular has remained in my mind. It was in late October,
at Bir Hamil. Bir Hamil has no claim to a place in history except
that it was near the dummy fortifications on which the Division
trained. I had come on with a small party in two trucks, to spend
the night close to the bir. There we were to wait and note how much
we could hear of the tracks and guns of the brigade which was to move
up in the darkness, ready to launch their attack at dawn.

We had hit the bir dead on, after a thirty mile run in the darkness
a pleasantly reassuring test of our desert navigation. There was
enough frost in the air to make my blankets and sleeping bag
welcome. I lay with my head on my haversack, staring at the sky.
It was crowded with stars, as if fistfuls of them had been hurled
against its black velvet dome. They stared down, clear and
unblinking, as if they saw not only every move but knew every
thought of us below. Reality, they seemed to say, is inescapable. But
if it contains battle, it also offers these moments of beauty, and
above all the chance of fulfilment. Perhaps it was just the tension of
the moment, and the knowledge that we would soon be going into
real action which stirred in me something close to exultation. I was
quickly jolted out of such musings. For was that not, very faint in
the distance, the sound of a motor vehicle? Indeed it was, and,
notebook in hand, I sat up and jotted down by the light of a
flashlight, '0115 hours . . . Faint sound of truck on bearing 330
degrees . . . 0214 hrs . . . motorcycle on bearing 187 degrees,
moving away.'

The shore at Baagush offered a gentler form of beauty, a gracious
fringe to the homespun of the desert. I slept in a bivouac tent on the
edge of the dunes at the back of a beach of white and pink and yellow

sand which curved round towards a slim headland. The sea was often a shining blue, crossed by twin lines of low white surf, but at times was green and rough, with a roar like distant gunfire. On nights when the moon was full its shining path ran across a corrugated sea to the very foot of my tent. It was easy to understand that twenty miles further west, at Mersa Matruh, this coastline had been a favoured spot for Antony and Cleopatra, when very different armies had gathered in their camps in their day.

Throughout October the autumn sun was still warm enough for bathing, and during the afternoons troops from the nearby brigades would fill the beach with sunburnt, lean, naked swimmers, their flesh looking very vulnerable beside the neat pyramids of stacked rifles and the steel helmets they piled on the sand. This reminder of the human being beneath the uniform, of the inevitable price which war was about to exact, has been portrayed, as has so much about men at war, by Tolstoi in *War and Peace*. The scene on these Libyan beaches that autumn was the same which Tolstoi describes as witnessed by Prince Andrew on the eve of Borodino, when he came upon his troops bathing in a pool, and noted the 'human flesh, white, firm and healthy, with muscles as hard as steel', destined he thought, soon to be *chair à canon*, soon to face the ravages of hostile bombardment.

Fortunately there was little time for such reflections, as preparations for a new offensive were now reaching their climax. By early November the coast road was jammed every day with long columns of supply trucks, and new guns and tanks and lorries. This bounty brought me one marvellous boon. Colonel Gentry had taken more note than I realised of my argument that I could not do my job properly on a motorcycle. Unexpectedly I was issued instead with an 8cwt pick-up truck, and allotted a driver, a burly former sheep drover from Southland. The pick-up was to serve us well. In a variety of camouflage colours, its sides in due course marked by bullet and shellfire, it was to be the Intelligence Officer's vehicle across North Africa to Tunis, and ultimately all the way up Italy to the end in Trieste.

24. Crusader

The Allied offensive, set for mid-November, had been given the somewhat grandiloquent code name of Crusader. This was also, rather confusingly, the name of the latest type of British cruiser tank, several hundred of which had reached Egypt in time to take part in the action. The officers who planned the attack and who were to form its top leadership were all new to the Western Desert. General Auchinleck had at the end of June been appointed C-in-C Middle East in succession to General Wavell, in whom Churchill had, wrongly, lost confidence after the Battleaxe defeat. No officer with experience of the 1940–41 desert victory had been sufficiently senior to command the newly designated Eighth Army. General O'Connor, who had brought a touch of genius to the conduct of operations against the Italians, had had the cruel misfortune to be taken prisoner, along with his successor, General Neame, during Rommel's sudden thrust towards Tobruk in March 1941. General Beresford-Peirse, who had then taken command of the Western Desert Force, was sacked after Battleaxe. This had brought General Sir Alan Cunningham to the head of the Allied desert forces. He had led the British and South African forces to victory in Abyssinia earlier in the year, and commended himself further to New Zealanders because he was the brother of Sir Andrew Cunningham, the Naval C-in-C in the Mediterranean whose ships had fought so valiantly in the battles for Greece and Crete.

General Cunningham had, however, not only no experience of the Western Desert, but he had never commanded tanks in any number, and certainly not in a mobile battle. Yet such were the vagaries of the British Army's command structure that he was to be pitted against the most spectacularly successful German tank commander the war had yet produced, General Erwin Rommel. Both Cunningham's corps commanders were also new to the desert – General Norrie, who was to command the three armoured brigades, grouped in 30 Corps, and General Godwin-Austen, a big affable man of considerable presence, who headed 13 Corps. He had served at Gallipoli, a valuable link with the New Zealanders now serving under him. Cunningham set up his Headquarters just along the coast from us at Baggush. There, in October, the title of the force under his command was changed from Western Desert Force to a name which was to go down in history – the Eighth Army.

General Messervy, the commander of the 4th Indian Division, with whom we were grouped in 13 Corps, had, however, fought in the Battleaxe campaign. One of Freyberg's first actions on reaching Baggush early in September had therefore been to go forward to Messervy's headquarters at Sofafi, close to the frontier, both to get the feel of the forward area and to draw on Messervy's experience. He took with him his ADC, Jack Griffiths; a liaison officer, Lieutenant Wild of Wellington; and myself. It was my first contact with Dick Wild, who was destined to rise high in the Division, becoming Brigade Major of the Armoured Brigade which was to be formed in 1942, and higher still in the law after the war, becoming ultimately, as Sir Richard Wild, Chief Justice of New Zealand. There were two future New Zealand Chief Justices in this Division in this campaign. The commander of the 6th Brigade, Harold Barrowclough, was to be Wild's predecessor in the post.

Messervy believed in having his headquarters well to the fore, and we spent a night in a curve in the desert some twenty miles from the great barbed wire fence which Mussolini had constructed, on the lines of Roman walls of two thousand years earlier, along the Libyan-Egyptian frontier. We were on the edge of a vast no-man's-land, with only an armoured car screen between us and the enemy, as we bedded down in the open in our sleeping bags, with Wild exchanging banter with Griffiths about the All Black tour of England in 1935 on which Griffiths had captained the New Zealand side. The next day, whilst the generals conferred, I studied the Indian Division's maps and situation reports, relishing this first real contact with the already fabled Western Desert.

Auchinleck gave Cunningham a general directive to destroy the enemy's armoured forces and drive the Germans and Italians from Cyrenaica, leaving Cunningham to decide how to do this. Early in October the Eighth Army commander unfolded his plan to the corps and divisional commanders and on 17 October General Freyberg passed on an outline of it to his brigadiers and senior staff officers at a conference in the small wooden hut amid the sandhills which served as his headquarters office. The plan was in two main parts. The three armoured brigades under 30 Corps, in which were

Link-up at Ed Duda between 19th NZ Battalion and 4th Royal Tanks from Tobruk

Watching a tank battle from a wadi

The mosque at Sidi Rezegh

General Freyberg talking by radio to the South African 1st Brigade Commander, November 30

grouped the cruiser tanks, and a number of new, light American tanks officially called General Stuarts (but for some reason always known as Honeys), would move out into the open desert some thirty miles on the enemy side of the frontier, and 'seek out and destroy' the enemy armour. The two South African Infantry Brigades, and the infantry and guns of the 7th Armoured Division's Support Group, would go with them, ready to give battle with the enemy troops besieging Tobruk, and to join up with a sortie by the Tobruk garrison. That infantry action would, however, wait until after the enemy armour had been defeated, a process which was assumed to be certain since we had a five to four superiority in tank numbers.

Meanwhile 13 Corps, with which we were to serve, would execute a left hook around the enemy strongpoints on the northern edge of the frontier. We and 4th Indian would cut off these strongpoints, and the enemy's fortified positions in Sollum and Halfaya and Bardia, and be ready either to storm them or to besiege them. A further role for which the New Zealand Division might be cast would be to move westward to join the fight to clear the enemy away from around Tobruk. This was seen as only a possibility. Freyberg, however, saw it from the outset very much as a probability. It was a task he was ready for, but one for which he was determined to keep all three brigades of the division together. Freyberg shared very strongly the World War I infantryman's belief in the importance of artillery, the guns which Napoleon had termed the monarchs of the battlefield. He stressed at this planning conference the importance of the Divisional Artillery acting as a co-ordinated unit, and not allowing itself to be split up into separate groups.

Freyberg also saw immediately one danger in the Army plan. With all three British armoured brigades committed to a battle against the German armour, the western flank of the New Zealand Division could be dangerously open to attack from the German 15th and 21st Panzer Divisions, should these decide to turn on us before facing up to 30 Corps. We and the Indians would have with us I tanks – Matildas and Valentines – of 1st Army Tank Brigade. But they could move only slowly, and could be outranged by the German tank guns. Freyberg therefore urged that at least one armoured brigade from 30 Corps should be detailed to protect our left flank. Godwin-Austen supported him strongly in this. Cunningham gave way on the point, and gave the 4th Armoured Brigade the double role of protecting the left flank of 13 Corps as well as joining in the armoured battle. It was a decision which was to emphasise the fatal flaw in the Eighth Army plan, the dangerous dispersal of the British forces, so giving Rommel the chance to destroy them piecemeal.

When the plan finally filtered down to our level, my impression was that it was a good one. The aim of seeking out and destroying the enemy armour was in accord with what we had been taught at OCTU, and what I had observed of war as a war correspondent. It was also free of the defensive mentality which had accursed Allied strategy on the Western front in 1940. It had the virtue, too, of identifying the enemy tanks as the main target, those deadly panzers which I had witnessed cutting such a swathe across Northern France in the spring offensive of that year.

As we moved into November signs of forthcoming action increased. War correspondents began to gather in the press camp set up along the coast from us, close to the caravans and wireless masts of Eighth Army HQ. Among the correspondents was Edward Ward. He showed me with pride the recording equipment with which the BBC had equipped him, a change from the days when he had reported alongside me from Finland and Belgium and France, and when he had had to seek out the nearest radio studio from which to broadcast. Now he had a caravan with a sound desk, on which his talks could be recorded on big round discs, like outsize gramophone records. He was not to have much chance to use it. Within the first few days of the offensive he and his caravan were to be captured by German tanks, and he was to be taken off to a series of harsh prisoner of war camps in Italy.

The Division rounded off its training with a very typically New Zealand occasion – a rugby football match on a Saturday afternoon. It was played against a team from one of the South African brigades at Baggush. The scene as the game ended could have been that on any of a hundred grounds in New Zealand, with the crowds moving slowly away, arguing earnestly about the game, and red-gold spurts of light showing in the dusk as cigarettes and pipes were lit. There were even a couple of dogs chasing across the field, being whistled at by their soldier masters. There were an astonishing number of dogs with the Division. They stared at you from the cabs of trucks, and ran beside the columns of marching troops, a reminder of the degree to which the units of the Division had become home to the men in it. Many of them had been together now for two years. This was a factor which contributed to the remarkably high morale with which the Division went forward to this new action. Gone now were any traces of post-Greece or post-Crete bloody-mindedness. This was a force eager for battle.

There were high level visitors, too. William Jordan, the ex-London policeman who had emigrated to New Zealand, and returned to London as High Commissioner, visited Freyberg's HQ. Known to everyone as Bill Jordan, he had used the powers of the High Commission to do a great deal for the 5th Brigade during its time in England, and he got a rewarding cheer from many in the brigade when, a very noticeable figure in a light grey suit and black Homburg hat, he stood by the roadside with the General to watch the troops move out from Baggush towards assembly areas close to the frontier. With Jordan was Colonel Park, the New Zealand Military Liaison Officer in London, in whose office I had enlisted fifteen months before.

Another visitor was the most senior Intelligence officer in the Middle East, Brigadier John Shearer, the Director of Military Intelligence at GHQ in Cairo. After a meeting with the General he came across to our Intelligence dug-out. Bell was away at the time, and it fell to me to answer his queries. What did we see as the main problems ahead? Knowing of the General's concern about our left flank, I answered, 'Defending ourselves against the Mark III tank if the German armour attacks us in the open desert'. He was confidently reassuring. 'You will have I tanks with you – and your 25 pounders. Don't underestimate the 25 pounder as an anti-tank weapon.'

Plans for the move forward were labelled as 'Div Exercise No 4', the fiction being that we were embarking merely on one more Sidi Clif or Bir Stella training scheme. But everyone knew that this was the real thing, and prepared himself in his mind for it. Security was tightened to ensure that no hint got out in letters or messages to base. The Maori Battalion raised one alarm which sent me post haste to their headquarters. Their cooks had noticed on the past three mornings pigeons flying overhead in a westward direction. Could these be carrier pigeons, carrying messages from a German agent in Alexandria? I passed the information on to Eighth Army, who were impressed by our assiduity, but sceptical as to its value. And since amid all the weaponry at our disposal, no such thing as a shot gun could be found, there was no way we could put the question to the test. But it was heart-warming to be with the Maoris at this moment, their faces eager for battle. With the heightened optimism which this pre-battle atmosphere engendered, I assured the Maori IO that Rommel might not stay to fight around Tobruk, but might withdraw to stronger positions to the west – a possibility the General himself had recently been canvassing.

25. To the Wire

On Armistice Day, 11 November, the Division began its move forward. 5th Brigade were the first to get under way. The next morning my pick-up truck took its place in the Divisional Headquarters column, behind the 15 cwt which carried Bell and the draughtsmen and clerks of the Intelligence section. I looked with sympathy at the detachment of Military Police who still had to use the accursed motor-cycles. Then we were off, along the tarmac road to Mersa Matruh, and then southwest down the sandy, rutted track which led towards the Siwa Oasis, and which had the grand name of the Siwa Road. Some twenty-five miles along this we turned westward and took up position in a wide stretch of open desert.

Here, over the next three days, the entire Division assembled, coming together in desert formation for the first time. We formed a small city of some 20,000 men, with 2,800 vehicles, spaced out over an area twelve miles by eight. As almost everywhere in North Africa, we were on historic ground. Alexander the Great may have passed close to the ground where we camped, for he met his death at Siwa, where his legions were swallowed up by the desert sands. If any Roman legions had followed in their time, their ghosts would have found our pattern of desert formation of interest, because it was formed on the same principles as were their own camps. When a Roman legion halted for the night, their bronze eagle standard would be thrust in the ground at the point at which their commander established his headquarters. From the standard each unit had a set position to occupy, with fortifications dug so many paces to each side, and guard posts, and supply points, set out at each halting place in exactly the same pattern.

We did the same. The big truck of Divisional Headquarters – the G (for General Staff) vehicle – with a large blue flag fluttering at its bonnet, would take up its position. Around it the other vehicles of the headquarters group would take their allotted places, each at 200 yards from its neighbour. Then the brigade groups would take up their positions, two on the side nearest the enemy, one to the rear, and with the fourth part of the great quadrilateral filled by artillery and supply troops. Within each brigade area the vehicles were similarly ranged in relation to the brigadier's command vehicle. Field guns, Bren carriers and anti-tank guns would move to the outer periphery, each knowing its exact place in relation to its neighbours, and each with its allotted task.

To give quick access to the Headquarters for despatch riders and for staff cars, a route was kept clear leading to the G truck, and named Anzac Avenue. At dusk compass bearings would be taken from the G truck to the General's car, alongside which his bivouac tent would be pitched, and the cars of the GI and other senior officers, so that messengers could find a way to them in the dark – an essential guide at night in featureless desert. In its main lines, this desert formation type of camp can be traced on the ground at a dozen points along Hadrian's Wall in Northumberland today. We had, however, one advantage over the Roman legions. We could maintain if need be these positions on the march, with each vehicle closing in to a somewhat closer distance, but keeping its same relationship with its neighbours.

The G office, the operational heart of the division, from which the General issued his orders, was in those days merely a three ton truck, on either side of which a canvas lean-to was erected to provide a pair of offices – on one side for the I staff, on the other for the Operations staff. These were equipped with trestle tables and folding wooden chairs and easels and wall boards for maps and a scattering of field telephones. Strict security was enforced by Colonel Gentry. Only staff officers directly concerned with controlling our own troops were allowed into the G, or Operations office. Bell might be occasionally called in there, but had no right of access, and I the and clerks and draughtsmen were rigorously excluded. This was to ensure that knowledge of the disposition of our own troops, and of future plans, should be kept to as few people as possible. From an Intelligence point of view this strict separation of function was a drawback, as knowledge of one's own side's plans and dispositions could give significance to what might otherwise seem unimportant detail in the picture one was constructing about the enemy. It was a limitation which was gradually to be lessened, though never completely removed in later campaigns.

On Thursday, 14 November, the General assembled all the officers of the division down to the level of company commanders and explained to them the plan of the battle ahead. He stood by the G truck, alongside a big map which Bell and I and the draughtsman had prepared, a powerful, erect figure in battledress, wearing canvas web ammunition pouches and belt and with the cord attached to his revolver round his neck.

It was an historic occasion, the first of many such pre-battle briefings which were to be held over the next four years. This was the first time General Freyberg had been able to assemble all the leading officers of the Division on the eve of battle. In Greece and Crete – and indeed in England in 1940 – we had been on the defensive, awaiting an enemy thrust, the timing and direction of which had been uncertain (or, in the case of Crete, unable to be communicated even to the brigadiers). Now for the first time we were taking the offensive, under a plan of our own side's devising, and we were moving into it as an integrated division, every man in it a New Zealander.

It was a key moment in the evolution of this extraordinary body, known as 'the Div' to those who served in it. The Div was to exert over the many thousands of men who passed through its ranks an influence as profound as that exercised by a great university. Comradeship, (that most inadequate word, with its undertones either of politics or sentimentality, to express the link amongst men in action) the essential cement amongst soldiers, does not in most armies extend much beyond a man's regiment or even his section or platoon. Seldom does it extend to any formation as large as a division, which in World War II numbered some 17,000 men, and which with supporting troops could rise as high as 20,000. But in the case of the 2nd New Zealand Division in the Middle East and Italy between 1941 and 1945 there existed a powerful sense of identity, of our being men of a particular tribe with its own attitudes, its own skills, its own interdependence, and above all its own pride. This quality owed much to our origins in a small country where we had shared common experiences, and indeed where many of us had known one another from childhood. But it owed a great deal to the leadership of this 51-year-old expatriate who had returned to lead his fellow countrymen in the second of the two great wars of his time.

Freyberg, radiating strength, confidence, and a courage which he took for granted not only in himself but in those around him, not only was, but looked, the leader. Never was that more the case than on this overcast, grey morning in the Egyptian desert, as he told the ring of officers, 'No battle is easy. This one promises to be a very tough one.'

He explained the Division's role clearly, warned particularly of the need to counter the German tanks, and to keep vehicles dispersed against air attack. It was not an adjuration to great deeds, but a careful explanation of tasks to men who, like himself, saw defeating the enemy as something like clearing the bush or driving a road up a mountainside – a job like any other. Only at the end did he allow himself a hint of emotion, when he concluded, 'The battle must be fought out to a finish, in the end ruthlessly. The spirit of the British Bulldog wins. You must prepare everybody for the battle ahead both mentally and physically.' Then he turned briskly to the next stage of the business, a demonstration of the laying of anti-tank mines.

The next day the entire Division moved forward in daylight a further forty-five miles westward, one of the rare occasions in the desert war in which it travelled as one single formation. We moved in lines of vehicles seven abreast, each vehicle two hundred yards from its neighbour, forming a vast column which stretched for nearly twenty-five miles. It was a clear, windless day, and the route lay for the most part over firm ground, so that there was little dust. On all sides trucks, Bren carriers, field guns, anti-tank guns, and staff cars lurched and bumped in one great moving fleet. It was an impressive spectacle. Early in the afternoon, above the sound of vehicle engines, we heard the sound of distant cheering, gradually growing louder. Up the centre of the column was moving a staff car, a Humber in desert camouflage colours. I recognised the General in it, with Jack Griffiths at his side.

The men in the trucks had recognised the General too and had begun to cheer. This was taken up in the vehicles around, and suddenly the whole column was cheering, with men waving from the backs of their three tonners, out of the cabs of trucks, from the carriers and the gun quads. As the General's car sped forward, the cheering sped with it. It was an emotive moment as, deep in the desert, with no one else to watch, these troops moving forward into battle cheered as if at a football match. It demonstrated not so much the popularity of the General – though that was one element – as of the men's confidence in him and in themselves for what lay ahead.

The next three stages of the move up to and through the frontier wire were to take place at night, to avoid attracting the attention of enemy aircraft. I was given the role of going ahead by day, and of stationing at intervals along the route soldiers from the Provost Corps. Each had a storm lantern, shuttered on one side but able to show a green light on the other. His job was to lie low during the day, and when night came to light his lamp and place it so that its beam would shine eastwards where it could be seen by our columns as they advanced, but would be invisible to the enemy in the west.

Eighth Army officers had been over the ground some weeks before, and had selected a route and the three staging places. We were given the map references for these. To my relief, for my experience of desert navigation was still scanty, the task of navigating our route was given to another officer. My responsibility was to pick, at intervals of half a mile, a point at which a lamp could be sighted so as to be readily picked up by the advancing columns and so ensure that an interlocking chain of these green points would mark the way forward in the darkness.

Our work for the first night's move went smoothly. We got away to an early start, a small party of two pick-up trucks and a lorry crowded with military police. It was clear and bright, so that the navigator could use his sun compass, and detected the course without difficulty. The ground was relatively open, and good vantage points for the lights were easy to select. At each one a soldier would clamber down from the truck, with his greatcoat as some protection against the night cold, rations in his haversack, and his hurricane lamp. But he would look a very lonely figure as, obeying his orders to keep out of sight, he would crouch down amongst the rocks watching us depart, leaving him utterly alone in this wild waste.

We reached the designated camping area in the early afternoon, leaving me ample time to complete the final stage of my work, which was to lay out a set of lights to guide each brigade to its area. With satisfaction I stood by my truck at midnight, picking up the first distant sound of engines, until it rose to a roar, like that of a cataract, a stone crusher, a factory in full blast, as the columns came closer, until the trucks themselves loomed up, seemingly endless in the darkness, filled with silent men.

The next day our difficulties began. The sky was overcast, so the navigation had to be by magnetic compass. This slowed our progress. The ground was more broken, with hollows and ridges which were low and readily passable by day, but which at night would present real hazards. With a strict ration of only one lamp per half mile, it was impossible to mark detours round them. Wolfe's dictum that war is an option of difficulties had been hammered into us at OCTU. I made my options as best I could, but I foresaw a rough ride for the brigades, particularly for the big quads towing the guns.

The laager area for the night, as we had drawn it out on our maps, was set close to a double cairn – an unusual landmark which should make it easy to recognise. It was with relief that in mid-afternoon, with still a couple of hours of daylight left, I saw a double cairn ahead. We had run our correct distances, and so I set about laying out the pattern of lights for the brigades, in an excellent laager area of open firm rocky desert. I was puzzled that one or two contours, and a cairn marked on the map did not seem to be on the ground, but I put that down to the fact that the maps of this part of the desert were known to be sketchy.

That done, I decided to use the brief remaining period of daylight to get a view of the area where we would have to lay the lights tomorrow, and drove to the top of a nearby ridge. To my surprise, another double cairn was visible. A check with the map disclosed the cairn and contours I had missed at the other site. To my horror I realised we had staked out a laager for the division some two miles south of where it should have been. It was too late to try to shift the lights. Even though the responsibility for the desert navigation had not been mine, I knew that, as the General Staff officer with the advance party, I must be prepared to accept a major share of the blame. Visions of being immediately sent to the rear, perhaps even of the ultimate ignominy of being sent back to New Zealand (a fate which had already been handed out to a number of those who had not measured up to the Division's standard) filled my mind.

Half an hour later Brigadier Gentry arrived in his car. I reported to him our error, and waited tensely for his wrath to descend. He did not waste time on anger. 'It looks a perfectly good alternative site. We will leave the brigades to take it up – and then we will see how many of them find they are in the wrong place. It will be a useful test of their map reading. But' – and here a note of steel entered his voice – 'see you get it right tomorrow.'

Only one brigade did in fact report that it had been placed out of its due position. The others were far more concerned with sorting themselves out after the rough passage they had had in the dark.

The last leg of these night advances was due to take us into Libya.

It was a cold, wintry, grey morning. Soon after ten we topped a low ridge and saw, some three or four miles ahead, what looked like a thick brown hedge stretching across the iron-grey sand of the desert. This was the frontier wire, the twenty yards broad series of barbed wire entanglements built by Mussolini as the modern equivalent of a Hadrian's Wall. It was brown with rust now, but impassable to vehicles. It stretched across the wide, tufted plain towards a small, empty redoubt, and then on into the distance. Beyond it was Libya.

Through my glasses I could see tiny black dots on the horizon which were the amoured car screens of 30 Corps. Excitement, indeed elation welled up in our tiny party as we raced towards the wire, across which, I was thankful to note, the going would be smooth for the advancing columns that night. Sappers were soon at work tearing a gap a hundred yards wide in the thick tangle of the fence, uprooting the metal stakes and dragging sections of wire to the sides. I laid my green lights up to it, and set in position the red and white lights to mark either side of the gap. Once the dark came it showed up from the Egyptian side, like a glimpse of Piccadilly Circus in peacetime.

Three miles north east of the gap, inside Libya, I laid out the brigade positions, this time punctiliously on target. By dusk Robin Bell had arrived, with a demand from the General for an estimate of the enemy's artillery strength in the eastern sector of Tobruk. This was new territory for us. Our study of the enemy had been concentrated mainly on the frontier area to which, under the Eighth Army plan, we were to move. But I had a mass of material about Tobruk from Corps and Army. I got to work on this by flashlight, lying half under my truck as protection against oncoming vehicles sweeping through the area. For a new hazard had emerged in these night moves. Anyone on foot, or worse still, asleep in the open stood a chance of being run over as the brigades advanced in the dark. I completed the estimate well after midnight, as the night air was filled once again with the thunder of trucks and carriers and guns bearing down on us.

I was puzzled by the General's sudden interest in Tobruk, which was right outside the sector allotted to us. It was the first sign of his belief that it was on the escarpment close to Tobruk, not in mid-desert, that the issue of this campaign would be settled – and that we would be drawn into that settling.

Away to the north throughout that night thunder rumbled and lightning flashed, signs of the storms which were turning the coastal

area into a quagmire. Our area remained dry, and we woke the next
morning – our first in Libya – to a cold grey day.

26. Battle is Joined

In the daylight the Division sorted itself out, with anti-aircraft and
anti-tank guns at the ready, and with slit trenches dug against the
air attack which, after Greece and Crete, we expected. But none
came. Two or three German fighters flew over us, high up, in the
early afternoon, but they had apparently been after other targets,
and kept disdainfully away from the bursts of anti-aircraft fire
directed at them from our Bofors. Nor were there any gun flashes,
or sounds of gunfire, which would have marked the great armoured
battle that 30 Corps was seeking some twenty miles ahead of us.

No such battle was in fact taking place. Eighth Army had taken
Rommel completely by surprise. He had, we later learnt, been
planning to launch an offensive of his own against Tobruk. It had
been timed for late November. When our move towards the frontier
began, Rommel was in Rome for a few days' leave, and to tie up
final details with the Italians, under whose command he was –
nominally – in North Africa. Our tactic of night marches had
worked, and our approach had gone undetected. Rommel had
returned from Rome only on 18 November, the day on which we
had crossed the wire. Reluctant to call off his attack on Tobruk, he
had dismissed the first reports of an Eighth Army advance as merely
a reconnaissance in force. He was reluctant to disengage his
armoured divisions from their task of guarding the flanks of the
assault on Tobruk – an assault he planned to launch at a point
opposite Sidi Rezegh. So we – and the British armour in 30 Corps
– faced a period of baffling inaction on this first day of our move
into Libya.

In mid-afternoon, the Division was ordered to move some twelve
miles further north-east. The move was made by daylight, with no
need for lights to be laid out, but it was to give me an anxious few
hours. As Divisional Headquarters moved forward, the signallers
reeled out behind their truck a field telephone cable, laying it over
the open desert. To maintain a link with 13 Corps, I was left at the

old site, with orders, once the call came through that the new HQ had been established, to bring on a rear party of signallers, cipher clerks and orderlies, due to travel in some half dozen trucks.

The desert seemed very empty once the vast cavalcade of the Division had moved off across the horizon, and I was left sitting by the field telephone amid the scrub and stone. It was almost dusk when the telephone at last rang from the new HQ site, authorising me to close down, and bring this rear party up to the Division. So long as the light held, our journey was easy going, for we had the telephone line to guide us. But we had gone barely a mile or so when the light faded, and we could no longer pick out the line of the cable amongst the tufted bushes. The only thing to do was to run on a compass bearing.

This was not easy. It was a pitch black night, with not a star showing, and there was a new and unexpected hazard. We had to travel across desert where two of the brigades had been in position. The ground was pitted with slit trenches some dug to a depth of four or five feet. They provided a constant hazard, a series of mini tank traps around which we had to snake and dodge our way. This not only slowed us up. It made navigation a nightmare, for maintaining anything like a straight course was impossible. We made very slow progress. We had too only the faint blue light, from slits in the lamp covers on our blacked out vehicles, to show up the ground. By nine o'clock, when my speedometer showed me we should have been very close to Division, there was no sign of anything but thorn bushes and rocks and utter darkness, so dark that it was impossible to tell where the sky ended and the desert's surface began.

At this moment a light showed ahead, for a brief instant. It led me into the basic error of desert navigation – that of departing from one's instruments. The light had been somewhat to the west of where the division, by my reckoning, would be. But I decided to run towards it. This I did, for some three miles, but without finding anything but open desert. I had to face the fact that we were lost.

At this point, a mile or so ahead of us, a yellow Very light sailed up into the air, followed by a green one. They could only be from German or Italian units. Very lights were used very sparingly by British troops, whereas – as Crete had shown – the Germans relied on them frequently. We were uncomfortably near to the enemy – and I was even more uncomfortably aware that in the trucks ranged behind me were copies of all the main army ciphers, and secret documents which would disclose at a glance much of what the Eighth Army knew about the enemy.

I decided to stop where we were until first light. Then I would run back three miles, along the course on which we had travelled on our wild goose chase – or, more exactly, our wild light chase. I formed the trucks into a small laager, posted two resentfully weary sentries, and warned the men not to light up any fires to brew tea.

It was a bitterly cold night, and I lay in my blanket wracked by anxiety, sleeping little, watching the northern horizon. Intermittently an occasional Very light would show and I could hear faint sounds of vehicles, and I thought of tanks. I had good reason, I later discovered, for this worry. I had halted just south of a German battle group of the 5th Panzer Regiment. They would have found our ciphers and secret documents a succulent morsel.

As soon as it was light I roused the sleeping troops – with considerable grumbling, because they were dead weary; forbade them, against even more grumbling, to spend time brewing up, got them embussed, and drove back three miles. There I left them in charge of the signals lieutenant, and set out in my truck north eastwards at right angles to the line on which we had advanced. After about a mile we topped a ridge and saw below us a huge concourse of vehicles with men moving about around them. Was this the Division, or were these the Germans whose lights I had seen in the night? I studied the scene through my binoculars. I could see guns in position, facing outwards. Behind these a black object rose up into the air, turning over and over, and falling back. A moment later it rose again. Was it, I wondered, some new form of German mortar or grenade? Then, studying it more closely, I realised that it was something very different. It was a rugby football, which someone was kicking up into the air. That could mean only one thing. It was the Division. I raced back, gathered in my convoy, and moved towards the mass of vehicles. As we approached I could see men running to man the guns, and swinging them to cover us. They were aligned on us every inch of the way until we got within the lines. It was a formidable sight. I would not like to have been enemy infantry or even tanks moving towards those gleaming guns, with their round dark muzzles, their gleaming barrels, and the night dew still wet on their wheels.

The day that followed was for the Division a further period without contact with the enemy, as we waited for the outcome of the battle between the British and German armour. Mid-morning brought the welcome sight of British I tanks moving between the rows of our widely spaced trucks and guns, as the two squadrons of

Valentines allotted to us from the 1st Army Tank Brigade arrived.
For many in the Division this was their first sight of a tank at close
quarters, and these monsters in their desert camouflage, many with
canvas canopies still above them, to give them from the air the
appearance of lorries, were reassuringly impressive.

Bell and I had little information about the enemy's whereabouts
to provide to Colonel Gentry, as he prepared for a conference
between the General and his brigadiers. Corps passed on to us news
that there had been a tank battle with the Italian Ariete Division on
the left flank of the British armour, in which thirty-five Italian tanks
had been knocked out, and 200 prisoners taken, and that German
tanks had been in an action with 4th Armoured Brigade to the
north-west of our position. It was these Germans who would have
fired the Very lights I had seen during the night. But there was no
news of any clash between the rest of the British armour and the
enemy.

The General conferred with his senior officers in the open,
alongside the G truck. It was to be the last time they would meet as
a group during the battle – and indeed the last time during the war
that they would all be together. Within ten days Hargest and the
artillery commander Brigadier Miles would both be prisoners,
captured in the thick of the fighting. Both were to make daring
escapes, and get to safety, only to meet death within a matter of
months, Miles in Spain en route to Gibraltar, Hargest as an
observer with the D Day landings in 1944.

Of the half dozen leaders of the division who gathered in the
wintry sun that morning, three had been civilians in peacetime, –
Hargest of 5th Brigade a farmer, Inglis of the 4th and Barrowclough
of the 6th Brigade lawyers. Three were professional soldiers –
Colonel Gentry, and Brigadier Miles, the CRA – commander of
the Divisional Artillery – of the New Zealand Army, Freyberg of
the inter-war British Army. The medal ribbons on their battledress
tunics proclaimed that all had seen action before 1939, Gentry, the
youngest, on the North-West frontier of India, the others in the
trenches of France and Flanders in World War I. Each in his
different way radiated a quiet yet steely aggressiveness, a burning
desire to get at the enemy without delay. Inglis, who had been a
machine gunner in the 1914–18 war, red faced, upright, his manner
assertive and yet friendly, was the only one who looked the fire-
eater. Hargest, crumpled and testy, yet showing no signs of his
Crete ordeal, spoke with a confidence born from many, many days

of battle. Miles, massive, calm, thoughtful, had the presence of a natural commander. Barrowclough was deceptively slight, bespectacled, precise, making it difficult to envisage him as the young platoon commander who at the age of twenty-one had won the MC in ugly trench fighting.

Gentry, with his sharp features, and spectacles with thick steel rims, looked more the scientist than the soldier. Indeed he brought something of the scientist's detachment to the problems of war, appraising each problem in a cool, analytic way, even though under his lighthearted manner was a fierce determination. He worked excellently with Freyberg. He respected the General's aggressive flair, his instinct for the enemy's weakspot, and was skilled at turning Freyberg's broad decisions into the practical terms of lines of advance, provision of supplies, selection of units. Because each man respected the other, Gentry was also able to probe and, where he deemed it necessary, challenge the General's ideas without arousing impatience or irritation.

If eagerness to get to grips with the enemy was a common quality radiated by these men – 'we are frothing to go' Freyberg told the corps commander – there were no raised voices, no striking of attitudes, no bravadaccio about this group. There was not a trace of Patton's histrionics, with his ivory-handled revolvers and his loud talk, or even of Montgomery's carefully calculated presentation of himself as the People's General. These New Zealand commanders were proud men, but not vain men. They were of a generation of New Zealanders who rated reticence, and modesty of manner, as virtues. The pioneer ethic, that you were to be judged by your deeds, not your words, that words indeed were somewhat suspect, was still strong. An old Scottish word, which occurs in the Waverley novels, was used to describe the vice of self-praise, of 'showing off'. To do so was to be a skite, an ugly word well fitted to describe a fault. A skite in our parlance covered not only the incompetent, the man who promised more than he could deliver. It applied also to the able man who boasted of his achievements, to the batsman who preened himself after scoring a century, or the school prize winner who implied that it had all been rather easy. It was the reverse of today's belief in publicity, in images and charisma. Your deeds should speak for themselves, good wine needs no bush were very much the attitude of the New Zealand of this day, and it was reflected in these New Zealand commanders of men in war.

Freyberg himself was of this view. He disliked, and avoided

publicising his personal background or achievements. Of the Division's work he would speak eagerly, but any journalist who sought to present him as a hero, or to get him to recall events in his past, got short shrift. During the years when I worked with him in the war and in my contact with him after the war, he very rarely referred to any of his World War I experiences, let alone his somewhat mysterious pre-war ventures into the Mexican civil wars. Like others on his staff, I quickly sensed that to question him on such matters would invite a rebuke, and none of us attempted to do so.

As the afternoon of 20 November wore on the sound of tank battles could be heard to our north-west, where 4th Armoured Brigade were under attack. But still the general situation remained obscure. The truth was that Cunningham's plan had gone badly awry. Instead of the three British armoured brigades of 30 Corps drawing the German armoured divisions into battle, the brigade had split up. One, the 22nd, had been committed by its ardent commander, Brigadier 'Strafer' Gott, entirely on his own initiative, to an attack on the Italian Ariete Division at El Gubi. He came up against the Italian tanks in hull-down positions, and against field and anti-tank guns in considerable numbers. Gott not only failed to take El Gubi, but lost some fifty of the new Crusader tanks, a wanton waste of these new-type tanks urgently needed to fight the German Mark IIIs.

Seventh Armoured Brigade, finding no enemy on its immediate front, had headed for Sidi Rezegh. It had easily overrun the airfield, but it did not have infantry enough to take the feature which really mattered, the Sidi Rezegh ridge on the edge of the escarpment, the key to Tobruk.

During this crucial day only one British armoured brigade, the 4th, had found itself fighting the Germans. Onto it had blundered – for Rommel was as much in the dark about his enemy's movements as was Cunningham – elements of both the 21st and 15th Panzer Divisions, causing the fighting we heard to our north west during the day. The German armour, had Rommel but known it, was well placed to finish off the 4th British Armoured Brigade the next morning. But alarmed by the news from Sidi Rezegh, the tactical importance of which he certainly appreciated, Rommel withdrew his armoured formations and sent them westward at first light.

Far from the British armour achieving its objective of seeking out

General von
tein in Tobruk after his

Map captured with
von Ravenstein

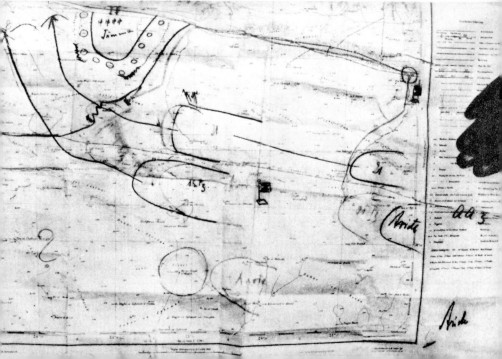

General Rommel in the Western Desert

The battlefield of Sidi Rezegh

and destroying the enemy armour, 30 Corps had got itself divided
into three segments, each a ready prey to the more experienced and
more skilled Panzer divisions. The first and key part of the Crusader
plan was on the point of disaster. Instead of the armoured
formations settling the issue, that task was now to fall to the infantry
and I tanks, and in particular to the New Zealand Division.
Freyberg's hunch that the heart of the battle would be around Sidi
Rezegh, and that we would be drawn into it, was about to become
true.

The true state of the armoured battle was, however, not known
to Eighth Army when the next morning we received orders to move
forward. These were still to carry out our original role of cutting off
and ultimately reducing the enemy posts along the frontier and
around Sollum and Bardia. We moved with alacrity. The Bren
carriers and light tanks of the Div Cav swept across Sidi Azeiz
airfield, rounding up prisoners and seizing stocks of yellow bombs.
Then, flanked by 4th Brigade, they moved onto the escarpment
overlooking the Via Balbia, that fine military road the Italians had
built to link Tobruk with the frontier.

We took the enemy completely by surprise. During the night 23rd
Battalion captured, almost without resistance, Fort Capuzzo, the
crenellated Beau Geste fort which had guarded the pre-war frontier.
The fort itself was of no use in a modern war, but the field
fortifications around it were strong, and it contained the telephone
exchange for all the units in the frontier area.

Divisional HQ was set up for the night north of Sidi Azeiz. I was
duty officer when, about midnight, a message arrived for the
General from 13 Corps. It was a cloudy, pitch-black night, one of
the darkest I had known in the desert. I had a bearing on which I
could find the General's car and bivouac tent, and woke him with
the message. 'Get Gentry at once,' he ordered. But no bearing for
the GI's tent had been left at the G truck, and I spent a nightmare
ten minutes stumbling about amidst the mud and the low bushes
before I found him. He conferred with the General, and then came
back to the G truck to send a message to Barrowclough. He was to
take his 6th Brigade and tanks allotted to it and move at once along
the escarpment in the direction of Sidi Rezegh. Our commitment to
the battle on the Tobruk perimeter had begun.

Throughout the next day, as the General urged Godwin-Austen
that the division as a whole should join Barrowclough in the march
on Tobruk, we sought anxiously for news of what was happening in

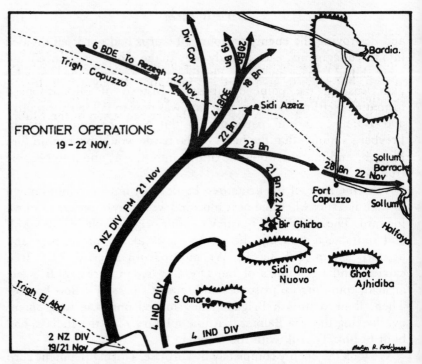

FRONTIER OPERATIONS
19 - 22 NOV.

the armoured battle away to our left. But little information came through, and what did arrive was at first misleadingly optimistic. Communications had failed in this desert battle as dramatically and as dangerously as they had failed on the first day in Crete – and with much less reason. No enemy air bombardment had cut the links between the armoured brigades and their commander at 30 Corps, nor was there any shortage of wireless sets. Lack of method and lack of training were to blame in what was to be the worst intelligence failure in Eighth Army's record.

What we could report, from the wealth of documents captured at Capuzzo and in 4th Brigade's attacks along the Via Balbia, was that the enemy forces in the frontier area were very much as had been forecast by Eighth Army before the battle. In the late afternoon I raced across the open desert in my truck to a Div Cav post on the escarpment west of Bardia to interview what we hoped would be a prime prisoner – a German tank driver. We thought we might have 21st Panzer Division coming up on us from the west, but the man proved only to be a tank maintenance man stationed at a nearby supply depot.

Soon after dawn the next morning I was on the other side of our sector, following on the heels of the Maoris as they attacked the barracks at Sollum. These were set on the edge of the escarpment, where it dropped sheer to the sea. The brief but sharp battle yielded a lot of Italian prisoners, but only one or two Germans. They were enough, however, to give me the information I sought, which was that the German Oasis Company was, as forecast, in this area.

Amongst the Maori officers was Tifa Bennet, a son of the Maori Bishop of New Zealand. It was the first time I had seen him since, nine years before, we had been students together at Otago University. Tall, good-looking, athletic, he was also a superb natural pianist. We had never needed to buy music for the piano in our college common room. Whenever a new record came out, Tifa would drop into the town music shop, listen to it a couple of times, and come back with every note of it in his mind.

Our reunion was curtly interrupted. We were studying, through field glasses, the wide curve of land below us to the east where the escarpment swung out into the desert, providing the Germans there with a very defensible line, when the whine of an incoming shell made concentration difficult. Other shells followed, smashing onto the roadway just behind us. Though it was a cloudy, cold morning, there must have been light enough to make our field glasses glint. It was the beginning of a bombardment from the many guns in the enemy positions on the flat which was to cost the Maoris severe casualties during the day.

On my way back I had time for a quick look round Capuzzo, the first time I had seen on the ground a place which we had studied intently from aerial photographs. The cameras had portrayed it exactly. I walked around its walls as if returning to a place I knew well. It was a sad little ruin, more like a stage set than a real fort, its stone walls ripped apart by shellfire as if they had been of lathe and plaster. But the cemetery with its German graves, each with a black wooden cross above it more like a military medal than a Christian symbol, was a reminder of reality.

The 5th Brigade Headquarters were on Sidi Azeiz airfield, ten miles further west. In a small camouflaged mess tent Hargest and his staff were breakfasting. He summoned me to join them in a superb meal of fried sausages and tomatoes. In a thick grey jersey which matched the greying hair at his temples, he sat like an old warrior chief amongst the members of his staff, most of whom were still in their twenties. He was concerned at the news that only the 6th Brigade had been ordered westward, and told me to pass on to the General his belief that the Division should not get divided up.

It was to be the last time I saw Hargest. Four days later, almost to the hour, and this same spot, tanks of the German 8th Panzer Regiment overwhelmed 5th Brigade Headquarters, despite a valiant fight by its few guns. Hargest, directing the fight to the end, standing by his blazing Intelligence truck, had to surrender. Rommel, who came on the scene soon afterwards, congratulated Hargest on the fight his men had made – and was offended when Hargest failed to salute him.

Hargest was taken to Bardia, and then on by submarine to Italy. He and Brigadier Miles, who was to be taken prisoner near Sidi Rezegh three days later, were placed in a Colditz-like fortress in Northern Italy. They tunnelled their way out, and made their way through France and across the Pyrenees with the help of the French Resistance. Miles fell ill and died in Spain, but Hargest got back to Britain. Unable at that late stage of the war to exercise command again in the field, he joined in the invasions of Northern France as an observer. There he died, hit by mortar fire in a jeep.

Hargest was not a complicated man. He was animated by a straightforward feeling – he was not going to allow anyone, let alone a German, make him do what he did not choose to do. He had not only courage, but determination to a rare degree. By the actions of such men are shaped a young nation's traditions and standards.

I got back to Divisional Headquarters to find gear being packed and vehicles assembled ready for a move. Orders had come through for the General to take 4th Brigade and one of the battalions of 5th Brigade (the 21st) and move westwards to join up with Barrowclough in the advance on Sidi Rezegh.

We were moving into the unknown, for information had not yet reached Freyberg, or Godwin-Austen at 13 Corps, that the day before, Saturday the 22nd, all three British armoured brigades had suffered huge losses in a battle with 21st Panzer Division just south of Sidi Rezegh. At the end of the day Rommel had not only driven 7th Armoured Brigade from Sidi Rezegh, but had destroyed so many British cruiser tanks that he now had at least twice as many tanks left as were in all three British armoured brigades. Later figures were to disclose that by this stage of the offensive the British had lost five hundred tanks to the one hundred lost by the enemy.

And matters were to get worse. For as we gathered that Sunday afternoon to begin our move, Rommel was marshalling his forces against the 5th South African Brigade, left exposed and vulnerable in the desert south of Sidi Rezegh. Had any dispassionate observer been able to survey the Western Desert battlefield that day, he would have classed our advance towards Tobruk as a rash folly. In the event it was to prove the action which swung the fighting ultimately in the British favour.

27. On to Sidi Rezegh

Divisional Headquarters, together with the 20th and 21st Battalions and their accompanying I tanks, formed one column, moving along the Trigh Capuzzo, a rough sandy track which led from Tobruk to Fort Capuzzo. Inglis took the other battalions of 4th Brigade and their I tanks along the Via Balbia towards Gambut, where there was an important Axis air base. Our convoy made slow progress, delayed at one point by enemy opposition, and we waited by our trucks as the infantry dealt with this. Then we went on in the dark, under a pall of black rain clouds. We went bumping on and on across rough ground, vehicles crowding in on one another as in a city traffic jam, or like frightened cattle herding together. Every driver was straining to keep his place, his eyes peering at the shape of the truck in front, his mind filled with one thing – determination not to have to drop out, and find himself at dawn surrounded by the enemy. At one point my truck lurched into a hole, throwing me against the steel dashboard and stripping the flesh from the bridge of my nose. I put my field dressing on it, but we could not, and did not, stop. Just after midnight we halted at our destination, a point called Bir El Chleta, half way between Bardia and Tobruk.

We were, though we did not know it, in a perilous position. Twenty miles to the west Rommel was gathering his forces and surveying his options at the end of one of the most decisive battles of the desert war. German historians have since given the fighting on 23 November the somewhat Wagnerian title of the Battle of The Sunday of the Dead, from Totensonntag, the name given to that day in the Lutheran calandar. That Sunday afternoon the combined might of 15th and 21st Panzer Divisions had annihilated the 5th South African Brigade in the open desert south of Sidi Rezegh airfield, killing and wounding more than 600 men, and taking 2,800 prisoners. The New Zealand 26th Battalion, advancing on the left

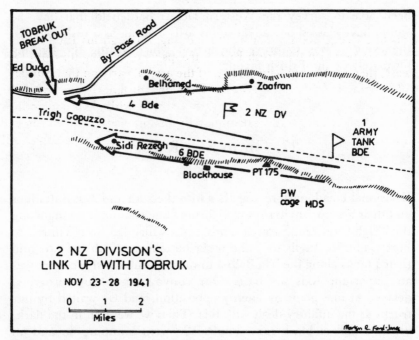

2 NZ DIVISION'S
LINK UP WITH TOBRUK
NOV 23-28 1941

flank of Barrowclough's 6th Brigade, has also come under attack, but had been able to hold the Germans at bay by the skilled use of their guns and by a counter-attack with the bayonet. It was the most complete victory the Axis forces had so far won in the desert. It put an end to 30 Corps's thrust towards Tobruk, and left Rommel with a superiority in tanks of at least two to one over the British armoured brigades.

Had Rommel turned his armour loose on us the next morning, we would have had a very rough time. But he decided instead to gather both armoured divisions together and to send them in a sweep south eastward towards the wire, close to where we had crossed into Libya five days earlier. Part of his aim was to strike at the Eighth Army supply dumps, part to remove the threat to his frontier positions. No doubt he was also influenced by his experience eighteen months earlier in France, when his 5th Panzer Division had spearheaded the German thrust across to the Channel ports. Bold movement by his tanks, regardless of the threats to their flanks, had stampeded the French, and brought swift victory. A similar thrust, it must have seemed reasonable to assume, would send the Eighth Army helter skelter back into Egypt, giving him time to restore his frontier line and to turn and mount the attack on Tobruk which he had so long planned.

A major influence on Rommel's mind was the patchy nature of his knowledge about what we were doing. Though his Intelligence staff warned him that fresh British troops were coming up from the east, they could only have known of the arrival early on that Sunday of Barrowclough's 6th Brigade. They had no knowledge that the further substantial force of the 4th Brigade with their Valentine tanks, and of Freyberg's Headquarters had moved to within fifteen miles of the Tobruk perimeter. This was because we had made our move during the hours of darkness, a tactic the Germans seldom employed, and in which few formations on either side were trained. Those night time manoeuvres on the approaches to Sidi Clif and Bir Stella were proving their worth.

So, with the destroyed tanks and lorries and guns blazing like funeral pyres on the battlefield of Sidi Rezegh, Rommel issued orders for his armoured divisions to move the next day towards the frontier. It was a crucial decision, one which was to lose Rommel the battle. Not only did he miss his chance to bring the full weight of his armour against our two infantry brigades, but he left us four vital days in which we were able to do great damage to his infantry around Tobruk.

None of this was yet apparent when we woke the next morning, Monday the 24th, at Bir El Chelta, and found close by the escarpment which we had studied so frequently on maps and air photographs. Abrupt, rock-strewn it rose, exactly as on the engineers' model, like the cliff from the dry sea of the desert. We woke also to an unpleasant reception. Soon after dawn shells began to land amongst the Divisional Headquarters vehicles. This set us digging slit trenches with some vigour, and there were no casualties. One man, a soldier from the Provost unit which had set out the lamps during the advance marches, did ask me where he could find the RAP – the Regimental Aid Post, where the doctor and his orderlies were based. Was he wounded? No, but it was the day when he was due to have his penicillin injection to complete his cure for syphilis. Anxiety marked his face when he found that there was no RAP nearby. Poor devil. It was bad enough to find oneself in battle, but to have that type of added worry was over the odds.

By mid-morning as the shelling slackened off, I saw the tops of a line of lorries passing along the escarpment. I climbed to its rim, and got a view over the vast tableland which stretched beyond it. Two or three miles away a line of vehicles was moving away south-eastwards, in the direction of Egypt. In the dust it was impossible to see what they were. I took them to be transport of the 5th South African Brigade withdrawing from Sidi Rezegh. We knew that the brigade had taken a heavy knock, but we had no idea at that stage that it had been destroyed. It was only some hours later that I realised I had witnessed the Afrika Korps heading for the frontier.

We had meanwhile a small battle in our own back yard. Germans had been located about two miles to the north, where another escarpment marked the line above the Via Balbia. Kippenberger's 20th Battalion moved out in their trucks to deal with them. As they neared the target in the morning sunshine they debussed and moved across the flat desert, with shells from our own guns bursting ahead of them. It was exactly like the attacks we had mounted on Sidi Clif and Bir Stella, except that this time the fire they met was real. But so too were the Valentine tanks in support, and the enemy soon retreated eastward.

As I drove forward in search of prisoners and documents the New Zealand infantry were already walking back in extended order across the desert, with Kippenberger standing in his Bren carrier in their midst. Everything looked so quiet and ordinary in the pale sunlight that it was hard to realise that death had attended these men and this place only a few minutes before. Kip's usually reserved face was lit with satisfaction, so I knew in a flash that all had gone well. His casualties had been slight, with only two men killed, and though the bulk of the enemy had escaped we had a useful bag of prisoners and had captured several guns, among them an 88 mm – probably one gun which had shelled us earlier. Most importantly we had cleared the ground between 4th Brigade on the Via Balbia and 6th Brigade on the top of the Sidi Rezegh escarpment.

We could now advance towards the Tobruk perimeter on a broad front, with the two brigades side by side. But to do this, it was essential to secure control of the Sidi Rezegh escarpment, with its view over the ground across which we must advance. This was proving far from easy. Throughout Sunday, as the great Totensonntag's battle raged on the open desert to their south, the 24th and 25th Battalions had been engaged in a bitter and costly battle to seize Point 175, on the escarpment. It was some two miles east of where two buildings – a rare sight indeed in the desert – showed up on the ridge. One was a square, squat building known to us as the Blockhouse: one, a white-walled building with a low dome which we called the Mosque, marked the highest point of Sidi Rezegh. The Blockhouse was in fact a crude shelter for travellers, and the mosque was the tomb of an Arab saint and his son. In this desert of few distinctive features, they served now as valuable reference points for warring armies, a role their builders could hardly have envisaged.

As Barrowclough advanced along the ridge on the morning of 23 November, he had no knowledge of the defeat of the British armour the day before, nor that the troops of the British 7th Armoured Brigade had been driven from Sidi Rezegh. Indeed his orders were to link up with 7th Armoured Brigade on to Sidi Rezegh as soon as possible. The immediate obstacle in his path, the low rise marked on the map as Point 175, its slopes covered with scrub and rock, showed no signs of being strongly held. Yet it was in fact a formidable German position, with strongly prepared entrenchments, occupied by seasoned troops well equipped with mortars, light and heavy machine guns and anti-tank guns, and with the tanks of 21st Panzer Division in support, held out of sight in wadis or below the ridge.

The New Zealand attack, by the 25th Battalion supported by Valentine tanks, went in on Point 175 just before midday on Sunday, 23 November. It was to be the start of six or seven hours of ferocious fighting at close quarters, in ground where there was little or no cover for attacking troops. At the end of it about half of the hillock was in our hands, but at a heavy cost. By nightfall some 100 officers and men of the 25th Battalion had been killed – the highest number killed in any one New Zealand battalion in a single day's fighting in the whole war – higher than in any one day at Alamein or Cassino. There were heavy casualties, too, in 24th Battalion, who were drawn into the action, and amongst the tank crews of the Valentine tanks, only two of which were in action at the end of the day. It was a savage forerunner of a type of fighting which all seven New Zealand battalions and their supporting arms in the area were to know during the week ahead.

On this next day, Monday 24 November, Barrowclough put in a fresh attack on Point 175, and seized it with relatively little loss. The main enemy forces had withdrawn across a deep wadi – the Rugbet en Nbeidat – and had taken up positions around the blockhouse and the Mosque. During the afternoon the General ordered Inglis to bring 4th Brigade forward, roughly abreast of Point 175. Divisional Headquarters moved forward also, along the Trigh Capuzzo. We had gone about ten miles, and had reached a point on the flat below a rise I estimated to be Point 175 when there was a burst of fire from the escarpment. An enemy post just beyond Point 175 had opened up with its machine guns. Since we had only one platoon, the Headquarters Defence Platoon, available for action, the order was shouted back from truck to truck for us to turn round and drive back half a mile along the route we had come. This about-turn, carried out by vehicles five abreast and a hundred yards apart, had never been thought of, let alone practised during our manoeuvres. But it was carried off without a hitch, and was to pass into the folklore of the division, a subject for both mirth and admiration.

Just east of Point 175 we settled in to what was to be our home base for the next four days and nights. We were on flat ground close to the edge of the escarpment, which rose some thirty to forty feet above us. A small rocky wadi curved up to the plateau. On the east side of the wadi a Mobile Dressing Station had been set up. This was a hospital of a dozen or so low brown canvas tents, one housing the Mobile Surgical Unit, and over the days ahead was to care for hundreds of wounded – British, German and Italian. Beyond it a prisoner of war compound was established. It was given the formal name of a POW cage, but consisted only of a stretch of open desert surrounded by a few coils of barbed wire. But it was guarded carefully by troops with Brens and rifles.

The prisoners taken in the attack on Point 175 provided an unpleasant surprise. They were from 2nd Battalion of the German 361 Afrika Regiment, a unit not on the list of enemy troops issued to us by Eighth Army before the campaign. At first I assumed it was a unit of one of the two panzer divisions which, apart from a few static groups on the frontier, were the only German formations thought to be in North Africa. But my questioning revealed that 361 Afrika Regiment was part of a German infantry division which had not hitherto been identified in the desert. This was called the ZBV Afrika (Special Purposes) Division, and had arrived in Libya very recently, sent to strengthen Rommel's forces for the attack on Tobruk.

The presence of a full German infantry division – the first of its kind in the Afrika Korps – marked a significant strengthening of the enemy forces in our path. We were no longer facing only Italian infantry around Tobruk. We now had to deal with German infantry – and, as the fighting for Point 175 had revealed, experienced German infantry. The other battalion of 361 Regiment – 1st Battalion – proved to be an odd but formidable lot. It was composed of former German members of the French Foreign Legion. Between the wars high unemployment in Germany had led a number of the more adventurous or more criminal types of German to enlist in the Foreign Legion. Their ranks had been enlarged after 1939 by left-wing Germans who had fought in the International Brigades on the Republican side in Spain, and who opted for the Legion rather than for a French internment camp. Shortly before this battle the commander of 1st Battalion 361 Regiment had told his men that this was their chance to prove they were good Germans. Whether this was their motive, or whether their previous training stood them in good stead, they certainly fought hard. Perhaps only in the ruins of Cassino two and a half years later were we to meet tougher resistance on the ground than along these three miles of the Rezegh Ridge.

This first encounter between New Zealanders and the ZBV Afrika Division was the beginning of a contest between two infantry formations which was to last until the final stages of the war three and a half years later. Within a few days ZBV Afrika was to be given a new title, that of 90th Light Division. This won fame as the crack German infantry formation of the Afrika Korps, particularly in the fighting at Alamein. We came up against them so often that when the end came for the Axis in Tunis in the spring of 1943, 90 Light refused to surrender to anyone but New Zealanders. In Italy, reconstructed as 90 Panzer Grenadier Division, they faced us again on many occasions, right up to the final Allied offensive on the Senio River in April 1945. Our contact was, in those later days of sophisticated psychological warfare, marked by an exchange of leaflets. They fired into our lines leaflets telling us that Europe's quarrels were none of our business, and that we should go home to our farms. We retaliated with leaflets telling them to do as they had done in Tunis, and surrender. In these long years of war it was a curious – and to a degree chivalrous – individual contest within the wide clash of huge armies.

On this evening of 24 November our forward troops were now about twelve miles from the foremost positions held by the Tobruk garrison. They had, three days earlier, made a sortie south-eastwards, moving out of their perimeter of anti-tank ditches and barbed wire and minefields, and fighting their way some three miles towards Sidi Rezegh. This had been intended as a step towards linking up with the 7th Armoured Brigade, whose tanks and Support Group had then been advancing on Rezegh from the south. But with the blunting of the British armoured thrusts, and above all with the annihilation of the 5th South African Brigade on 23

Tobruk commander, General Scobie, had told his troops to halt and dig in, to await our arrival. Freyberg's orders from 13 Corps were now to link up with Scobie's forces, and open a corridor into the fortress from the east. A ridge called Ed Duda, between Sidi Rezegh and the Tobruk positions, and directly ahead of the line of 4th Brigade's advance, was set as the junction point.

The Tobruk sortie had revealed the existence of other units of the German Afrika Division, so that when the General conferred that night – Monday, 24 November – with Inglis and a tired but resolute Barrowclough, Bell was able to give them an estimate of eight enemy battalions in the eastern Tobruk sector, with a total of some 120 guns. This was a formidable nut to crack, even though there had been no sighting during the day of enemy tanks in the area. General Freyberg's instinct was that Rommel had withdrawn his armour westwards, to rally in renewed strength. His instinct was in part right. Rommel had indeed left this part of the battlefield, but to move east, not west. The next day for the first time information reached us from 13 Corps that the panzer divisions had struck south eastwards, scattering 30 Corps before them, and had then turned northwards towards Sollum.

As a first move towards linking up with Tobruk, Barrowclough was told to seize the next obstacle on the escarpment, the enemy positions around the Blockhouse, and Inglis was ordered to advance below the escarpment, along and to the north of the Trigh Capuzzo. By midday both these objectives had been attained, though on the escarpment 6th Brigade had once again had heavy casualties in attacking across the open ground under withering enemy fire.

Early in the afternoon I visited 6th Brigade to see what documents and prisoners the attack had yielded. Above the escarpment the plateau stretched away, flat, drab, immense. Tufted with dark low bushes, it opened out under a glowering low sky. An occasional truck moved against the wide horizon. Half a mile ahead a group of Stuart tanks, damaged and abandoned, stood like an ochre-coloured metal megalith. Parts of Otago and Southland had tussock-covered landscapes of similar sweep and emptiness. But they usually had a mountain on the horizon to lift the spirit, and their grasses, though coarse, could sustain livestock. These plains, *morne et triste*, arid and waterless, seemed fit only for the use to which they were now being put, for war.

The cost of the morning's fighting was marked on the slope beyond Point 175. That evening I noted down what I had seen. I have the record still, in pencil on the coarse brownish Army paper:

> They lay amid the tufted bushes, with the bayonets of their rifles thrust
> into the ground to guide the burial parties, the New Zealand dead. They
> had the same waxen look as I had seen on the bodies of the Russian and
> Finnish dead strewn in their hundreds in the snows of Lapland, looking
> smaller in death than in life, with their clenched hands and their false
> teeth and the brown blood dry on their wounds. They lay as they had
> fallen. Some were thrown back by the bullets, one buried his face in the
> sandy dust.
>
> There was no one I knew amongst them – the 24th were drawn from
> Wellington and the districts around it – so I felt only a generalised, not
> a particular sorrow at the sight of these men whose cold clay lay now
> upon this cold hard desert.
>
> Three smashed Valentine tanks, their tracks burnt away, hung on the
> skyline. A corporal in the uniform of the British Tank Corps was
> salvaging gear from them. 'They had a bad knock,' I commented. 'They
> sent us to our death, sir,' he replied, quietly. 'Only three of us got out
> of it – my mates and myself, out of twenty-seven men in the troops.
> And we got away only by running like hell.'
>
> His voice trembled on the edge of tears. He turned away and went
> grimly on collecting the gear of the dead men and smashed tanks. One
> of the men with him paused to bend over a New Zealand body alongside.
> It was of a man with his bullet pouch open, his pack still on his back,
> the mess gear and a packet of biscuits showing. Near it lay a photo of
> some mosque in Cairo with, written on the back, 'Went here last
> Sunday. I am second from the left in the group.'

The reference to false teeth may need some explanation. Perhaps
because dental care for children was rare in New Zealand before the
mid-twenties, or perhaps because of something in the diet, many
New Zealanders at this time had poor teeth. 'We knew we were up
against New Zealanders,' one German prisoner was later to say to
me. 'They are the chaps with false teeth and wristwatches.'

I gathered in a pile of documents from 6th Brigade and went on
to 26th Battalion stationed a mile or so out in the desert. Their
trucks loomed suprisingly large against the skyline, like a group of
skyscrapers, rather as I imagined New York's skyline might look
from a distance (as later I was to find that it did). Colonel Russell
Page, the commander of the 26th, was poring over a map spread on
the bonnet of his car. A strongly built, vigorous man of middle
height, he was a schoolboy hero of mine. His father had been the
gym instructor at the secondary school I attended, Southland High
School. Rusty Page had been our head boy, captain of the Rugby

XV and of the First Eleven, and had won a scholarship to Sandhurst. There he had played rugby for the Combined Services, and had returned to be an artillery officer in New Zealand's tiny Regular Army. Now, in this desert on the other side of the world, it was pleasant to find myself with him again, and I gave him my smartest salute. He was pleased with the way his Southland and Otago men had borne themselves against the tanks on Sunday, and in ground attacks since then. Two days later he was to be virtually out of the war, so severely wounded that he had to be sent back to New Zealand, though he was to recover and have a distinguished post-war career in the New Zealand Army.

28. Belhamed

I got back to Div HQ just in time to get caught up in the only air raid on the division at this stage of the campaign. We had been so well protected by the RAF since we crossed the frontier that this attack in the late afternoon by Stukas took us completely by surprise. The bombs thudded in lines across the flat desert, coming closer and closer. Several fell amongst our vehicles, one within a few yards of the G truck, but caused no casualties. The Army Tank Brigade HQ about half a mile further east was more unlucky. Seven men were killed there and twenty wounded. I photographed the burning vehicles from my truck as Bill got busy deepening our slit trenches.

That night, Tuesday, 25 November, attacks were launched in the dark by 6th Brigade to capture the remaining enemy positions on Sidi Rezegh, now centred near the Mosque, and by 4th Brigade to seize Belhamed, a low ridge between us and El Duda. They were to be attacks with the bayonet, under cover of darkness, the first use in the desert of this tactic which was to become the hallmark of the Division. The attack on Belhamed was to be made by the 18th (Auckland) Battalion, and the 20th (South Island) Battalion. In the hope of securing an early identification of the enemy on Belhamed, I joined 20th Battalion as they gathered on the start line, ready for zero hour at 9 p.m.

The next day I snatched a moment to set down the scene.

They lined up outside their trucks in dark. It was overcast and cold, and the tufted desert bushes were damp to the hand. Beyond Rezegh and towards Belhamed the German Very lights went up, white and red and green, cold, mysterious, frightening at first. Away to the east, too, where there shouldn't have been any of the bastards they soared up. And suddenly, far ahead, red and green and gold tracers cascaded up, and the searchlights roamed white and stiff and lost.

'Jesus, look at that. Like a bloody fireworks display.'

'Tobruk barrage.'

Tobruk: over there, under that barrage, was Tobruk, besieged now for six months. We were on the edge of it now, with the last few miles to go, across towards Belhamed and Duda and we were there.

Under their steel helmets the set neat New Zealand faces were losing their normal half quizzical, half cynical expression and settling into the mould of the man about to fight – hard, intense concentration, the utter concentration of a man about to walk side by side with his own life, as if it were a separate person alongside him, and you wondered if he would get hit and then you knew it would be yourself and for the moment fear clutched at you.

Men in battledress, in grey jerseys, with that strangely domestic kit of men going to fight – haversack on back with towel, mess tin, spare pair socks, enamel mug. Bayonets fixed and the platoons deploying as if on manoeuvre. The light dying away now, and it was just the dark, with Rezegh ridge sharp against the sky and an occasional flash of a big gun from Tobruk.

By the headquarters truck four prisoners huddled, grey, miserable, cold in their hideous Afrika Korps uniforms. One whimpered with a wound.

'Someone ought to do something for that bastard. It's time they looked after his wound. Anyway someone ought to take them away.'

'He'll get attention in time. Anyway serve him right to take it for a bit.'

'Hell, he's just a human being anyway, even if he is a Hun.'

A squatting figure among the guards spoke up. 'Hell, let the bastard wait. I've been a prisoner of theirs in Crete. Let the bastard wait.'

The prisoners did not stir. Then one got up, walked a few yards, and began to pull down his trousers. The guard watched him, his hand ready on his rifle.

Then the whistle went and the line moved off. No tanks went, no carriers, just the four waves of men abreast, their bayonets fixed, walking silently ahead in the darkness. They looked a tiny force, thin, too thin a group in this great desert waste. The company commander walked in front, compass in hand, with a runner behind him counting the paces. On either side men were fanning out, and the bushes breaking underfoot, and dark figures against the sky and it is dark and heavy going.

The 20th had over a mile to go to the edge of Belhamed, and it was nearly half an hour before the darkness was broken by lines of tracer bullets, and by Very lights cascading suddenly upwards and, faintly but unmistakably, the high yell of men charging. It was another half hour before an infantryman, a field dressing wrapped round a wound on his left arm, stumbled out of the darkness escorting a pale and frightened young German soldier. I interrogated him quickly. He was a sapper, from 900 Engineer Battalion, fighting as infantry. This meant that Belhamed was not strongly garrisoned, and should fall easily enough – which it did.

In their parallel attack on Sidi Rezegh 6th Brigade had on the contrary met very tough opposition. When dawn came the enemy was still holding out around the Mosque, in strongly fortified positions, some of which were of concrete. Amongst the enemy documents captured during the night was a real find – an Operation Order issued by Lieutenant-General Karl Boettcher, the German in command of that sector. It showed that the troops fighting so tenaciously around the Mosque included not only Germans, but also Italians of the 9th Bersaglieri Regiment, who, contrary to our expectations, were to fight with great determination and courage.

In the early morning at Div HQ I interrogated two more prisoners from Belhamed, a young sapper, almost beardless, still just a youth, and his officer, a grizzled veteran. The officer made a formal protest. Our troops had, he said, not only forced his men on Belhamed to show them where they had laid a minefield, but had forced them, under levelled rifles, to lift some of the mines. Quietly the officer insisted, 'That is against the Geneva Convention. No captured man can be forced to engage in any action against his own side.'

Seeking a justification, I said, 'Many of our men fought on Crete, where the Germans used wounded New Zealanders as cover, and they remember that.'

The officer nodded. 'I can understand that. But it is well to observe the laws of war. After all, in war sometimes one side wins, sometimes the other. By tonight you may be the prisoner, and I the free man.'

I turned to interrogate the young sapper, who was being guarded by a New Zealand Provost officer, a former Territorial who had volunteered for this war even though he was well into his forties. Alongside him, and the veteran German officer, the young German looked no more than a boy. War, I suddenly thought, is a matter of boys against boys, directed by their fathers.

The author interrogating a German prisoner during the battle of Sidi Rezegh

Staff officers confer on Sidi Rezegh. The author at right

Shell fire amidst Divisional HQ vehicles

The end on Belhamed, December 1, 1941. General Freyberg — the central figure — watches the 6th Brigade gun line being overrun

When in mid-morning I drove across to 4th Brigade HQ, now close up under the lee of Belhamed, the news from the 20th and 18th Battalions on Belhamed was discouraging. They were under heavy artillery and mortar and machine gun fire, but so hard was the ground that digging any sort of protection was difficult. Wounded were being brought back in what seemed a steady stream. But Brian Basset, Inglis's lionhearted Brigade Major, was undismayed. He put down the field telephone into which he had been talking, and turned to me, his wide face cheerful. 'Everything under control,' he said. 'We've got twenty-four Blenheims coming over in half an hour, directed onto the enemy on our front.'

True enough in half an hour the hazy blue sky filled with the drone of aircraft, and we could see the RAF markings on the bombers as they flew overhead in close formation, and heard the crump as they dropped their loads. It was an historic moment – the first occasion in which close air support had been given to New Zealand troops in this war. In later years in Italy, when we could whistle down instant dive bombing attacks from fighter bombers circling overhead, I used sometimes to think back to this attack. But if it was an historic moment, it was also a tragic one. For the bombers had hit, not German troops, but our own – the men of the 1st Essex Regiment advancing towards Ed Duda, causing more than thirty casualties.

One of the many inefficiencies of the planning of Crusader had been a failure to establish any direct signals link between the Tobruk garrison and the New Zealand Division. Messages could reach us only through 13 Corps. News that the Tobruk garrison had launched its breakout to Ed Duda had not yet reached us. But this was not known to Basset or myself that morning, as we watched with delight our own bombers join in battle for the first time on our side.

29. Rommel Returns

Freyberg's orders for the next night were straightforward. Barrowclough's 6th Brigade was to complete the conquest of Sidi Rezegh. Inglis was to link up with the Tobruk forces on Ed Duda. Both objectives were achieved. On Sidi Rezegh the last enemy forces were overwhelmed around the Mosque, or forced down the escarpment in one more night attack, but only at a very heavy cost in dead and wounded to 6th Brigade. Ed Duda had, by contrast, been reached by 4th Brigade with very slight losses.

Inglis had devised a superbly simple plan. He lined up the Valentines of 44 Royal Tanks and told them to advance at top speed in the darkness, towards Ed Duda, with 19th Battalion in their trucks following. It succeeded brilliantly. The tanks swept aside all opposition, and with an hour and a half they were on the edge of Ed Duda, firing the green Very light signals agreed as a sign of recognition. The link between the advancing Crusader forces and Tobruk had been made, and by dawn a corridor was being cleared through the minefields to allow vehicles to pass in and out of the fortress. We had done the job we had been sent to do five days earlier.

It had been a job done at heavy cost. All four battalions of 6th Brigade had suffered terribly in their five days of fighting, all of it across open ground, in the face of heavily armed and well fortified enemy positions. Both 18th and 20th Battalions and 4th Brigade had been hard hit in their exposed positions in Belhamed. And the full bill had not yet been paid. Even as Brigadier Barrowclough in the sunshine of that Thursday morning, surveyed, from the Sidi Rezegh mosque, the ground below, stretching towards Tobruk, and as Inglis grouped his forces to protect his end of the corridor, away to the east Brigadier Hargest and the survivors of the attack on 5th Brigade Headquarters were being marched off towards Bardia and imprisonment. Equally ominously Rommel had ended his foray towards the frontier, and had ordered 15th and 21st Panzer Divisions, and the Italian Ariete Armoured Division to return towards Tobruk.

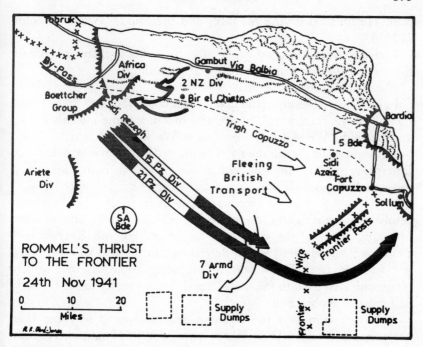

ROMMEL'S THRUST
TO THE FRONTIER
24th Nov 1941

That afternoon the sound of gunfire suddenly reached us at
Divisional Headquarters from a new direction, from the west, from
along the Trigh Capuzzo, to our rear. It was the low, distinctive
rumble of a tank battle, menacing and unmistakable.

The Intelligence Officers at 13 Corps had gained knowledge of
Rommel's move largely by listening in to the enemy's wireless
messages. With 13 Corps were a number of German and Italian
speakers who, guided by signals experts, tuned in to the enemy
wireless sets. Though much enemy wireless traffic was in code, in
the urgency of battle it was usually in clear providing a valuable and
immediate source of information. I was on duty in our side of the
G truck early on the morning of Friday, 28 November, when an
urgent message from 13 Corps reached us. It gave confirmation that
the power of the Afrika Korps was about to be unleashed against us.
It was an intercept of an order sent by Rommel to the two German
armoured divisions. It read: '15th and 21st Panzer Divisions are to
rendezvous at Point 123456 (the exact map reference is not in my
papers) destroy the New Zealand Division and advance on Tobruk.'
I took it across to where the General's bivouac tent was pitched. He
was washing in a green canvas basin. I read the message out to

him. He finished drying his face, and then said, 'Where is Point 123456?'

I tried to sound in good heart. 'By my reckoning, sir, it is about the second tussock from where we are standing.'

'Read the message again.'

I did so. 'Destroy the New Zealand Division,' he said thoughtfully. Then a note of cheerful defiance came into his voice, and he said, 'We won't let 'em, Cox. We won't let 'em.'

I glimpsed, in that moment of swift, yet instinctive response, an innermost quality in this essentially reserved man, his truly indomitable spirit. It was a quality which went beyond courage, though courage was an essential element in it. It was the steely resolve of a great fighter, the perfect counterpart to the unhesitating attacking spirit of the men who had captured Sidi Rezegh and Belhamed, the element which determines in the end whether wars are won or lost. There was a buoyancy about it, too, which communicated itself to me, and I strode back eagerly to the G truck to report to Robin Bell

A further sign that the German armour was close came that morning when an NCO and three men from the Headquarters staff of 21st Panzer Division were brought in as prisoners. They had blundered into a Tank Brigade outpost on the Trigh Capuzzo during the night, having come from the east. They were well trained, and would say little, but their documents made plain what their unit was. When I had finished questioning them the NCO, a youthful-faced man in his early twenties, asked me whether they would be taken into Tobruk. I gave him no reply, but the question lingered in my mind. Why should it matter to him by which route they were taken to the captivity which now surely awaited them?

To be ready to meet the threat of the enemy armour, Freyberg set about widening the corridor into Tobruk. At two o'clock that afternoon a tank and infantry attack was organised against the one remaining enemy stronghold on the flat between Sidi Rezegh and Ed Duda. From the slope of the escarpment close to the Blockhouse we watched, as from a grandstand, the Valentines move forward, the infantry debuss from their trucks and advance, rifles held at the high port. It looked almost artificial, as if it were being staged at a military tattoo, as tanks manoeuvred, and brown spurts of earth were thrown up by the shellfire, and grey figures emerged from slit trenches with their hands raised, or lay in crumpled groups amidst the low bushes, and the Bren carriers rounded up lines of prisoners.

These were all Germans, mostly from 155th Infantry Regiment. Their commander, Colonel Mickl, was amongst them, the highest ranking German I had yet interrogated. I identified him from his documents, but he adamantly refused to answer any questions, and angrily stalked off under guard towards the prisoners' cage.

This compound, on the plateau above Div HQ, now had more then 900 prisoners in it, a mass of grey-coated men, mostly squatting on the sand, seeking shelter from the cold wind, with a few standing in groups, and one or two moodily alone. The officers kept apart, pacing up and down, talking and occasionally gesticulating. There were a number of Italian prisoners now, Bersaglieri from Sidi Rezegh, mostly round-faced peasants, and mostly only too eager to talk, their swift words swamping the scanty Italian I had acquired on shipboard.

Close to the cage, the MDS was busy with wounded, both British and German, being brought in from the afternoon's fighting. Two ambulances stood by the surgical tent, marked by a red lamp. From within it a call went up: 'Stretcher bearers, stretcher bearers,' in singsong tones. Walking wounded, their bandages very white against their drab uniforms, gathered in groups or sat amongst the tufted bushes. Over it all was a cold, grey hostile sky.

We ate our supper, early, in the dusk, before the night came in its swift way. We were sitting at a trestle table at the back of the C mess truck, close to the foot of the escarpment, when I suddenly saw a truck drive to the edge of the escarpment, and the driver and three men jump out and take cover down the slope. The next moment a Bofors gun further along the escarpment started to pump out its shells towards an unseen target on the plateau beyond. Then white and gold tracer bullets began to spray out over our area. I ran back to my truck to get the rifle I had acquired, over and above my regulation revolver. Bill was already in his slit trench, rifle ready. On the plateau the firing continued, and then, as the dark settled in, I heard cheering, and faint but unmistakable, shouts of '*Deutschland über Alles*'. It could mean only one thing. The Germans had released the prisoners – and the MDS must now also be in their hands. I realised then why the NCO from 21st Panzer had been anxious to know whether he would be sent into Tobruk or held in the desert. He probably knew this raid had been planned.

We waited tensely for troops to move down the escarpment against us, but none came. The Germans were not night fighters. A dozen or so men from our defence platoon moved up the escarpment and took up position on its edge. Meanwhile, in the last fading elements of light, a cavalcade of vehicles appeared from the east, along the Trigh Capuzzo – three ton trucks, signal lorries, and a number of curious caravans, wooden structures erected on truck chassis. It was 13 Corps HQ. Having found themselves virtually in the front line, facing the advancing German armour on the Trigh Capuzzo, they had wisely decided to utilise the newly opened corridor, and moved into Tobruk. A hour or so later we too move back towards 4th Brigade, putting about a mile between us and the escarpment.

30. A General is Captured

The next morning brought a major coup – the first German general to be taken prisoner in World War II. Soon after first light an outpost of the 21st Battalion on Point 175 saw a staff car moving westwards some 200 yards away. From the flat caps of the officers in it they recognised it as German, and opened fire. Three men jumped from it, and were taken prisoner. One proved to be a general. He was hurried back to 6th Brigade and on to Divisional Headquarters.

I found myself facing a man of middle age and middle height, with neat, sharp features, receding hair, a firm mouth and a quiet, self composed manner. He had an Iron Cross around his neck, and another decoration which I did not recognise (it was the World War Pour Le Mérite, which despite its name, was a high German decoration equivalent almost to a British VC). He had given his name, when questioned at 6th Brigade, as Mueller. I had checked carefully through the lists of German officers supplied to us by Eighth Army but there was no General Mueller among them. It seemed highly unlikely that a new officer of such high rank could have arrived in Africa and been given a top command in the middle of a battle, but under my questioning he held adamantly to his story. It seemed all the more improbable because Mueller – the equivalent of our Miller – is a common German name, just the one at which one would grasp when seeking an alias.

Bell told me to escort the prisoner to General Freyberg. In his red-banded cap, with four rows of medal ribbons on the tunic of his battledress, Freyberg looked a formidable figure as he stood alongside his staff car. Our prisoner halted before him, clicked his heels together with well drilled formality, bowed, and, as was the German custom of being introduced to someone, gave his name.

'Ravenstein,' he said.

'But you said your name was Mueller?' I queried.

'So it is,' he insisted.

'Why then did you say Ravenstein?'

He shook his head. 'You have misheard me,' he said.

But I had heard enough. I knew, from my Baggush studies, that the commander of the 21st Panzer was Major General von Ravenstein. I told General Freyberg that I was sure that our prisoner was the commander of 21st Panzer. I got confirmation of this when I searched his belongings (they included an orange, nuts, and a pair of nutcrackers), and found amongst them a pair of pyjamas with on them the laundry mark V.R.

It was an important identification, for amongst the papers found in von Ravenstein's car had been a map with the enemy positions, and indeed the enemy intentions, marked on it. Drawn directly onto the map, in thin blue pencil strokes, were lines which showed the present placings and proposed lines of advance of the three enemy armoured formations – 21st Panzer, 15th Panzer, and Ariete. These showed that 21st Panzer was where we expected it to be, on the Trigh Capuzzo immediately to the east of us. An arrowed line led from its present position through where we were placed, and on through Belhamed towards Tobruk. Its fellow German armoured division, 15th Panzer, was shown in the desert south of the escarpment. Its route, marked by another arrowed line, would be westwards across the plateau, then onto the escarpment at Sidi Rezegh, and down across the flat ground towards Ed Duda. At the top of the map a big loop, with half a dozen symbols for field guns, and nine small circles which I took to indicate minefields, showed the German positions to the north of us besieging Tobruk on its eastern flank. Scrawled in this section was the name 'Summe'. This puzzled me. Only later did I work out that it must have stood for Summermann, who was commander of the newly named 90th Light Division.

This was rich booty indeed. Here, under our hand, was Rommel's plan of attack for the day. It was a plan he was to follow closely. Even as Ravenstein was being presented to Freyberg, 15th Panzer

were moving westwards, south of Point 175 where von Ravenstein
had been taken prisoner. The commander of the Afrika Korps,
Lieutenant-General Cruewell, who was travelling with 15th Panzer,
modified the plan in one respect. Instead of attacking our positions
on Sidi Rezegh, he directed 15th Panzer further west. In the early
afternoon it made its way down the escarpment and proceeded to
attack Ed Duda, at the same time calling upon 21st Panzer to press
its attacks along the Trigh Capuzzo – again as predicted on the
map.

   These moves were clearly set out on the captured document. How
far they were deduced from it I had no means, at the time, of telling.
The map had passed immediately from the Intelligence unit to the
Divisional Operational staff, who made their own interpretation of
it. I never saw it again. Nor did Bell, who set off to escort von
Ravenstein into Tobruk. The official New Zealand War History of
the campaign surprisingly expresses the view that this map, and the
other documents in von Ravenstein's possession, 'were not the
blessing they were deemed'. It argues that von Ravenstein had
missed an early morning conference with Cruewell and

> knew nothing of later modifications to Cruewell's plan to drive with both
> panzer divisions abreast straight through the New Zealand Division.
> The Ravenstein papers drew all eyes at Divisional Headquarters to the
> eastern flank in imminent expectation of the tremendous assault forecast
> in bold crayon lines on the captured map, though at that very time the
> major partner in this threatened enterprise, 15th Panzer Division, was
> already miles west of Sidi Rezegh and swinging round to attack Ed
> Duda.

It is difficult to reconcile this interpretation of events with the
evidence of the map itself. A photograph of it, shown in the Official
History, makes clear that it does *not* show any plan for a
'tremendous assault from the east' for a 'drive with both panzer
divisions abreast through the New Zealand Division'. Only 21st
Panzer is shown as given this task. The wide detour by 15th Panzer
across our southern flank, and its swing northwestwards towards Ed
Duda, is clearly marked. Nothing on the map indicates that any
other formation than 21st Panzer would attack the Division from the
east. If the deductions which the Official Historians describe were
drawn from this map, then they were inaccurately drawn. It clearly
showed a threat to 6th Brigade on Sidi Rezegh as well as to 4th
Brigade and Divisional Headquarters on the Trigh Capuzzo.

The two main enemy thrusts mounted that morning were writ large in the confident blue lines on that captured map. If too much attention was paid to the eastern flank, the Ravenstein map could not – or should not – be blamed. Indeed except for a move by the Ariete Division later in the day on to Point 175, all the main enemy attacks on the division during the day came from the east. The attack of 15th Panzer on Ed Duda as marked on the map, was witnessed by von Ravenstein and Bell as they made their way through the corridor towards Tobruk. Von Ravenstein sat on the edge of a slit trench and watched the tanks of his fellow Panzer commander gain a grip on part of Ed Duda – a process which encouraged him to say to Bell, 'Tonight you will dine with me in my mess.' But the attack on Ed Duda was halted, and Bell and his prisoner got safely into Tobruk.

Had Bell's departure with von Ravenstein from the Division been delayed by about half an hour, the German commander would have faced the chance of being killed by the shells of his own division. From mid-morning onwards we came under steady shell fire at Divisional Headquarters from the guns of 21 Panzer from the east and of 90th Light from the north. We spent much of the rest of the day diving in and out of our slit trenches. I shared mine with a splendid black beetle who obviously enjoyed the warm corner, in sunshine and out of the wind, which the trench provided.

In the intervals of this, I had to deal with a new responsibility placed on me by the departure of 13 Corps to Tobruk the previous evening. They had left behind their Intercept Unit. This consisted of seven or eight caravans – each a simple wooden walled hut built on the chassis of a three ton truck – in which a number of German and Italian speakers listened in to the enemy wireless traffic, or as much of it as could be picked up through the constant static. These eavesdroppers were mostly anti-Nazi or anti-Fascist refugees, many of them, despite their khaki battledress, of a most unmilitary appearance. They would have seemed more in place in the corner of a Vienna cafe than out here in the Libyan desert. Several looked Jewish and I wondered whether, if they were taken prisoner, their uniforms would be enough to save them from a concentration camp. Apparently abandoned by their previous masters at 13 Corps, they looked justifiably anxious, all the more so as their high walled vehicles were very vulnerable to shell fire.

They were of little value to us, as the intercepts had meaning only to someone with a more detailed knowledge of the wider enemy situation. The problem was the more difficult because of the German practice in the desert of setting up ad hoc groupings of troops, tanks and guns, and giving these the names of the officer for the moment in command, so that we had at various times a Stephan Gruppe, a Knabe Gruppe, a Boettcher Gruppe. There was now – I noted to my annoyance – a Mickl Gruppe, obviously commanded by the colonel we had briefly in our hands only for him to be released by the raid on the prisoners' cage. The experts who could provide the swift analysis of the intercepts had, however, gone on into Tobruk with 13 Corps.

Much of General Freyberg's time was taken up on this Saturday in trying to get the 1st South African Brigade to move up from the south and join us on Sidi Rezegh. Its commander, Major General Pienaar, had been placed under Freyberg's orders. The South Africans were some twelve miles away, across the plateau, and their troops and guns would have been an invaluable, indeed a decisive reinforcement, particularly to the 6th Brigade, whose ranks had been terribly depleted by a week of almost continuous fighting. One battalion, the 21st was reduced to only 91 men out of 800. In the early afternoon a South African armoured car got through to Div HQ, providing with its wireless a direct link with the South Africans. Freyberg spoke on it to Pienaar, adopting a code name which was unlikely to deceive the German intercept service. 'This is Big Boy calling Big Boy,' he announced. His orders were clear. Pienaar was to move up to Point 175 with all speed.

Pienaar was not alone in the desert. Close by were the two remaining British armoured brigades, with some 120 cruiser tanks, supported by strong artillery units. Ahead of them only the Italian Ariete Division could bar the way, as 15th Panzer was committed against Ed Duda and 21st against our eastern flank. Yet such was the confusion within 30 Corps and Eighth Army that the British armoured brigades wasted the day milling around in hesitant and ill-directed actions – at one stage they even shelled 6th Brigade on Sidi Rezegh – and the chance was missed.

Pienaar, with the recollection of the terrible fate of 5th South African Brigade before his eyes, understandably held back. This not only denied us the reinforcements which could have turned the battle, but led to a fateful misunderstanding. On Point 175 the 21st Battalion had been told to watch out for the South Africans advancing from the south. When, late in the afternoon, trucks and lorries appeared from that direction, the forward posts of the 21st thought that the reinforcements had arrived, and got up out of their trenches to greet them. They were met by fire from what was a column of the Italian Ariete Division, which moved on to overrun Point 175, seizing back for the Axis this rise which had already cost us so much blood.

This swift change in the fortunes of war presented us the next morning with an Intelligence problem right on our doorstep. We woke to see on the escarpment around Point 175 a mass of trucks with two or three tanks amongst them. Was this at long last the South Africans? Had they utilised the darkness to link up with us? Or was this an enemy convoy? I got out the silhouettes of enemy tanks which we had been issued with, and tried to match these against the outline of the tanks on the skyline. But none of these showed up clearly enough to give a certain identification. I thought they might be Italian M 14s, but we had had no contact so far with any Italian forces, and I could not be sure. The General, with this tempting target in front of him, did not want to turn our guns onto it if there was the least chance it was the South African 1st Brigade, the more so since our ammunition was short. He turned to Major Bonifant of the Divisional Cavalry who had rejoined us with a troop of outdated light Mark VI tanks – the type used in the attack on Galatas – whose thin armour could barely withstand a rifle bullet, let alone an anti-tank shell.

'Bonifant,' the General said, pointing to the escarpment, 'we aren't sure who those chaps are. We want you to find out.' Bonifant, a livestock auctioneer in civilian life, but a warrior by instinct, was into his tin can of a tank in an instant, and off across the desert towards the escarpment. The Italians – for these were vehicles of the Ariete Division – were fools enough to fire on him, telling us what we wanted to know. A moment later, its engine boiling like mad, the Mark VI came down the escarpment in a cloud of dust, its mission done. No cutter of Drake's facing up to the Spanish Armada ever did a job with more verve.

A moment later the skyline erupted with flames and dust and smoke as our guns opened up. This bombardment smashed several trucks, and chased the rest away. But Ariete's infantry and gunners were by now well dug in on Point 175, providing the South Africans with one more excuse for not joining us. They never did. Nor did the British armour, now amalgamated into one composite brigade under Brigadier Gatehouse. They wasted another day skirmishing around the fringes of the Ariete Division. This left Rommel's main tank force, 15th Panzer, time to reorganise after its abortive attack on Ed Duda. (It had been forced in the dark to give up such ground as it won). By mid-afternoon the Germans were in a position to bring their tanks and lorried infantry, supported by the deadliest of their desert weapons, their 88mm guns, against Barrowclough's thinly stretched and weary forces on the Sidi Rezegh ridge.

From the east the guns of 21st Panzer had brought Div HQ area once again under shell fire throughout much of the morning, filling the air with the stench of explosive and the pinging of metal fragments. The ground was soon littered with small jagged pieces of metal. Two of the intercept vehicles were hit, and I got permission to move them a mile further west, close to where 6th Brigade Headquarters were now placed on the flat below the mosque. As I guided them there in the late afternoon I could hear the sounds of heavy gunfire from the plateau beyond the mosque. Fountains of earth, black smoke at the top, yellow sand below, were thrown up by shell bursts. Lines of tracer showed against the blue autumn sky. It was clear that a heavy battle was under way. This was indeed the case, for 15th Panzer were mounting an assault which was to overrun 24th Battalion and half of 26th Battalion, and drive us off the ridge around the Mosque. I questioned two dazed men from the Ariete Division. Their tank had been hit by a 25 pounder shell. One of the crew had been killed, another blinded. The survivors wanted only to go home. Brightly coloured pictures of Catholic saints were in their diaries.

I was back at Divisional HQ when news came through of 15th Panzer's attack. Major Moffatt, a quiet former schoolmaster who was IO at 6th Brigade, telephoned it to me soon after five o'clock. I took it across to where General Freyberg and Gentry and Miles were eating their evening meal at a trestle table in the open. Miles' face reflected deep concern, as if he had a premonition of his own capture the next day. Gentry told me to guide him to 6th Brigade HQ. We found Barrowclough and his staff watching the flames rise from a German tank which had been hit as it tried to make its way down the escarpment towards them. Between the thump of the guns we could hear men digging new positions at the foot of the escarpment. Brigadier Barrowclough, tense but as calm as if he were presenting a case in court, urged Gentry to get the Division drawn back onto the Tobruk perimeter. That would be the only way of preventing the rest of 6th Brigade from being overrun the next day. Sidi Rezegh was lost, except for one strongpoint around the

Blockhouse. The flames and smoke from the blazing tank, rising against a clear sky from which the light was fast fading, gave powerful emphasis to Barrowclough's words.

Back at Divisional Headquarters I found that plans had been drawn up for a last ditch stand the next day, but on our present positions. No authority had come from the higher command for us to fall back on the much stronger line of the outer defence of Tobruk. Under these plans, only a small Battle Headquarters would remain with Freyberg and Gentry. The rest of us were to move into Tobruk that night. So I made my way back to the Intercept vehicles, and guided them towards the corridor. About ten o'clock we set off behind Ed Duda, along the narrow lane cleared through the minefields. It was a slow, bumpy drive in moonlight, with ahead the anti-aircraft barrage flaring up above Tobruk, and with German Very lights illuminating at intervals the line of the Sidi Rezegh escarpment, where tanks still burned redly. Shells swished over in the dark. At one stage we overtook a soldier of the Provost Corps struggling and jolting his way forward across the broken ground on a motor cycle. I felt for him. Then we moved onto a well made road, and were quickly over the last ridge and onto the drab, grubby desert on the outskirts of the smashed white buildings of Tobruk town.

The next morning Bell and I sought out 13 Corps, anxious for news about the Division. It came through slowly, and was at first all bad. The expected German attack at dawn had overrun Belhamed, causing heavy losses among 20th Battalion, forcing the 18th and part of the 19th Battalion into Tobruk. The German tanks had made their way right into the gun lines of the 6th Field Regiment, slaughtering the gun crews and destroying the guns. It was in this gun line, directing fire to the last, that Brigadier Miles was taken prisoner. General Freyberg and Colonel Gentry watched from close at hand. John White caught this scene in a memorable photograph. It shows the General in greatcoat and steel helmet, like a great totara tree on a storm-wracked New Zealand hillside, outlined against the blazing guns and trucks. His driver, rifle in hand, stands nearby. Only when the gunners a hundred and fifty yards away began to put up their hands did the General and Gentry withdraw to the shelter of the 4th Brigade positions. But the Germans did not press their attack further, and during the night the remnants of 4th and 6th Brigades and Divisional Battle Headquarters got away under cover of darkness and made their way back to the frontier wire. The battle of Sidi Rezegh was over.

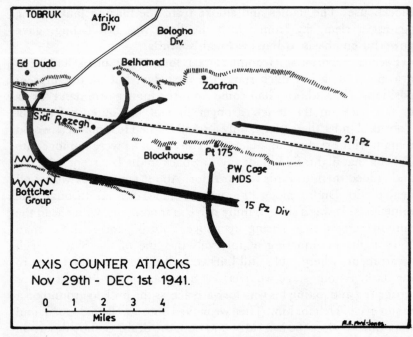

AXIS COUNTER ATTACKS
Nov 29th - DEC 1st 1941.

0   1   2   3   4
Miles

Rommel for the moment held the field, but this was to prove for him even more a Pyrrhic victory than Crete had been for Student. Rommel made one more thrust towards Bardia, but the column he sent was skilfully ambushed by the Maori 28th Battalion. The Germans and Italians had now lost so many troops, particularly around Tobruk when the Afrika Korps tanks had been away at the frontier, that they no longer had infantry enough to hold the ground they had regained. Rommel drew back, first to a line at El Adem, west of Sidi Rezegh, and that at Gazala, thirty miles west of Tobruk. Sidi Rezegh Ridge, and Point 175 and the blockhouse and the mosque were once again in British hands. Yet even at Gazala Rommel found his position precarious, as he decided to pull right back to El Agheila, at the foot of the Gulf of Sirte, giving up every square yard of territory he had gained since he made his first advance nine months earlier. The Crusader offensive, despite our early defeats and our huge losses of men and materials, had in the end proved a British victory. We had relieved Tobruk, and forced the enemy out of Cyrenaica.

31. From Tobruk by Sea

I had six days in Tobruk, long enough to gain a detestation of its brackish water, and its rubbish dump appearance, with broken lorries, rusty wire and old petrol cans littering the bare, worn desert. In the mess of 70th Division British officers talked hunting. 'Damn rude fellow that MFH of the Portman was. He used to make a hell of a scene if you broke any of his rules, saying, "Any more of that, and I'll take my hounds home." Pretty damn tough when you'd paid your two guineas for the day and your train fare and for getting your breeches cleaned, just because some damn woman hadn't stopped when he said so.'

On the western perimeter I visited the Free Czech Battalion which formed part of the garrison. I had been in Prague during the Munich crisis just over three years earlier, and had witnessed the extraordinary spectacle when a general mobilisation was called on the night of 23 September. The talks between Chamberlain and Hitler at Godesberg had broken down, and war seemed inevitable. Soon after ten o'clock the mobilisation order had been broadcast over the Czech radio in the six languages of the polyglot Republic – Czech, Slovak, German, Hungarian, Ruthenian and Polish. Its effect was immediate. In cafés and restaurants waiters and chefs took off their aprons, donned their coats, and set off to the barracks. Late night shop-keepers closed their premises, cars in the streets were halted by police and asked to carry men to their assembly point. Soon the blackout streets were full of men, each carrying his small suitcase, hurrying to railway stations or barracks.

I had shared with the Czechs that evening the sense of relief that they were going to be allowed to make a stand against this enemy who threatened their very existence. Six days later I shared their bitterness as news came in that at Munich we had betrayed them, and ourselves. Shame flooded through me when the London papers reached Prague, their headlines exulting in 'peace', but which meant for Prague peace with imprisonment. It was at that moment

191

that I resolved that when war ultimately came, I would enlist rather
than remain a journalist. Now in dugouts on the edge of a barren
Libyan wadi, I met men who remembered that night of mobilisation,
and who now said to me sadly, 'We only wanted to fight. Why
couldn't you let us do it?' These men in the Western Desert knew well
that they were the lucky ones. They had a chance now to fight, away
from the Gestapo terror which darkened the lives of the men and
women trapped now within the borders of the Third Reich.

The next day I was told to report to the docks at 10 p.m., to
command the escort of nine hundred German prisoners being
shipped to Alexandria. The column of prisoners in their long grey
overcoats and the peaked caps of the Afrika Korps stretched along
the quayside in the dark. They were filing aboard a small Greek
cargo vessel, clambering down into its hold under the guard of
British military police. Enemy planes were droning overhead, and
searchlights probed the cloud cover. The bombing began as the last
hundred or so prisoners shuffled across the deck and made their way
one by one down the iron rungs of a ladder to the hold. The space
below was already crammed with men, and the senior German
officer was protesting to the British Provost Major that conditions
were intolerably overcrowded.

Suddenly the anti-aircraft guns on the naval vessels in the harbour
and in positions on shore opened up, their roar mingling with the
whistle and shriek of falling bombs. Shrapnel began to whine and
ping onto the deck and superstructure. The Provost Major was in
no mood for further argument. His men hustled the remaining
prisoners down in the hold. When the last three of four could find
no room below, and clung onto the ladder, his sergeant brought the
butt of his rifle briskly down onto their knuckles. They yielded their
grip and fell. The Greek sailors quickly lowered into position the
heavy wooden covering beams, and locked these into position.

The Provost Major's final instructions to me were clear. 'You can
take a couple of the beams off tomorrow, to give them some air, but
on no account are you to allow any of the prisoners on deck. They
stay below till you get to Alexandria the day after tomorrow.'

When I had the beams removed the next morning, a stench of
vomit, faeces and urine rose from the hold. The men in it were
packed so tight that most of them had to stand, and the white faces
which were turned up to me seemed to be a solid mass. Several sick
or exhausted men were stretched out on the floor close to the
bulkheads, some straddled by the legs of other prisoners. Pools of

General Freyberg and the author

German POWs on deck on ship from Tobruk. Guard at left with rifle

Escort vessel alongside POW ship

excrement mixed with vomit on the floor. I decided to modify the Provost's instructions, and to allow two men at a time to climb the ladder onto the deck. There they could use two benzine tin buckets for their sanitary needs, emptying the contents into the sea once they were finished, before making way for the next two.

This seemed to me an acceptable risk, even though I had only twelve guards on board – eight New Zealanders, mostly clerks from Divisional Headquarters, and four South Africans. We had no automatic weapons, only rifles. I divided these forces into watches of four, and set two men on a raised part of the deck with loaded rifles, with orders to shoot at the least sign of trouble. Close on our starboard side we had also an escorting Royal Navy corvette. Though it looked not much bigger than a small tug boat, its two-pounder pom-pom gun was a comforting sight. I realised that if nine hundred Germans, or a substantial portion of them, could get loose they might – even though unarmed – be able to overpower us by sheer weight of numbers, seize our weapons, and direct the Greek captain to turn the ship northwards towards Crete. But the risk of this could be contained so long as the number of Germans on deck was strictly limited.

It was a relatively calm day, with a steady but not unpleasant swell, and the system functioned smoothly enough for me to risk increasing the number of prisoners on deck to four at a time. I had in any event another matter to think about. During the morning the frigate advised us that two nights before Italian torpedo bombers had sunk a comparable cargo ship carrying wounded troops and some prisoners. Amongst the prisoners, I learnt later, was von Ravenstein. After two hours in the water he was hauled aboard the escorting corvette, and set ashore the next day at Mersa Matruh, clad only in an army blanket. Robin Bell had been aboard the corvette, which had escaped unharmed in a second torpedo attack. Our own escort vessel warned me that we would be in the main danger area, within reach of enemy airfields in Crete, in the late afternoon.

By early afternoon the sun was out, the sea blue, and there was almost the atmosphere of a peacetime cruise. The German prisoners, leaning on the rail to draw a last breath of clean air before climbing down to their stinking pit, mingled with the off duty guards. I got out my camera to record this moment. As I lined up the scene in my viewfinder I suddenly realised there was an undue amount of field grey amongst the khaki. I counted the Germans on deck. There were fourteen in all, lying on the uncovered areas of the hold covers or sunning themselves on the deck. I hurried down and got their numbers back to the manageable four. Even so, anxiety nagged at me until shortly before four o'clock I ordered the covers to be replaced and clamped down.

As this was done I caught a snatch of talk between a German NCO and an officer at the foot of the ladder. '*Keinen Machinen-Gewehrn* . . .' I heard – 'No machine guns.' They had, I realised, spotted the fact that we had no automatic weapons, and that it might be worth trying to rush us. I saw the reason then for the Provost Major's orders – and the rashness of my disobedience of them, however humanitarian my motives. I kept the hold battened down from then on, with two guards watching it throughout the night – the time when a breakout could have been most effective.

Just before dusk, the Italian bombers came in, two of them moving at us out of grey clouds which had now gathered. They were biplanes, each with a big yellow torpedo slung under it. They circled slowly above us, disdainful of the corvette's pom-pom, which fired away like a toy cannon, and of the few rifle shots we could put into the air above us. The captain had put the ship into a laborious zig zag, with all the speed he could raise.

The first torpedo passed just behind our stern, greeted with shouts and a burst of fire from the four South Africans. They had brought aboard a jar of South African brandy, and were now, I realised, all drunk. Since I could not spare New Zealanders to put them under arrest I let them be. The second torpedo passed between the corvette and ourselves, racing through the water alongside us. We watched it thankfully disappear into the waves. Then the planes were gone, and the dark came on, the dark of the night of 8 December. I remember the date because during the afternoon the ship's radio had picked up a BBC broadcast with the stupendous news that the Japanese had the day before attacked Pearl Harbor, and the Americans were in the war. I had been talking to a young German infantry captain when this information reached me. He was a fine figure, dignified even in captivity. He had been captured on Sidi Rezegh, and was sincere in his praise of the troops he had faced. I told him of the news from America. His face hardened. 'So Roosevelt and the Jews have had their way,' he said, with sudden vehemence, his face savage. I was thankful I had the power to order him back immediately into the hold.

We had no more alarms in the night, and the next morning the white beaches and the low shorelines of the Western Desert were on our starboard bow. By midday we were at Alexandria, with red-capped military police waiting on the quayside, and with a Polish officer in green uniform and a flat-topped, gleaming helmet on hand, no doubt to find if any Poles were amongst the German prisoners. I thankfully handed over my charges, gathered my eight New Zealanders, decided that the hangovers the South Africans were suffering were punishment enough for them, and drove off in a three tonner to the transit camp at Amariya.

One last blow was in store for four of my weary party. They were sitting with their backs against the canvas canopy of the three tonner when another truck, coming from the opposite direction, passed very close to us. The steel poles holding up its canopy struck against the back of our men, hitting them a brutal blow. Two were in particular agony. I turned the truck round, and told the driver to take us to the military hospital in Alexandria, where they were admitted at once. The other four and myself made our way gloomily out on the tarmac road to the transit camp.

It had a big officers mess tent where, after I had had a shower and a shave, I sat down to write a letter to my wife. A voice said quietly, 'Hello, Geoffrey.' Standing alongside me, erect and in battledress, with Rifle Brigade tabs, was George Millar. He had been a correspondent for the *Daily Express* with me in Paris. Eighteen months ago we had escaped together from France. On the SS *Madura*, the P & O liner which had brought us from Bordeaux, we had both decided to quit journalism and enlist, and we had both done so within a few days after the ship docked at Falmouth.

A fair-haired, Bonnie Prince Charlie Scot, George Millar was that evening at Amariya on the threshold of extraordinary adventures. Within six weeks he was to be taken prisoner, as Rommel thrust back towards Tobruk from El Agheila. After several escape attempts from Italian camps, he got away from a German camp near Munich, made his way across France and over the Pyrenees. He then parachuted back into France, to become a Maquis leader in the Besancon area, winning for these exploits the DSO and the MC. But all that lay hidden in the future, as we drank Stella beer, and talked late into the night.

32. Forgotten Battle

Sidi Rezegh is the forgotten battle of the Desert War, neglected by historians as they hurry on to write yet one more study of Alamein. This is understandable, as Crusader was a very complex campaign, with battles taking place, often simultaneously, across a wide and largely featureless desert, making the fighting as difficult to follow as is a game of American football to the uninitiated. Even to those who knew the terrain it is difficult to discern and evaluate from the official histories all the swirling currents and backwaters, the ebb and flow of fighting of those grey November days. Nor can the course of the battle be traced on the ground, because for nearly twenty years now Libya under Colonel Ghadaffi has been a forbidden land to foreigners.

Alamein was by contrast fought in one limited area, where the desert narrows to a forty mile wide bottleneck between the Qattara Depression and the sea. In this sector – less than half the distance between Bardia and Tobruk – the two armies, Axis and Allied, were face to face, the most convenient form of battle for historians to describe. It was a battle, too, with coherent direction from the centre, which Crusader was certainly not, and was in any case sure of its place in the history books because it was, at long last, the decisive encounter of the two year Desert War.

Yet Crusader was an extremely important campaign. Tobruk was relieved, and Rommel's drive towards the Suez Canal was postponed until the summer of 1942, so allowing the Allied strength in the area to be greatly augmented. Crusader was an Allied victory, albeit a messy one, in which our success owed much to Rommel's blunder in charging off to the frontier after his spectacular victory at Sidi Rezegh on The Sunday of the Dead. But it also owed much to the counter-thrust of the 2nd New Zealand Division towards Tobruk on that same day, and to the hideously bitter and costly fighting of the subsequent week amid the rocks and scrub of Sidi Rezegh and Belhamed. The battle of Sidi Rezegh ranks – or should rank – high in the annals of the New Zealand Army in World War

196

II. For it was not only a battle in which the fighting qualities of New Zealand troops was crucial to the outcome, but it was one in which the influence of their commander on the wider strategy of the campaign was very important – perhaps decisive.

Even in the early planning stages of Crusader General Freyberg had realised that control of the Sidi Rezegh ridge was the key to the relief of Tobruk, and that the struggle for it might prove the heart of the campaign. He was ready, and indeed eager to move towards Rezegh from the moment we crossed the Wire. As we moved northwards to cut off the enemy frontier positions, he had 6th Brigade poised on our left flank, able to get under way the moment the call came. When the opening armoured battles ended in disaster for 30 Corps, and General Cunningham at Eighth Army considered cancelling the whole offensive, Freyberg's was a powerful voice against withdrawal. When he heard talk of this, he told General Godwin-Austen, 'You can't withdraw. You haven't even begun to fight.' This robust attitude was an invaluable buttress to Godwin-Austen's own instinct, which was to go forward rather than back. When the order came on 23 November for General Freyberg to establish a link with the Tobruk garrison he was able to move westward swiftly because he had trained his troops for night movement across the desert. Indeed the only formation in the Eighth Army in Crusader which made use of the cover of darkness both to move and to attack was the 2nd New Zealand Division – and that was because Freyberg had seen far enough ahead to train his troops in these tactics.

Of the many actions which Freyberg took in World War II there was none which he considered more important, or more right, than the advance westwards towards Tobruk on Sunday, 23 November. 'If we had not done so, the battle of Alamein would have been fought a year earlier – and without the Sherman tank,' (the American tank which at last gave us an Armoured Fighting Vehicle to match the German Mark III) he said on a number of occasions later. The date remained firmly fixed in his mind. Three years later, in Italy, when the Division was moving forward to join in the attack on Faenza, I took the daily Intelligence Summary across to the General. 'Did you notice the date?' he asked me. I looked at it. It was 23 November, and realised what he meant. 'Sidi Rezegh' was all I needed to say to bring a slight smile of recollection to his face.

Early in 1945 the Division faced a particularly unpleasant problem, that of storming the stop bank of the River Senio, a high earthern rampart thickly sown with mines which threatened to cause heavy casualties among the attacking infantry. Driving back from one planning conference, I commented to the General that it seemed a particularly difficult problem. He answered quietly, 'It's not as difficult as the one which faced us at Sidi Rezegh on 23 November. Nothing the Division has faced since then was as dangerous as that. We cracked that one – and we will crack this.' (As indeed we did, by a bombardment so intense and so precisely placed that the infantry were able to pick their way through the minefields along the narrow paths the Germans had left for their own patrols in the soft earth.)

The danger to the Division in the desert on 23 November 1941 and during the days which followed would have been much greater, and the outcome much more in doubt, had Rommel not rushed off to the frontier on the morning of 24 November. But even that action was in its way a tribute to Freyberg's instinctive daring. For Rommel did not contemplate the possibility that any British general would have made such a bold thrust as this along the Trigh Capuzzo and the Via Balbia directly towards Tobruk. It was as daring a move as any Rommel himself made, and was the work of a commander of comparable verve and nerve.

General Freyberg's attitude was all the more important because the virtual collapse of the command structure of the Eighth Army, once the fighting became confused, threw greater responsibilities onto him and onto his Brigadiers than was the case in later desert campaigns. Freyberg's immediate superior, Godwin-Austen at 13 Corps, remained cool-headed and clear-headed throughout, his only error being his failure to give clear orders to the division on the night of 30 November/1 December to fall back on the Tobruk perimeter. Indeed it is a measure of the inexperience and clumsiness of the Eighth Army command mechanism that neither Godwin-Austen nor his Chief of Staff, the admirable Brigadier Harding, came forward on that night to see and decide for themselves.

In the event the hands of 13 Corps were tied by the instructions reaching them from the Army Commander, who was utterly out of touch with the battle. Indeed the only role which the High Command of Eighth Army played in the battle of Sidi Rezegh was to call upon Freyberg and the 2nd New Zealand Division to go on fighting, whilst themselves doing virtually nothing to bring to our aid the very substantial infantry and tank forces available to them. Though Cunningham had been sacked on 25 November, and

replaced by General Ritchie, the generalship displayed at Eighth
Army and at 30 Corps remained lamentable. Ritchie was resolute
to the point of stubbornness, but never had the means nor showed
the capacity to command a fast moving battle – as he was to
demonstrate even more spectacularly when he lost the great tank
battles of the Cauldron and Knightsbridge in the summer of 1942,
opening the way for Rommel into Tobruk and up to Alamein.

General Norrie, having lost the first armoured battles of Crusader
by committing his forces piecemeal, feeding them into Rommel's
mincing machine in neatly consumable portions, now saw his role as
keeping in being, rather than committing to battle, the new tank
reinforcements which had reached him. The British armoured
regiments had in these early battles gained such a sense of inferiority
about the quality of their tanks in a fight with the German Mark IIIs
that their hesitation to join battle anew is understandable.

This attitude explains, though it does not excuse, Norrie's failure
to use his tanks to escort the First South African Brigade to join us
on 30 November. Even less does it excuse Norrie's refusal to allow
Brigadier Gatehouse to join in the battle in which the 4th Brigade
and the gunners suffered so severely on 1 December, and which led
to our withdrawal from the field that night. Gatehouse, with some
100 cruiser tanks under his command, many new and in tip-top shape,
had arrived on the escarpment near the Mosque that morning just
as the main German panzer onslaught was going in on 20th Battalion.
The German flank was wide open to attack, and Brigadier
Barrowclough pleaded with Gatehouse to send his tanks forward with
the 6th Brigade infantry in support. But Gatehouse had been given
orders merely to cover a New Zealand withdrawal, and Norrie was
too far to the rear, and Ritchie too far out of touch to countermand
these. So Gatehouse ordered his tanks to turn round and withdraw,
leaving the New Zealanders to carry on the fight alone.

It was a decision which appalled many of the British tank
commanders. One, who had been on the Intelligence course with me
in Cairo, told me later of his feelings. 'As we came down the
escarpment to the New Zealand positions, men leapt up from their
slit trenches and fixed their bayonets, ready to join in the attack.
They were gaunt and exhausted but full of fight. They crowded
round our tanks, patting the armour plating, their faces lighting up
at this chance of getting at the enemy. When the orders came
crackling over our wireless sets for us to withdraw we could hardly
bear to look at these men. I felt nothing but shame.'

To Brigadier Barrowclough this decision was particularly bitter. He had carried much of the burden of the battle for Sidi Rezegh. He had had to face his first day's fighting alone. On Sunday, 23 November, when he mounted the attack on Point 175, and when 26th Battalion fought its own corner of the Sunday of the Dead battle, he was without the backing of the staff and structure of the Division. Even after General Freyberg had arrived with 4th Brigade, and had strengthened 6th Brigade by adding 21st Battalion to it, each brigade had had to fight very much its own separate battles, 6th along the ridge and the 4th across Belhamed towards Ed Duda. Day after day Barrowclough had faced the hard task of sending into the attack, across open ground where only the shallowest of trenches could be dug, the officers and men with whom he had trained and lived for months past. Shortage of ammunition prevented the artillery support which was available in most later battles. The I tanks which had seemed invulnerable against the Italians proved easy targets for the more powerful German anti-tank guns.

It is the measure of the men under his command that they did not hesitate to answer the calls he made on them – and it is the measure of Barrowclough that he did not hesitate to make these calls, as his duty and the situation demanded. Only close scrutiny of his quiet, reserved face, as he came across to the G truck for the evening conference with Freyberg, could reveal in its furrows and tenseness the strain which these decisions – frequently taken under shell or mortar or machine gun fire – placed on him. Yet when I saw him on that last Sunday evening, with the enemy tank blazing on the escarpment ridge a few hundred yards from his Headquarters, he was calm as if about to deliver a judgement from a court bench.

Brigadier Inglis was, by contrast, cheerfully and extrovertly belligerent, ready with views not only as to how to fight his own brigade battle, but also as to the role the Division as a whole should adopt. He became convinced, the moment the German armour returned to Sidi Rezegh, that commonsense demanded that we should fall back onto the new, outer defences of Tobruk, and together with the garrison form a solid position on which Rommel could break his teeth. Every time I went across to 4th Brigade to interrogate a prisoner or collect documents he would expound this view to me, for relay to Gentry. It was a view all the more effective because this defensive move came from a man of such an aggressive nature. But it was a view which could not prevail, because we were caught in the clamp of the Army Commander's order that the corridor into Tobruk must be kept open – though there was no one now to pass through the corridor, which had indeed merely become a vulnerable sally-port from which there were no forces to sally.

One reason for the inadequacy of the High Command during Crusader was the lack of clear and recent information on which decisions could be based. Quite as much as in the early fighting on Crete, and on a much larger scale, the Crusader offensive was marked by a breakdown in communications which blinded those at the top as to the true situation in the front line – or, in the case of Crusader, the many and varied front lines. General von Ravenstein, soon after his capture, made a comment that the desert was the tactician's paradise and the quartermaster's nightmare. To the Intelligence officer it was both paradise and nightmare. It brought the boon of copious in-depth information about the enemy, as the cut and thrust of mobile warfare led to each side overrunning the positions or capturing the vehicles of the other, bringing a rich bounty of documents and prisoners and material. Before the campaign ended, the Intelligence services of each side had an extraordinarily detailed knowledge of the other. But offsetting these gains was the nightmare of maintaining communications between rapidly moving units across wide spaces. The open desert areas were, curiously, often unsuitable for radio transmission. Moreover the wireless sets of the time were frequently inadequate and at night worthless. This prevented the flow of information essential to enable commanders to guide large scale operations. As a result the Crusader offensive became Balkanised into a series of localised battles, fought desperately by units who were at best in only limited contact with others on their side.

Fortunately this was as true of the Germans as of the British – and in the case of the Afrika Korps the scarcity of information was compounded by Rommel's reliance on his own instinct rather than on the evidence of his Intelligence Officers. Both sides as a result made serious blunders because of their ignorance of the enemy. Rommel's failure to observe our advance towards Tobruk on 23 November was a striking example of this. Had he been aware that two New Zealand brigades were within a few miles of his armoured formations that evening and the next morning, he would almost certainly have turned on us before he raced away to the frontier. Similarly had Eighth Army known that Ariete on 19 November were solidly entrenched at El Gubi, they would not (and should not) have allowed 22nd Armoured Brigade to break its teeth on vain attacks there. Again on 29 November had the Eighth Army appreciated that the main German armour was committed to attacking Ed Duda, ten miles away to the west, they could have sent the 1st South African Brigade northwards to help us without any major risk. But neither side had the necessary information at those key moments. It was as if the campaign was being fought in a mist which blotted out all long range scrutiny, leaving only scenes at short range to be perceived with terrible clarity.

On the British side this poor intelligence was exacerbated by inexperience and incompetence. Tactical reconnaissance from the air was inadequate. Specialist interpreters of air photographs were not attached to any forward divisions. Most reprehensibly of all, wireless links were not established between neighbouring formations, and codes were not available for direct interchange of information between, for instance, our division and the Tobruk garrison. When on the morning of 27 November the Tobruk garrison captured Ed Duda, they could not let us know this direct, although there were only two miles between their forward positions and ours. Scobie from Tobruk had to send all his messages to Freyberg through 13 Corps. This was why Brian Basset had no idea, when he called for the air strike that morning, that he was setting in train the bombing not of the Germans he had been informed were on Ed Duda, but the British who had captured it during the night.

Our own Divisional Intelligence work during Crusader was, by comparison with later campaigns, a somewhat rough and ready affair. Bell and I were a two-man band. Later Divisional Intelligence staffs had the services of a specialist interrogator, with no other duties than to cross question prisoners; of two air photographic interpreters (known as the Mae West unit from the initials of its full title – Mediterranean Air Interpretation Unit); and a flow forward from Corps and Army of detailed and recent material, much of it based no doubt on Ultra.

Nor had Intelligence work at NZ Divisional Headquarters, in November 1941, yet evolved into the pattern which was to serve so well throughout later battles. In particular two methods which were to prove invaluable in securing a clear picture of the enemy had not yet been introduced. One was the production by the Senior Intelligence Officer – the G III (I) – of a daily (at least in battle) Intelligence Summary. This was a typed and cyclostyled document, usually about a page and a half of foolscap in length, containing the latest information about the enemy, and his intentions, and his weapons. This was circulated at least down to battalion level. Its main object was to provide all senior officers with the best information available on which to shape their fighting. But it had a valuable further function for the Intelligence staff. Having to gather together and evaluate every twenty-four hours a picture of the enemy was a useful discipline for the IO and the G III (I), requiring them constantly to update their own knowledge and their own appreciation. Above all, it provided them with the occasion on which to think about the information reaching them, to put themselves constantly and regularly, as far as possible, into the minds of the Germans or Italians opposing them.

We did put out occasional I Summaries during Crusader, but these were not signed, or even finally prepared by Bell. They went out over Gentry's name. That gave them added force, but amidst his other duties it was impossible even for such a very able Chief of Staff as Gentry to spend time on evaluating and pondering over the evidence about the enemy opposite him. Yet that is a key function of divisional military intelligence. The resulting I summaries issued during Crusader were neither full enough nor recent enough.

The other piece of machinery which had not yet been evolved was the presentation, by the G III (I), of the latest information about the enemy, to the General's regular planning conferences. During Crusader these conferences, which in due course became a key and characteristic element in Freyberg's method of command, were held only intermittently and not, as in later battles, as part of the daily routine. At them in 1941, Gentry, or the General himself, tended to summarise what was know about the enemy, drawing on information gleaned beforehand from Bell. In later campaigns, the pattern became firmly established that planning conferences were opened by a statement by the G III(I). This not only provided for the Intelligence staff the further valuable discipline of getting its information and its thoughts clear about the enemy. It also gave us a seat, as of right, at these conferences – and as a result put us in the picture as to what was being planned by our own side, information largely kept from us during Crusader.

Even so, we could claim that much of the essential information about the enemy reached Gentry and the General during Crusader. We were able to identify the most important German reinforcements, the ZBV Division, very quickly. We had, from 13 Corps, forewarning of the return of 21st Panzer and 15th Panzer, and were able to support this by interrogation of prisoners from 21st

Panzer on the morning of 28 November. We saw through von Ravenstein's alias, and validated this map. The major gap in our work was our inability to foresee the attack by 15th Panzer from the south against 6th Brigade on 30 November. But that was something which called for the wider resources of 13 Corps, particularly in interpreting the material intercepted by the Intercept Unit – and they had by that time put themselves virtually out of touch, within the Tobruk fortress.

Ultra was of little direct value in Crusader. Auchinleck got no hard tactical intelligence from the special messages from London based on Ultra[1] It did provide a valuable confirmation of Rommel's thrust to the frontier on 24 November, but this merely made plain what was becoming apparent on the ground. It picked up and passed on to Cairo the orders issued by Rommel for his attack on us on Sidi Rezegh and on the Tobruk forces on Ed Duda on 29 November. But GHQ did not get this information to us, and in any event it had already been overtaken by the local intercept I had taken across to Freyberg early that morning. Similarly on the morning of 1 December Eighth Army received warning from Ultra that Rommel intended to resume his attack on us that morning. But there was no way in which this could be relayed to General Freyberg, and by then the battle was already joined.[2] Yet indirectly Ultra had a considerable influence on the battle. It made plain on several occasions Rommel's anxiety about his shortage of petrol and, as the fighting continued, about the erosion of his tank strength, particularly during his dash to the Wire. This knowledge undoubtedly helped to stiffen Auchinleck's resolve at a time when others were losing their nerve. Before the campaign, too, Ultra had played a very valuable role in identifying convoy sailings, so enabling British submarines and aircraft to inflict heavy losses on enemy shipping.

Sidi Rezegh was far from being the only hard fought battle of Crusader. The tank battles between the British and German armoured formations, the largest of their kind in which the British Army had ever been engaged, had seen high casualties, and many acts of gallantry. The infantry and gunners of the Support Group and of the 5th South African Brigade had been exposed in open desert to the full force of the German armour, at an horrific cost. The 2nd Black Watch had fought a magnificent but costly action in the break

---

[1] Lewin op. cit. p. 169
[2] *The History of British Intelligence in the Second World War.* Vol II p. 310.

out from Tobruk. On the frontier the 4th Indian Division, which had already sustained heavy casualties against the enemy positions at Libyan Omar, fought stubbornly against the raiding columns of 15th and 21st Panzer, as did the New Zealand 23rd and 28th Battalions outside Bardia. Mobile units called Jock Columns, (after Colonel Jock Campbell of 7th Armoured Division) snapped constantly at the heels of the enemy. The remaining cruiser tanks of 22nd Armoured Brigade and 4th Armoured Brigade blocked for an afternoon Rommel's return towards Tobruk on 27 November, only to give up the ground at nightfall – as was then the drill with British armoured units – to withdraw to a night laager five miles to the south.

But the advance of the 2nd New Zealand Division's two brigades to Sidi Rezegh and Belhamed was the lynch pin of the campaign. Our thrust held the Crusader plan together at a time when General Cunningham at Eighth Army was contemplating a full scale retreat to Egypt. Our final stand on 1 December exacted from Rommel a cost in men and tanks which he could not afford. Freyberg's decisions, and his resolution, combined with the fighting qualities of the men under his command, snatched victory out of possible – indeed probable – defeat.

The fierceness of the fighting at Sidi Rezegh was reflected in the casualty figures. The number of New Zealanders killed, wounded or missing in the Crusader campaign was 4620, greater than that of any other Eighth Army division. More New Zealanders died or were taken prisoner than in any other of the hard fought campaigns in which the Division was to be engaged, more even than at Alamein or Cassino or Orsogna. General Gentry (as the GI at Sidi Rezegh was to become) has recorded that 'the 2nd New Zealand Division later became more skilful, especially in the higher ranks, and was probably more effective, but it is doubtful that it ever fought again with the same fury and determination as it did in that short and confused campaign'.[1]

In the closing stages of the war I had a fascinating glimpse into how the battle of Sidi Rezegh had seemed to the enemy. In Rome in March 1945 I talked at length with Colonel Mario Revetria, who was then an officer on the General Staff of the reconstituted – and by then pro-Ally – Italian Army. At the time of Crusader he had been Chief Intelligence Officer of the Italian forces in Libya. He

---

[1] *The Relief of Tobruk* (NZ War Histories) by W. E. Murphy. p. 521.

claimed that the Italians had been convinced early in November 1941 that we were about to attack, but that Rommel would not listen. 'His mind was set on taking Tobruk,' Revetria said. 'The Germans had a great fault in Intelligence matters. They were apt to believe that the British were going to act in the way they wanted them to act.'

Revetria was definitely of the opinion that the New Zealand advance on Sidi Rezegh had tipped the scales, and forced Rommel to abandon his plans to attack Tobruk, and withdraw to El Agheila. Our move had taken even the Italians, whose Intelligence was better than that of the Germans, by surprise. The first knowledge that Revetria had had of events around Sidi Rezegh was when Westphal, Rommel's Chief of Staff, sent for him and asked that a regiment of the Italian Trieste Division should go the Belhamed at once. Revetria said to Westphal, 'But you already have 200th Regiment of 90th Light on Belhamed. What has happened to them?'

Westphal drew a cross on a pad in front of him, pointed to it, and said, '*Vernichtet*' – 'Destroyed'.

33. Year's End

When we returned to Baggush after Crusader we had the benison of letters from New Zealand, but also a heavy new anxiety – the knowledge that our homes there were now exposed to the threat of the Japanese advances in the Pacific. I went off for a week's survivor's leave to Cairo in a sombre mood. On the coast road just east of Alamein we passed a column of new arrivals, a Free French battalion, with a girl driving an ambulance – the first woman I had seen in the Western Desert. Some of their troops were Tahitians, conscripted into the Gaullist forces when the French colonies in the Pacific joined up with the Free French. Tahiti had, in the inter-war years, seemed to us in New Zealand as a neighbouring paradise, mainly no doubt because of its legend of eager brown-limbed girls beside a turquoise and blue sea, the place of Rupert Brooke's 'whispering scents that stray about the idle warm lagoon'.

It seemed wrong that young men from that background, with

their open Polynesian faces, and the red cross of Lorraine on their khaki sleeves, should be heading now for these barren and harsh Libyan wastes. Within a few months most of them would remain there, killed in the epic siege of Bir Hacheim.

In Cairo I was told that Major Randolph Churchill wished to see me. Randolph Churchill was Auchlinleck's Head of Public Relations, and had run into a storm of criticism in Britain because of his handling of news of the Crusader operations. The trouble was not of his making. All he had done was to hand on to the public the wildly over-optimistic estimates of British successes in the early tank battles, those same estimates which had reached us in the field. But when these proved to be wrong, and when Rommel sent 30 Corps and Eighth Army stampeding eastwards in his rush to the Wire, there was an almightly row in Parliament and in the British press. Some of this was due to Randolph Churchill's personal unpopularity at Westminster, where he had become an MP only by being awarded a safe Tory seat under the wartime Parliamentary truce. Some of the attacks were no doubt aimed at the Prime Minister by those who dared not attack the father but were willing to have a go at the son. But the outcry had been strong enough for Randolph Churchill to feel concern, and the need to strengthen his staff.

I came face to face for the first time with 'this notable figure, with his heavy leonine head, his thick greying hair, his husky voice and big shoulders' (to quote Alan Moorehead) in his office in the GHQ building in Cairo's Garden City. Churchill told me that he wanted me to become his second-in-command, with the rank of major, and with responsibility for all dealings with the British and foreign press. It seemed to be my fate that I should emerge from battle only to be enticed by offers of soft jobs in Public Relations. I gave to him the same reply as I had given to Peter Fraser – that I had joined the army to be a soldier, not a publicist. But he insisted that I dine with him that evening, and hear more about the post.

Over Shepheard's rather tough roast chicken, Randolph deployed at first his considerable charm. He had sounded out the British war correspondents. They were unanimous that I was the ideal man for the job. Maintaining public morale at home, particularly now that we had a war with Japan on our hands, was enormously important. I could contribute far more in the Public Relations field than in an infantry division. It would mean a substantial rise in pay, and contact at a high level with those who led our war effort.

When I stuck stubbornly to my refusal, he showed an uglier side;

I was a soldier, under orders. He would damn well see that
tomorrow orders were issued to me to take on this task, which he had
cleared with the Commander-in-Chief. When I countered that I was
in the New Zealand Army, subject to their orders only, he got
angrier still. 'I'll ring up Bernard Freyberg and get him to show you
where your duty lies,' he thundered. This did not worry me. I was
sure Freyberg would not order to the rear someone who wanted to
stay at the front.

We continued the argument over a second bottle of champagne
– Randolph was clearly pulling out all the stops – in his bedroom
upstairs. We had been joined now by a White Russian girl, the
friend of one of Randolph's brother officers. She was not the tall,
black-haired, black-eyed type of White Russian whom I had known
in pre-war Paris, but a quiet, rather demure girl who, I suspected,
was hoping to find a husband among the Guards or Cavalry officers
thronging wartime Cairo. She sat quietly by, both amused and
bemused as Randolph tried a new tack. 'I know the *Daily Express*
pays those of its staff who have enlisted a retainer during the war.
If you don't take this job I will cable Max Beaverbrook and get him
to stop your retainer.'

I had a counter to this. Shortly before Crusader offensive began
I had written to the *Express*, saying that I no longer wished to take
the retainer. Though Beaverbrook had done wonders as Minister of
Aircraft Production, he had been a major appeaser before the war,
and I had no intention of returning to his employ after it. As I put
it to myself I did not want to die with Lord Beaverbrook's cheque
in my pocket.

Blocked on this line of approach, Randolph conceded defeat, and
became less truculent and more maudlin as the level of champagne
in the bottle was steadily lowered. We spoke of another Expressman
whom Randolph knew well. Unkempt, ill-dressed, with none of the
class background so important in those days, my former colleague
exercised a formidable attraction for even the most elegant and
snobbish of women. 'How does he do it?' Randolph queried angrily.
'I have far more to offer, but women never take to me like that.' It
struck me then, and even more later, as a curious plea, for
Randolph had had at least one celebrated romance when little more
than a schoolboy with the Ohio beauty Kay Halle – who was still
a beauty when I met her in Washington in the mid-nineteen fifties.
But by this time we were both fairly drunk, so no doubt neither
Randolph's words nor my recollections of them rank as valid

evidence. I retained enough grip on my senses however to leave without yielding to Randolph's pleadings and cursings at me to take the job. If he bore me any ill will, he never showed it. When, twenty years later I became Editor of Independent Television News, Randolph put me on the list of those in the media he rang up regularly to chide and abuse – but always in a way basically friendly.

A few nights later I talked again late in to the night in a room in Shepheards, this time with Philip Jordan, of the *News Chronicle*. We had been colleagues on that paper five years before. He was now on his way back to Britain after six months in Russia. I was keen to learn from him about the military situation there, but even more about political developments. Was Stalinism being modified under the pressures of war? Would their common fight alongside us, and even more alongside the Americans, make them more democratic, give communism the human face (to use a later expression) for which many of us hoped? Jordan had been a stalwart man of the Left, ardently on the side of the Republic during the Spanish Civil War. I hoped his answers to these questions would be a firm 'Yes'. If the fact that the Red Army was in the field meant that fewer New Zealanders would be stretched out on slopes like that of Point 175, I wanted to believe the best of them.

But Philip Jordan, if a man of the Left, was also above all a man with a passion for facts. And the inescapable fact about Russia in 1941, as he had observed it, was that it was a brutal dictatorship, and would remain one, and indeed become even more of one in war. He saw no chance of Stalin's regime softening either because of the alliance with us, or when victory came. To delude ourselves that they were a democracy was to betray anyone who truly believed in democracy. I heard his views sadly, and probed them hard. But he held firmly to them – and I respected them. They were to provide me with an invaluable point of reference in the months ahead, when we were engulfed in a wave of uncritical pro-Soviet feeling engendered by the common struggle.

One point, however, Jordan's news from Moscow was highly acceptable. He had discussed with General Zukov, then a figure little known in the West, the book I had written about the Russo-Finnish war. Zukov had confirmed that my account of how the Red Army had met its early defeats, and had learnt from these defeats to secure its later success, was broadly true – as later historians have confirmed.

Most stimulating of all, however, during these days in Cairo was the time I spent with Bill Williams in the Intelligence staff offices at GHQ. Captain E. T. Williams, to give him his full ranking, had been a don at Merton College, and a friend of mine before the war. We had canvassed together against Quentin Hogg in the Oxford by-election soon after Munich. He had enlisted in the King's Own Dragoon Guards, an armoured car regiment. As commander of the foremost armoured car patrolling the front in March 1941 at El Agheila, he had been the first British soldier to sight Rommel's forces in North Africa. His unit had come face to face with the German 33 Recce Unit.

Whilst we were in Tobruk I had found, in a bundle of captured German documents, the diary of the German commander of the foremost car in this encounter. He had described how the British cars moving westwards along the tarmac road and the Germans moving eastward had come upon one another unexpectedly, and had passed each other like traffic in a Berlin street. '*Wie in der Friederichstrasse*,' he noted. It was a beautifully written diary, with sketches amidst the text, including one showing this incident, and I am sorry I did not pocket it. Someone else alas did take it, and it never reached Williams at GHQ in Cairo. Both Recce units had exchanged only desultory fire, but had swung wide out into the desert, anxious to get away and report the highly significant news of their sightings.

When the British were driven back, Williams ended up in Tobruk. From there he was sent by boat to Egypt, where Brigadier Shearer, realising that his combination of Oxford scholarship and military experience could be useful in Intelligence, gave him a post on the General Staff. Now, from a large, bare room in what had been a luxury flat, Bill Williams presided over the production of the daily GHQ Intelligence Summary. He was keen to bring into the somewhat rarefied air of GHQ someone with experience of recent desert fighting. So I found myself attached for a period to his unit, helping to assess and present the day's information from the battlefronts.

I worked at a big table alongside an officer from the Highland Light Infantry, Lieutenant Stuart Hood. He had a troubled time ahead of him. In early July 1942, when he was serving with 13 Corps, he was taken prisoner during Rommel's thrust to Alamein, and put into a camp at Mersa Matruh. Hood escaped during the night, seized a jeep, and with two others drove out into the desert.

Unable to get back to the British lines before daybreak, they immobilised the jeep by removing the distributor head, and hid in a nearby patch of camel thorn. When darkness came they made their way back to the jeep, only for Hood to find the distributor head had fallen from his pocket. In the intense darkness of the Egyptian night they could find no trace of it, though they searched on their hands and knees, yard by yard. They were still searching when, at first light, an Italian patrol captured them.

Hood had a year in Italian camps and, after escaping in 1943, a further year with the partisans. He came back through our lines in the summer of 1944. Sixteen years later I met him in another context. He became Editor of BBC Television News, my direct rival at the time when I was Editor of ITN.

Of the many documents which passed through my hands in those days in GHQ, two remain in my mind. One was a report on an agent landed by submarine in Italy. A Maltese by origin, he had had a series of nightmarish escapes from the hands of the Italian secret police, who would certainly have subjected him to brutal torture had he been captured. But the Naval Intelligence Officer who controlled him from Alexandria had little interest in such adventures. His sole comment was, 'His reports are unclear. He should be recalled and put through a course – and then sent in again.' It sounded callous, but practical.

The other document covered only a page and a half, but was a consummately clear, thoughtful and well argued forecast of what the next German moves would be in transporting equipment and troops to North Africa – an excellent example, I thought, of the value of employing good academic minds in Military Intelligence. The name at the foot was new to me, but I recalled it later. It was that of a Major Enoch Powell.

I was back at Baggush for Christmas, a subdued occasion under grey skies, alongside a grey and stormy Mediterranean. Ted Shand invited me to Christmas dinner with the officers of 4th Brigade. Their mess was a huge square dugout, roofed over and forming an underground room. There were many new faces, to replace the heavy losses the battalion had suffered on Belhamed. Colonel Jim Burrows had taken over as CO, replacing Kippenberger, who had been promoted brigadier to replace the captured Hargest at 5th Brigade. I noted afterwards:

Everyone frankly glad he's alive, unashamedly glad, outwardly at least unworried by the death or injury of others. Beer, and singing the ballads of beer drinkers to a mandolin. There was one minor fracas, when one of the few unpopular officers got truculent in his cups, and declared that all the best had gone, and only the worst were left. But this was soon settled, and we were back to the ballads, just as if we were in a coach coming back from a hard won football match.

After Christmas I returned to the Senior Common Room atmosphere of the GHQ Intelligence section in Cairo. Out of working hours the city continued to offer its dolce vita life. At Madelaine Mansour's the parties were as agreeable as ever, even though there were gaps in the ranks of the regular attenders, for the officers of the cavalry regiments had suffered heavily in their tanks in Crusader. George and Katy Antonious were on a visit from Jerusalem to her sister, who was married to Sir Walter Smart, the famed Oriental Counsellor at the British Embassy, and there were good dinners and good talk at the Smarts' Cairo home. At midday the winter sun shone warmly on the tables in Groppi's garden, and on the lawns of the Gezireh Club.

All this was abruptly ended for me when I received orders to report back at once to the Division at a new base at Kabrit, close to the Suez Canal, just north of Suez itself. I found I was to be Intelligence Officer to Brigadier Kippenberger, on a highly secret operation which was being prepared. This involved a seaborne landing behind Rommel's lines at El Agheila. The 5th Brigade was to move by sea and to be put ashore on the coast of Tripolitania, at the foot of the Gulf of Sirte, to the west of the narrow bottleneck where Rommel had taken a stand. At the same time General Freyberg would lead a force of lorried infantry and guns from the 22nd Guards Brigade through the rough going of the wadis and sandhills on the inland flank. Together we would link up, cut off Rommel, and finish him once and for all.

The planning was done in one of the Nissen huts in the encampment at Kabrit. A plaster model of the area had been built, and set out on a trestle table alongside aerial photographs of the coastline. The hut's contents were so secret that only those of us caught up in the operation had access, and a sentry with fixed bayonet stood always at the door.

For Kippenberger, in his new role as brigadier, it was an important command. But from the outset he was deeply worried about the practicability of the plan. As we walked away from the hut one morning, after a briefing by a naval officer who had seemed by no means certain that his boats could get us close to the shore, he

said quietly, 'I don't like this at all. We would be sitting targets –
or more exactly, slowly wading targets. What is more we might not
get any of the supporting arms ashore, and the Long Range Desert
Group tell me the going inland is very rough.' Later in the war he
told me that he thought it was quite wrong for the General to have
put himself and his reputation at risk in leading the land section of
such a risky venture.

But Kippenberger's warnings did not prevail. Someone in GHQ
was sure this was the way to win the war in the desert, and so we
prepared to go ahead. Fifth Brigade trained at landing operations in
the Bitter Lakes on the Canal, and I studied the air photographs and
the model until I felt I knew every contour. Fortunately Rommel
came to our aid. A week before we were due to embark in the
troopships at Alexandria, Rommel began a new drive eastwards,
scattering the inexperienced 1st Armoured Division in his path.
(This was the drive in which George Millar was taken prisoner.)
Ten days later Rommel was back on the Gazala line just west of
Tobruk. We were indeed lucky for when the Division advanced to
El Agheila early in 1943, after the victory at El Alamein,
Kippenberger inspected closely the area in which we were due to
land. A naval officer who surveyed the offshore waters with him
confirmed that virtually none of our supplies or supporting vehicles
or weapons could have got ashore. We would have waded into a
massacre.

That, however, still belonged in the days ahead, when, on 31
December 1941, I stood for the last time by my bivouac above the
beach at Baggush. The Division was seeing the Old Year out and
the New Year in in some style. From the battalion areas along the
coast Very lights and captured enemy flares were rising into the
skies, and tracer bullets were curving up in a dramatic – and no
doubt very costly – fireworks display. There was even the sound of
an occasional twenty-five pounder in action. In the Ops dugout the
phone rang repeatedly, as anxious commanders of neighbouring
units asked if we were under attack.

The celebrations died quickly away, but whilst they lasted they
had been a sight to remember, almost as vivid as that of Bristol
and Cardiff under the German bombers twelve months earlier. All
in all, it had been a full year.

Appendix: The Crete News

Shortly before this book went to press, I came across some diary notes, which I had long thought to be lost, about the Crete News. They add some vivid detail about the paper's production. They take up the story from the point, on page 62, at which I found the printing shop barred and padlocked.

Across the wooden doors of the printing shop stretched an iron bar held in place by a padlock. 'This is a hell of a way to start a paper – with a lock out,' commented Taylor. 'We haven't even had time to form a union, yet they have gone and locked us out.' George had no suggestions to make other than the excellent one that we should adjourn to the cafe. Here he got onto the ancient telephone and began to make frantic inquiries. At this moment a drunken soldier in the room above the cafe hurled a huge mirror out of the window. It cut clean through the canvas awning and exploded on the pavement amid the tables with a report like a bomb. Two Greeks were hit by fragments, one getting a huge cut above the eye. Everyone thought an air raid had started, and dashed out of the square. Only George, unruffled, continued his wild shouting into the telephone at the back of the cafe. He returned, oblivious of the blood and mess, drained off his brandy, and gave us his news. The printing shop had been deliberately locked up by the proprietor who was either scared of reprisals later from the Germans, or who was a Fifth Columnist. In any case he had fled to the hills, taking the key with him.

There were more details of the arrest of the Greek soldier compositor, who had absconded.

I drove to the Greek Army H.Q., explained the situation, and secured the services of two villainous-looking Greek military police, armed to the eyebrows. When Alexei saw us arrive with the policemen and with our own weapons he turned as pale white as the white-washed wall behind him. But he was Greek enough to be indignant. In a mixture of Greek with a few scattered words of English, he called upon the neighbours to witness his indignation. He was a free man, and would not be arrested. He was willing, and indeed honoured, to work on a British paper. But come under guard? No. That he would never do. But we had got beyond considering anyone's susceptibilities. Barry Michael bundled him

214

into the back of the truck and we sat over him with our rifles as we drove back to the press.

Still shouting furiously, Alexei allowed himself to be ushered into the shop and even took off his coat and took up a typeholder. Then, arguing and protesting, he set to work, until he saw that one of he police was standing guard outside. At this he flung down his typeholder, folded his arms, and shrieked in English 'No, no. I will not'. Another flood of Greek followed, and George pushed his grey felt hat onto the back of his head and burst into tears.

I went to the door and motioned the policeman to leave. He shrugged his shoulders at the crowd which had gathered and took up his carbine and strolled away. Alexei watched him go and then, his eyes still blazing, turned to us, shook hands all round and said 'Friends now, good friends. Police no good, never good the police'. Then without any further fuss he set to work.

The sheer labour of setting by hand a single sheet paper emerged as something enormous. The Greeks worked willingly, but entirely by eye, so that we had to type out extremely carefully every line of copy., and it was only then that I realised how easily one letter can be confused for another. E's were continually turning up as C's; s's in some peculiar way always got in back to front.; b's and d's were a certain bet for misplacement.

There were maddening mishaps, too. Taylor had been working on the longest story for the front page, mounting up to three half columns of close set small type. As he carried it carefully across the room the door of the shop opened, and the assistant printer, a fool from some distant village, stepped in. He flung open the door just far enough to knock Taylor's arm. The type, four hours of concentrated work, spilt on the floor. For a moment there was near murder in that Canea back street. But Nico, the head printer, came to the rescue. Without emotion he got straight down on his knees and started gathering the type up, and dissing it so that it could be reset. As he did he spoke quietly to George, who translated – 'Tell the New Zealanders to go and have a drink'.

By two in the morning we finally had the first number printed. Wearily we trudged the three miles up the hill, and put half a dozen copies of the first number on the doorstep of the General's residence. It was one of the most satisfactory moments I have known. We felt fine as we stood there on the edge of the ridge, looking over the great sweep of beach and the dark hills towards Suda Bay where, as we watched, the anti-aircraft guns suddenly opened up, splashing red shells towards unseen bombers.

Index